Marvellous Fantasy

Marvellous Fantasy
Edited by Jørgen Riber Christensen

AALBORG UNIVERSITY PRESS

Marvellous Fantasy
Edited by Jørgen Riber Christensen

The publication of this book has been
generously supported by the Department
of Communication and Psychology and
the Department of Language and Culture,
Aalborg University.

© Aalborg Universitetsforlag, 2009

Layout: Kirsten Bach Larsen
Cover: ZUCCEZ ApS

Review by Michael Skovmand,
associate Professor, Aarhus University, Denmark

Printed by Toptryk Grafisk, 2009
ISBN: 978-87-7307-962-1

Published by:
Aalborg University Press
Niels Jernes Vej 6B
9220 Aalborg
Denmark
Phone: (+45) 99 40 71 40, Fax: (+45) 96 35 00 76
E-mail: aauf@forlag.aau.dk

www.forlag.aau.dk

All rights reserved. No part of this book may be
reprinted or reproduced or utilized in any form or
by any electronic, mechanical, or other means, now
known or hereafter invented, including photocopy-
ing and recording, or in any information storage or
retrieval system, without permission in writing form
the publishers, except for reviews and short excerpts
in scholarly publications.

Contents

Jørgen Riber Christensen
Fantasy Definitions and Approaches   5

Lene Yding Pedersen
Harry Potter and the Ending Hallows   17

Jørgen Riber Christensen
Certain Regressive Tendencies in Rowling and Tolkien
Fantasy and Realism   45

Dorthe Andersen
L-spaceTranstextuality and Its Functions
in Terry Pratchett's Discworld   61

Torben Rølmer Bille
Sword & Sorcery The Barbarian Archetype
and the Conan Tales of Robert E. Howard   79

Steen Christiansen
The "Rat" in Fraternity China Mieville's King Rat   107

Camelia Elias
There is a text in 'The Balloon'
Donald Barthelme's Allegorical Flights   125

Kim Toft Hansen
Identifying the Junction
The idea of Reason in Fantasy   143

Gunhild Agger
"The Snow Queen" and the White Witch   167

Jørgen Riber Christensen
Peter Pan from Barrie to Disney   193

Ole Ertløv Hansen
Fantasy A Cognitive Approach   221

Martin Knakkergaard
Browsing the Suggestive Catalogue: Music in Modern
Fantasy Films   231

Anders Bonde
Distant Lands of Danger and Pleasure Musical Exotica
as Devices for Feminization in Xena: Warrior Princess   259

Index   285

Jørgen Riber Christensen

Fantasy
Definitions and Approaches

Before the first stage performance of *Peter Pan* at the Duke of York's Theatre in London in 1904, James Barrie and the director were concerned about the audience's reception of the play, particularly about the crucial point in the action when the fairy Tinker Bell has swallowed poison that Hook intended for Peter Pan. At the end of act 4, Peter Pan says about Tinker Bell:

> Her light is growing faint, and if it goes out, that means she is dead ! Her voice is so low I can scarcely tell what she is saying. She says – she says she thinks she could grow well again if children believed in fairies ! (*He rises and throws out his arms he knows not to whom, perhaps to the boys and girls of whom he is not one.*) Do you believe in fairies ? Say quick that you believe ! If you believe, clap your hands ! (*Many clap, some don't, a few hiss. Then perhaps there is a rush of Nanas to the nurseries to see what on earth is happening. But TINK is saved.*) Oh, thank you, thank you, thank you! (Barrie 1928, 72)

Barrie's worries about the risky audience participation of the performance are expressed in the printed stage directions with its repeated "perhaps." Before the opening night the members of the theatre orchestra had been instructed by the director Dion Boucicault to clap their hands in the secrecy of the orchestra pit if the audience failed to do so. This was not necessary. The audience's reaction was so strong that their clapping made Nina Boucicault, the actress who played Peter Pan, burst out crying so that she had to run off stage. (Davies)

However, the seconds between Peter Pan's emotional exhortation to the audience and the audience's reaction are significant. This hesitation, which is part of the reception of the play, is one of the characteristics of the fantasy genre. In this essay, hesitation -- along with the concept of primary and secondary worlds and the concept of the endlessly receding horizon -- will be the defining traits of the genre of fantasy.

Fantasy is a genre that is not easily and clearly defined. In fact it may be an element of the definition of the genre that its demarcations from other genres are dissolved or dissolving.

As may be inferred from the above anecdotal description of the opening night of *Peter Pan,* the discussion of the genre fantasy in this chapter will be based on the relationship between reader or audience and text, and as such it is influenced by reader-response criticism. Though Tzvetan Todorov, as seen in his book *The Fantastic: A Structural Approach to a Literary Genre,* may, with good reason, be called a structuralist scholar, it is in the act of reading that he defines the genre "the fantastic." Todorov examines two related genres, the uncanny and the marvellous. Where the uncanny can be defined as a text in which the reader at the end decides that the laws of reality are intact and can explain the occurrences of the text, the marvellous, on the other hand, can be defined as a text in which the reader decides that the laws of reality cannot be employed to explain the occurrences of the text, and, therefore, that the supernatural exists in it. (Todorov, 41) It is on this (in)decision of the reader's that Todorov concentrates when he examines and subsequently defines the genre "the fantastic." The crucial point is the brief moment when the reader of a text has to make up his or her mind as to whether the text belongs to the uncanny (e.g., horror) or the marvellous (e.g., a fairy tale). This hesitation in the act of reading is what Todorov uses to define the fantastic. This hesitation is produced when genre demarcations start to dissolve.

DEFINITIONS AND APPROACHES

Todorov puts the reader's hesitation on par with a character's hesitation when both have to decide between the uncanny and the marvellous. This analogy and connection between reader and character are more than just the reader's identification with the fictional character, as the character's cognitive insecurity becomes part of the reader's cognitive insecurity, causing hesitation. In this case the theory about the fantastic is analogous to the theory of the neighbouring genre, horror, as it can be found in Noel Carroll's *The Philosophy of Horror*. In this work one of the defining characteristics of horror or the experience of the uncanny is when the reader's cognitive skills fail in the face of a monster, a failure the reader shares with the hero/victim of a text about monsters, the figure who experiences the same monster first hand. (Carroll, 18, 34)

Some texts may be able to maintain the reader's hesitation throughout the book and even after the reader has finished reading the text. Todorov mentions Henry James' *The Turn of the Screw* as an example of this type. (Todorov, 43) However, most texts are unable to do this, and therefore Todorov establishes two transitory subgenres between the uncanny and the marvellous: the fantastic-uncanny and the fantastic-marvellous. These two subgenres are able to maintain the hesitation for long stretch of time, but ultimately the reader must decide whether the laws of reality in them are valid or not. Todorov points out that it is exactly between the two subgenres that the fantastic exists. It must be noted that the fantastic is not identical with the genre fantasy; the point here is that the hesitation that takes place on the border between two genres is part of the definition of the fantasy genre.

Where Todorov's description and definition of the fantastic with its hesitation are tied to a temporal aspect of reception, Lucie Armitt points to a spatial aspect when she employs Louis Marin's article "Frontiers of Utopia: Past and Present" to define fantasy using the concept of the endlessly receding horizon. Marin reads the view from and of the Sears Tower, he reads More's 1516 *Utopia*, and he examines the etymology of "horizon" and "frontier." The point of origin of Marin's essay is reception, and in Marin's arguments we meet the cognitive insecurity already noted in Todorov and Carroll. The visitor's gaze from the observation deck of the Sears Tower to "the spatial frontier of the horizon where gaze and earth seem to coincide" (Marin, 397) is not stable and firm: "This process of totalization at work through the beholder's gaze is nevertheless displaying its practical weakness, its cognitive uncertainty, its ontological trouble from its beginning to its end." (Marin, 398) The cognitive result is "a tension between frontier and horizon, totality and infinity, limit and transcendence, closure and liberty." (Marin, 406) A similar sense of duality can be seen in Marin's examination of the word "frontier." This word means not just a limit that separates two countries, but also a fringe or border with a well-defined edge inward towards the country and an outward and amorphous edge towards the other, the foreign, unknown, and limitless. Marin writes Utopia is situated in such an in-between area: "This is the merging place of Utopia, a neutral place, an island in between two kingdoms, two states, the two halves of the world, the interval of frontiers and limits by way of a horizon that closes a site and opens up a space, the island Utopia merging in the "indefinite." (Marin, p. 411) It is tempting also to place fantasy in this in-between area with its spatial challenge that is also a cognitive challenge that creates signification in reception.

The spatial receptive categories in Marin's analysis of *Utopia* are not necessarily new. As early as 1938 and 1939, Tolkien uses the same metaphors in what is the clearest definition of fantasy. It is to "On Fairy-Stories" we must turn for Tolkien's critical paratexts about his fiction. In "On Fairy-Stories" there is the concept of primary and secondary worlds.

As early as in the first paragraph of "On Fairy-Stories," Tolkien writes about "shoreless seas" and himself as "a wandering explorer" (Tolkien, 11), and in Tolkien's discussion of the genre of fairy-stories he is quick to dismiss character as a defining trait of the genre; instead, place, location, or setting is defining: "stories about fairies too narrow… for fairy-stories are not in normal English usage *about* fairies or elves, but stories about Fairy, that is *Faërie*, the realm or state in which fairies have their being." (Tolkien, 16) Travelling between the realm of men and the realm of fairies is what creates the stories. Tolkien writes: "Most good 'fairy-stories' are about the *aventures* of

DEFINITIONS AND APPROACHES

men in the Perilous Realms or upon its shadowy marshes. (Tolkien, 17) The most important aspect of Tolkien's definition of fairy stories is the double concept of the primary and the secondary worlds. Again, here there is a movement between worlds, but in this case the reader's and not the character's travel between his or her own world (the primary world) and the secondary world of the fantasy story. This travel takes place in the reception of the texts, and the ticket to it, so to speak, is the willing suspension of disbelief, an ability that Tolkien does not attribute exclusively to children. The validity of the ticket to the secondary world is not only a skill on the part of the reader. Tolkien writes that the skilled story-maker becomes a creator (or "sub-creator") of the secondary world that has the quality, which allows the reader to enter it. (Tolkien, 40-41)

The definition of the genre of fantasy is a combination of time and space, which takes place in the reception of fantasy texts. The combination is double. The reader is hesitant to leave the primary world and enter the secondary world, and this delayed travel into the secondary world is indeed significant. We never really reach the realm of Faërie as the horizon of this secondary world is forever receding. It is the "being on the way" in reading that matters. The joy and reward of reading fantasy are reaching out for, but never reaching, Faërie.

This book is the result of the cooperation between several departments at Aalborg University, Denmark. As such the book as a whole offers an interdisciplinary approach to the genre of fantasy. Scholars from fields as diverse as English language and culture, media studies, cognition science, Danish literature, and music have contributed to the book. A former student and candidate, Dorthe Andersen, and a scholar from Roskilde University, Camelia Elias, have also been invited to add their insights to *Marvellous Fantasy*.

"Harry Potter and the Ending Hallows" was written *in medias res* -- immediately before the last Harry Potter book was published -- and its author, Lene Yding Pedersen, employs this unique position and its point of view to examine and define the genre(s) of the series. She also answers the question of why it was so important for the readers and fans of Harry Potter to predict the outcome of the series. The element of participation is important: fan fiction, official and unofficial web sites are combined with Rowling's own core texts to describe Harry Potter as both a literary and cultural phenomenon within fantasy. To explain Harry Potter as a cultural text and to show how popular fantasy texts are consumed, constructed and reconstructed the chapter discusses concepts such as primary worlds, real fictional worlds, secondary worlds, secondary secondary worlds, and mediated worlds.

"Certain Regressive Tendencies in Rowling and Tolkien: Fantasy and Realism" by Jørgen Riber Christensen examines the Harry Potter books and *The Lord of the Rings* in order to discuss whether or not fantasy is regressive and without connection to contemporary reality. The chapter focuses on the family discourse in the Harry Potter series and on the modernity discourse in *The Lord of the Rings*. The methods employed are Georg Lukács' prescriptive theory about critical realism, Thomas Ziehe's concepts of narcissism, Carlyle's and Arnold's cultural critique, and Marin's description of fantasy as an endlessly receding horizon. The chapter concludes that there is a connection between fantasy and realism, and that fantasy is not a mere escapist attitude to contemporary social life and historical issues.

"L-space: Transtextuality and Its Functions in Terry Pratchett's *Discworld*" by Dorthe Andersen argues that there would be no Discworld without transtextuality, and further that transtextuality in Pratchett's work exists both at the surface and deep within the thematic contents of the texts. The chapter provides a useful survey of Gérard Genette's terminology, and it applies terms such as parody, pastiche, allusion, irony, and dead metaphors to Terry Pratchett's *Discworld* witch sequence: *Equal Rites, Wyrd Sisters, Witches Abroad, Lords and Ladies, Maskerade,* and *Carpe Jugulum.* The chapter, which is based on its author's master's degree thesis "Bewitching Writing," Aalborg University 2006, is also key to a large number of transtextual or intertextual references in the novels analysed. Dorthe Andersen concludes that Pratchett's use of transtextuality serves both humour and reflection, and that Pratchett's fantasy is subversive in Rosemary Jackson's sense of the term as it interrogates the real through the unreal.

Torben Rølmer Bille's near-encyclopaedic chapter about low fantasy, "Sword & Sorcery: The Barbarian Archetype and the *Conan*

DEFINITIONS AND APPROACHES

Tales of Robert E. Howard," offers a detailed survey of the Conan character across all media (books, films, comics, television, and computer games). The chapter discusses the Gothic aspects of the genre's collage setting and the protagonist's ancestors in the Victorian quest romance. The genre's explicit taboo subjects and its publication roots in pulp magazines are made significant. The creator of Conan, Robert E. Howard, and his writing career and style are described in detail, and a survey of the critical response that he received, both academic and popular, is included. The ideological aspects of the Conan figure are so pervasive that they in no way can be ignored. Torben Rølmer Bille employs the approach of cultural critique, and he contextualises Robert E. Howard within the frontier mythology, the American Dream, and Social Darwinism; he rejects the claim that Conan is an expression of protofascism.

Like other chapters in this book, Steen Christiansen's "The 'Rat' in Fraternity: China Miéville's *King Rat*" is concerned with ideological aspects of fantasy; but in contrast to other essays, the subject of Steen Christiansen's article is a fantasy writer that is politically and ideologically left wing. Like Rosemary Jackson and Lucie Armitt, China Miéville sees the narrative structure of most works of fantasy as one with a closure that establishes order and harmony in the end, and transgressions from the social order are cast as the villain. Miéville's *King Rat* employs the myth of the Pied Piper in a modern London setting and the metaphor of pests to explore the life of the metropolitan homeless in a fantastic form. One aspect of this fantastic form is mapping, known from many other works of fantasy, with the dual universe of London above and London below. The radical cultural critique makes the fantasy of Miéville subversive, and it is not escapist and nostalgic as other works of the genre. Steen Christiansen argues that the subversion in *King Rat* is double. There is the social critique as well as the subversion of genre conventions.

Camelia Elias' "There is a Text in the Balloon: Donald Barthelme's Allegorical Flights" provides its reader with a much-needed and useful distinction between fantasy and the fantastic when she writes: "Whereas fantasy in critical discourse can be aligned with allegory, in which a supernatural world can be said to stand for a figurative representation of our real world, the fantastic has the potential to occur within the world that we know." With Todorov as the point of departure, this distinction is expanded into an epistemological investigation of these two central terms. The concept of knowledge and storytelling is exemplified in the myth of the Biblical Fall and in Scheherazade's stories. Here Camelia Elias' gendered and witty point is that man knows (or rather wishes to know) and that woman knows (but does not tell). Finally, the meaning of a giant balloon appearing in the sky over New York in Donald Barthelme's 1968 short story "The Balloon" is discussed in light of the chapter's epistemological understanding of fantasy.

In his chapter "Identifying the Junction: The Idea of Reason in Fantasy," Kim Toft Hansen juxtaposes what may seem two dissimilar genres -- fantasy and crime fiction -- with the intention of demonstrating how the two have more in common than meets the eye. Kim Toft Hansen's discussion has its parallels in other chapters of this book about fantasy's relationship to realism, but here the core of the argument is the western epistemological framework of the Bible with its Old Testament of a mythical or fantastic nature and the more realistic New Testament. The approach is not only theological. Various literary critics, notably Northrop Frye, are included in Hansen's exposition. Using the concept of modality of fiction, Kim Toft Hansen ties the fictional and fantastic world to the "real" world again in order to demonstrate the junction of realism, reason, and fantasy. This theoretical foundation, which also includes a cultural historical aspect, is then employed in depth in an analysis of Simon R. Green's detective story *Hawk & Fisher*, which takes place in the fantasy world of Haven.

Gunhild Agger's "'The Snow Queen' and the White Witch" points to a connection between C.S. Lewis's *Narnia Chronicles* and Hans Christian Andersen's fairy tale "The Snow Queen." Structurally, Andersen's 1845 tale with its double universe is regarded as a very early form of fantasy, foreshadowing later developments; with regard to theme and characters Gunhild Agger demonstrates through a detailed reading of "The Snow Queen" how time, sexual symbolism, and adolescence are treated similarly in both Andersen and Lewis. "'The Snow Queen' and the White Witch" also contains a survey of

DEFINITIONS AND APPROACHES

the international evolution of the fantasy genre and its narrative structure, and the chapter discusses the lines of demarcation between fairy tales and fantasy. A particularly rewarding aspect of Gunhild Agger's chapter is her discussion of what constitutes an "immortal" literary character, such as the Snow Queen, and how these literary characters migrate through literary history.

Jørgen Riber Christensen's chapter "Peter Pan from Barrie to Disney" is a historical reading of many different versions of Barrie's *Peter Pan* from the last one hundred years. Riber Christensen's hypothesis is that Peter Pan is a cultural text that has adapted itself to changes in the mental setup of generations of audiences, and that these interpretations and versions of the Peter Pan text and its characters have worked both on a therapeutic as well as an ontological level. The sociological and psychoanalytical approach of the chapter is inspired by Bruno Bettelheim, and the chapter correlates the different versions of Peter Pan with the child's development and role in the family from the classical Oedipus conflict through narcissism, tweening, changing gender roles, and the dissolution of the nuclear family.

"Fantasy: A Cognitive Approach" by Ole Ertløv Hansen is a narratological and theoretical introduction to the cognitive processes that are involved in the reception of fantasy texts. Hansen's premise is that fantasy texts mirror the mental, cognitive processes of the mind that are connected to dreaming and imagining: Fantasy is remediation of these processes. The chapter outlines relevant developments within narratology from the Russian formalist Vladimir Propp through the Jungian-inspired Joseph Campbell to Christopher Vogler's later Hollywood screenwriting method based on Campbell. Concepts such as prototypes, templates, and procedures belong to contemporary cognitive film theory (David Bordwell), and the chapter discusses these and other perceptive categories and functions that come into play in the reception of fantasy texts. In his conclusion, Ole Ertløv Hansen stresses the close connection between, and perhaps even identity of cognitive processes with, the aesthetic and narrative forms of fantasy.

Martin Knakkergaard's "Browsing the Suggestive Catalogue: Music in Modern Fantasy Films" analyses the music for the films *The Lord of the Rings: The Fellowship of the Ring* (2001) and *Harry Potter*

FANTASY

and the Philosopher's Stone (2002). These thorough analyses are based on the tenet that music is integrated inseparably into the film experience as a whole, and the chapter deals in some detail with the signification creating processes and effects of music as such. These processes are a combination of psychological, pragmatic, semiotic, and cultural factors. Martin Knakkergaard's close readings of the music in the two films add a much deeper understanding of them than readings without the inclusion of their music would have been able to provide. The musical historical angle of the chapter brings special insights to an understanding of the films. For instance, one of the findings of the analysis of *The Fellowship of the Ring* is in tune with another chapter in this book, "Certain Regressive Tendencies in Rowling and Tolkien." Martin Knakkergaard concludes that the use of archaic musical language in the film does not bring the past to the present, but rather suggests the opposite movement – from the present to the past.

The question whether music contributes affectively to the gendered reading of the narration in the fantasy television series *Xena: Warrior Princess* is answered by Anders Bonde in the chapter "Distant Lands of Danger and Pleasure - Musical Exotica as Devices for Feminization in *Xena: Warrior Princess*." The trend of tough female protagonists or action chicks in series such as *Sabrina, the Teenage Witch* (1996-2003), *Buffy the Vampire Slayer* (1997-2003), *Ally McBeal* (1997-2002), *The X-Files* (1993-2002), and *Xena: Warrior Princess* raises the interesting issue whether the case is simply one of gender reversal, or whether this tendency is more ambivalent. Anders Bonde's detailed and thorough study of the use of music (themes, underscoring, incidental and leitmotifs) in *Xena: Warrior Princess* discusses this issue. The empirical reception studies of Philip Tagg of "manly" or "womanly" stereotypes in music are combined by Anders Bonde with historical investigations of the otherness of woman in Western music depicted through the exotic and Orientalism. A substantial part of the chapter consists of anthropological studies of Bulgarian indigenous music with its gendered positions of singing and ululation and the playing of bagpipes in the Balkans, Greek Thrace being the homeland of Xena. Based on this analysis Anders Bonde argues that *Xena: Warrior Princess* represents a new kind of musical femininity.

References

Armitt, Lucie. *Fantasy Fiction*. New York: Continuum, 2005.
Barrie, J.M. *The Plays of J.M. Barrie*. London: Hodder and Stoughton, 1928.
Carroll, Noel. *The Philosophy of Horror*. London: Routledge, 1990.
Davies, Russell. "Opening Nights: Peter Pan Takes Flight." BBC Radio 4, 23 December 2006.
Marin, Louis, "Frontiers of Utopia: Past and Present." In *Critical Inquiry*, 19, no. 3. (Spring 1993): 397-420.
Todorov, Tzvetan. *The Fantastic. A Structural Approach to a Literary Genre*. New York: Cornell University Press, 1973.
Tolkien, J.R.R. *Tree and Leaf Smith of Wooton Major: The Homecoming of Beorhtnoth*. London: Unwin, 1977.

Lene Yding Pedersen

Harry Potter and the Ending Hallows

Anticipation

It is now only a few weeks to the release on July 21, 2007 of *Harry Potter and the Deathly Hallows*, the final instalment of J.K. Rowling's seven *Harry Potter* books. Writing a chapter on Harry Potter at this time allows for an examination of particular aspects of the literary and cultural phenomenon which Harry Potter has become. Combining literary analysis with cultural studies, this chapter aims not to predict what will happen in *Deathly Hallows*, but to describe the complexity of *Harry Potter* as a cultural text, which is being constructed and reconstructed at this moment. On December 22, 2006, *Deathly Hallows* reached number one on the Amazon.co.uk chart only eight after customers could preorder the book, and before neither release date nor price were announced. By mid-July 2006, approximately 1,843,000 preorders of *Deathly Hallows* had been placed on Amazon worldwide.[1] Globally, the air is filled with expectations and prefigurations, and the context of this chapter can be summarised with the word *anticipation*.

From official quarters this sense of anticipation is felt in the release marketing campaigns, which have been going on since the release day was announced on 1 February 2007, and the author herself, J.K. Rowling, has contributed to it all as well. At its website, Bloomsbury

---

1 http://www.amazon.co.uk/Harry-Potter-Characters-Games/b/ref=sv_w_h__4/202-9396445-1104642?ie=UTF8&node=470448. Accessed July 11, 2007.

Press, which owns the British rights to the series, has set up quizzes, questions, etc., and lucky fans can, for example, win an invitation to a *Deathly Hallows* midnight reading by Rowlings herself in London on July 21.[2] Scholastic Books, which owns the American rights to the Potter series, has also initiated a series of *Deathly Hallows*-related downloads, content, and quizzes; among them, a seven-question series of bookmarks, released one at a time, asking what will happen in *Deathly Hallows.* (Who will live and who will die? Is Snape good or evil? Will Hogwarts reopen?).[3] These questions also form a poll in which fans may engage, both by voting on the website and by discussing the questions in the "Discussion Chamber Message Board." Rowling herself has a very active website, where she provides information about the Potter books and about herself.[4] She updated her website diary on May 14 with a comment on potential unofficial spoilers for *Deathly Hallows*, referring to a similar warning at the unofficial fansite www.the-leaky-cauldron.org.[5] To protect her readership, she states that "I want the readers who have, in many instances, grown up with Harry, to embark on the last adventure they will share with him without knowing where they are going." At the same time, however, in both the "diary" entries and the "rumours" entries, she keeps the pot on the boil by commenting on rumours regarding what will happen in *Deathly Hallows.* (She even includes a NAQ (Never Asked Questions). Rowling also keeps her fans informed about the events taking place on July 21, such as the midnight reading in London. Both publishers and author are therefore actively involved in generating expectations regarding the plot of *Deathly Hallows* and the release of the book as a cultural event in which author, publishers, and fans participate.

In unofficial places fans are waiting for the release of *Deathly Hallows* in eager anticipation. What will happen in the novel is discussed

---

2   http://www.bloomsbury.com/harrypotter Accessed July 11, 2007

3   http://www.scholastic.com/harrypotter/home.asp Accessed July 11, 2007

4   http://www.jkrowling.com Accessed July 11, 2007

5   http://www.the-leaky-cauldron.org/ Accessed July 11, 2007

extensively, and events are planned for the release night. At the abundant unofficial websites and discussion fora, rumours are distributed, discussed, or debunked, and various theories circulate. Fan fiction is written about the end of the series, interviews by Rowling are scrutinised, clues and red herrings in the first six novels are analysed, and plot structures are discussed and projected onto the end of the series.[6] An unofficial Harry Potter festival, "Sectus 2007." will be held in London July 19-22 with a variety of events from the reading of academic papers, discussions and debates to themed sports and games. Of course, a reading room has been set up, where delegates can read *Deathly Hallows* at a "reading party" when the book is released at 00.01 (one second after midnight).[7] In addition to the officially launched initiatives, the unofficial websites and events also play an important part in the creation of the expectations for the final *Potter* book, both as the end of a seven-volume fantasy series and as a broader cultural phenomenon.

It is within this cultural framework of general anticipation that this essay examines the Harry Potter phenomenon, that is, from a point in time where the final book is still not released and where the air is still filled with excitement, rumours, theories, and expectations. After July 21, this atmosphere will inevitably have changed: even though not all books have yet been made into films, and even though the releases of the coming films will have their hype, readers and viewers will by then know *how the story ends.* In the light of this, this chapter seeks to outline aspects of the Harry Potter phenomenon as they manifest themselves in June/July 2007 with the aim of illustrating the proportions of the Potter phenomenon – both as a literary phenomenon, which has brought not only children's literature but children's *fantasy* literature to the fore over the past ten years, and as a cultural phenomenon manifesting itself primarily on the Internet. Through a discussion of Harry Potter as "satirical fantasy," this chap-

---

6 Examples of well-established unofficial sites: http://www.the-leaky-cauldron.org/, http://www.mugglenet.com/, http://www.harrypotterfanzone.com/, http://www.hpana.com/ , http://www.immeritus.org/ (includes fan-art). Accessed July 11, 2007.

7 http://www.sectus.org/index.php. Accessed July 11, 2007.

ter expands the analysis to include other aspects of it as a cultural text. It demonstrates that "Harry Potter" is a "literary-turned-cultural phenomenon," which – when viewed from a cultural studies point of view – shows how popular texts such as Harry Potter are consumed, constructed, and reconstructed far beyond the covers of the novels themselves. This essay also examines narrative notions of "endings" (both from a genre point of view and an existential point of view) and uses that as a basis for discussing if or to what extent the phenomenon of Harry Potter will "end" with the seventh and final book.

A Bit of Potter History

The beginning of the Potter phenomenon is by now well-known: the young unknown author and single mother, Joanne Rowling, got the idea for the Potter character on a train from Manchester to London; wrote *Philosopher's Stone* at cafés with her daughter asleep in her pushchair; was rejected by several publishers before Bloomsbury in August 1996 decided to publish the first *Harry Potter* book. (www.jkrowling.com; Eccleshare, 7-14) The first hardback edition of *Philosopher's Stone* numbered 500 copies. Since then, the Potter books have been an ever-growing success: The print run of the first editions of *Chambers of Secrets* and *Prisoner of Azkaban* were 10,150 and 10,000 copies, respectively, and the first hardback run of *Goblet of Fire* was 1,000,000 copies.[8] All of the books published up to now have received one or more literary awards.[9] The first six books sold 325 million copies, and they have been translated into 65 languages (as of June 2007). According to *Forbes* magazine, J.K. Rowling is now the second richest woman in global entertainment – the richest is Ameri-

---

8   www.bloomsbury.com. Accessed July 11, 2007. Bloomsbury no longer releases first print run information, but the first printing of *Deathly Hallows* is said to be 12,000,000 copies (http://product.ebay.com/Harry-Potter-and-the-Deathly-Hallows_ISBN-10_0545010225_ISBN-13_9780545010221_W0QQfvcsZ1389QQsoprZ59049480#ProdDesc. Accessed July 11, 2007)

9   http://www.bloomsbury.com/harrypotter/default.asp?sec=1. Accessed July 11, 2007.

can talk show host Oprah Winfrey[10] — and in *The Sunday Times* Rich List 2007, Rowling is the thirteenth richest woman in Britain. (The Queen is number 21).[11] The success of the Potter books raises the question of what it is about the Harry Potter books that makes them so successful and/or what it is about contemporary culture that has turned these books into such a phenomenon. The first of these two questions indicates a literary approach to the Potter books, whereas the latter implies a cultural studies approach, and both approaches can be found in the reception of Harry Potter.

Harry Potter as Fantasy Fiction

In a much quoted commentary in the *New York Times* July 7, 2003, A.S. Byatt criticises the Harry Potter books for not possessing the literary qualities of earlier or other contemporary examples of fantasy fiction, and she uses Tolkien's notion of "secondary worlds" when she claims that Rowling's world is a *secondary* secondary world "made up of intelligently patchworked derivative motifs from all sorts of children's literature – from the jolly hockey-sticks school story to Roald Dahl, from 'Star Wars' to Diana Wynne Jones and Susan Cooper." And she concludes about this world that it "has no place for the numinous. It is written for people whose imaginative lives are confined to TV cartoons, and the exaggerated (more exciting, not threatening) mirror-worlds of soaps, reality TV and celebrities." Byatt ends her commentary thus:

> It is the substitution of celebrity for heroism that has fed this phenomenon. And it is the leveling effect of cultural studies, which are as interested in hype and popularity as they are in literary merit, which they don't really believe exists. It's fine to compare the Brontes with bodice-rippers. It's become respect-

---

10 T*he Independent* 20 January 2007. "Rowling ranked the second richest woman in global entertainment" http://news.independent.co.uk/uk/this_britain/article2169251.ece . Accessed July 11, 2007.

11 http://business.timesonline.co.uk/tol/business/specials/rich_list/rich_list_search/ .Accessed July 11, 2007.

> able to read and discuss what Roland Barthes called 'consumable' books. There is nothing wrong with this, but it has little to do with the shiver of awe we feel looking through Keats's 'magic casements, opening on the foam/Of perilous seas, in faery lands forlorn.' (Byatt, "Harry Potter and the Childish Adult," *New York Times*, July 7, 2003)

Not only does Byatt criticise the *Potter* series for not being true to the genre of literary fantasy; she also attacks the ways in which literary and cultural studies make no distinction between "high" and "low" art and culture. Her critique of cultural studies seems a bit one-sided with regard to *Harry Potter*. Instead of practising the kind of cultural analysis that levels everything and where values do not exist (which seems to be Byatt's notion of cultural studies in this commentary), I wish to demonstrate that *Harry Potter* utilises and actualises literary genres, most specifically the fantasy genre, and that reading these literary genres is important for the ways in which *Harry Potter* works as a cultural text. Thus, it is not a question if Harry Potter is "good" or "bad" literature, but of acknowledging the cultural functions of the literary genres for the construction of the Harry Potter phenomenon.

Steven Barfield has suggested that, instead of being an example of the kind of fantasy in Tolkien's tradition or an example of the fantastic in Todorov's sense of the word, the *Potter* series is an example of what he calls "satirical fantasy." Barfield's argues that, instead of being situated between the mimetic genre and the fully marvellous genre, which is where Todorov places the fantastic, the *Potter* series relies on a kind of "expanded, albeit unstable, realism." (Barfield, 27) The world of the *Potter* series is distinguished by the "extraordinary ordinariness" of its magical world. (Roni Natov in Barfield, 26) Barfield sees this magical world as a "quasi-secondary world," which is much closer and more familiar to the real world we live in than the typical "secondary world" of fantasy fiction.

The magical world of the Potter series is explicable because it relies on an *expanded* set of natural laws. Even though the magical world of the Potter series differs from our "natural world," it still relies on natural laws and "naturalistic" rather than "supernatural" explanations (curses, for example, need to be learned and studied). And even though this magical world is impossible in terms of our present real-world knowledge, Barfield, ironically, reminds us of all the energy the wizards put into hiding, for example, the dragons from the Muggle world, which again places the magical world closer to our own. Barfield's use of the concepts of "expanded realism" and "quasi-secondary world" challenges Todorov's definition of the fantastic because it undermines the binary opposition of "supernatural" and "naturalistic" explanations as well as the need in fantasy fiction for strong secondary-world characteristics. Instead of a "proper" secondary world or "fantastic" hesitation between the mimetic and the marvellous, the magical world of the Potter series presents a satirical comment on our real world, "which comically point to the deficiencies in our real world and challenge them without any clear political or metaphysical framing narrative that would allow the reader to see a way forward." (Barfield, 30-31)

In 2004 Barfield expected future Potter books to continue the course of approaching our reality (Barfield, 30), and if we look at the opening of *Halfblood Prince* (book 6), Barfield's prediction appears accurate. Here the story begins with an encounter between the magical world and the fictional real world. Former Minister of Magic, Cornelius Fudge, appears in the Prime Minister of England's office to discuss current critical issues. The increasing problems with Voldemort are now affecting the Muggle world (the fictional real world) and not only the magical world: in the past week a bridge has collapsed, two women have been murdered, a damaging hurricane has ravaged the West Country, the weather has been unusually misty and cold, and people have seemed more miserable than usual. Fudge reveals to the Prime Minister that it is all the work of Voldemort and his followers: Amelia Bones, one of the women killed, was really a very gifted witch; what looked like a hurricane in the West Country was indeed the work of Death Eaters and Giants (*Halfblood Prince*, 18-19); and the mist is the result of Dementors (who drain hope and happiness out of people) breeding, and now the wizarding community feels obliged to involve the Muggle world. At the meeting with Fudge is the newly appointed Minister of Magic, Rufus Scrimgeour, who wants to takes measures against Voldemort, also in the Muggle world, by increasing the security and protection of the Prime Minister, as "'it will be a poor lookout for the Muggles if their Prime Minister gets put under the Imperius Curse,'" as he puts it. (*Halfblood Prince*, 22) Therefore Scrimgeour has placed a highly trained Auror as the Prime Minster's new assistant, without the Prime Minister knowing that his new highly efficient secretary is really a wizard (until Scrimgeour tells him so). The interaction between the magical world and the real world is again emphasised here, both by events and characters existing and acting in both worlds, and by the mirroring in the magical world of a real world logic: Fudge was forced to resign as Minister of Magic due to his inability to improve the current situation – just as the Prime Minister is accused by his political opponent of being responsible for all the terrible incidents currently happening in England. All in all, the opening of *Halfblood Prince* emphasises the way in which the clear boundaries between the magical world and its logic and the real world and its logic are blurred, or how the magical world relies on an expanded set of natural laws and real world logics. Thus, it confirms Barfield's prediction that the books would approach our reality, and we should therefore be cautious of their use of genre.

Other critics have likewise emphasised the way the *Potter* series relies on the fantasy genre as well as other genres. In an article appropriately titled "Generic Fusion and the Mosaic of *Harry Potter*," Anne Hiebert Alton outlines the genres that she sees as underlying the Potter series. She discusses the genre characteristics we see in the *Potter* series of pulp fiction, series books, mystery, *Bildungsroman,* school stories, realism, fantasy, adventure tales, and quest romance. Like Barfield, she points out how the books make use of generic fantasy elements, but that these elements are combined with realism. Rather than constructing a pure fantasy world governed by generic fantasy principles from the fantasy genre, the fantasy appears in the detail, such as in the owl post, live photographs, hippogriffs, and flobberworms. (Alton, 155) Furthermore, Alton emphasises the quest element usually found in fantasy, where a noble-natured hero with faithful companions faces dangers, and where the plot climaxes in the final battle against the main opponent – which is what Rowlings has promised will happen in *Deathly Hallows*.

Of the genres discussed by Alton, the mystery genre is of particular interest for the expected conclusions in *Deathly Hallows*. Throughout the series the underlying mystery concerns the identities of and relations between Voldemort and Harry Potter, and much of the suspense and expectations surrounding *Deathly Hallows* rely on the need for a solution to this mystery. Each of the first six books presents their specific mysteries, which are generally solved at the end of each (Alton, 144), but it is this underlying mystery that may be said to keep the series moving toward a final resolution. Alton also sees the combination of fantastic plot elements with a realistic narrative as a generic aspect of mystery. The generic aspects of detective fiction, which Alton considers a subgenre of mystery, appear in the use of false and true clues related to both the underlying mystery of the whole series and each book in itself. Alton ends her discussion of the Potter series' underlying genres by stressing that:

> [b]ecause of their conscious or unconscious awareness of the various genres fused in the books, readers gain the delight of recognition as they read something that feels familiar in form: they know the conventions of the game or the story before they begin, and thus they are looking for the tags, or signs, of fantasy, or pulp fiction, or the school story, or detective fiction. As they read the story (or progress through the game), they not only find these tags but also start to anticipate how Rowlings will include others specific to the genre they are reading. (Alton, 159)

Thus, the use of literary genres in the *Potter* books does not only structure the individual novel and the series as such; it also functions as a way for readers to anticipate what will happen later in the story and how the plot can be constructed. In so far as this chapter wants to demonstrate how the cultural phenomenon of Harry Potter is manifested at a particular point in time (summer 2007), the question of literary genres and Alton's view of their functions become highly relevant: much of the anticipation and expectations for the final book rely on genre awareness, and if we consider all the rumours and speculation on the official and unofficial Harry Potter websites, we see that readers do indeed look for genre tags and conventions when they discuss the series in general and *Deathly Hallows* – and how the story will end – in particular.

HarryPotterSeven.Com

'Fan critics' have offered their own guides to the final book and how the story will end. The website the-leaky-cauldron.org, a well-established unofficial Harry Potter site, has a section called HarryPotterSeven.Com, which comprises a comprehensive fan guide to the final book in the series "from some of the most knowledgeable fans online." The aim of the guide is to "[wrap] up almost a decade of speculation as we head to the moment when speculation ends," and it features essays, round-ups, predictions clues, hints, and tips. As a whole, the guide offers three different strategies for determining what will happen: 1. ask the author, 2. check for literary genres, 3. check narrative structures of the first six books. Relying on the first strategy, one essay in the guide presents and discusses what Rowling has said about book 7 by giving hints and clues across ten years of interviews.[12] These hints and clues are ranked according to importance (from "high importance" to "unimportant to the big picture") and commented on. Of high importance is the fact that Harry has his mother's eyes; that we will find out more about Dumbledore (who will *not* "do a Gandalf" – he is truly dead); and that it is of great importance that we do not know if Snape is evil or not. However, we are also told that Rowling often teases the reader. (She is quoted as having said that she does not lie about the books, but that she might have given "misleading an-

---

12 Lisa Bunker and Deborah Skinner, "Hint, Hint: Jo Rowling Speaks about *Harry Potter and the Deathly Hallows*". http://www.the-leaky-cauldron.org/#static:bookseven/hinthint. Accessed July 11, 2007.

swers unintentionally or [she] may have answered truthfully at the time and then changed [her] mind in a subsequent book.")[13] So even though Rowling's statements in interviews and elsewhere are seen as the best way of predicting the end, one should still be careful when reading them.

Focusing on the second strategy, Emily Bytheway [sic], in an essay called "Divination Made Easier – A Few Guidelines to Making Prediction for Book 7," lists four guiding principles for predicting what will happen in *Deathly Hallows* if one is interested in being able to "point to a list of predictions written a week before the book comes out and say 'See! I was right!'"[14] Her principles are: 1. stick to generalities (the opposite would be to create elaborate scenes of, for example, the final confrontation between Harry and Voldemort – as is done in fan fiction (se below), 2: focus on the books (instead of comparing them to other similar stories – as literary critics constantly do), 3: pay attention to genre (Bytheway mentions the young adult genre, fantasy, mystery, and romance), 4: keep an open mind (which means: be prepared to be wrong). Bytheway thus refrains from asking the author and instead focuses on the books themselves and their inherent genres as means by which fans can predict the end of the story.

The final "prediction essay" in the fan guide uses the third strategy. It discusses how the plotting strategies for each book may be found in the plotting strategies for the series as such. Rowling has repeatedly emphasised that she had the plot for the entire series planned before book 1; and that consequently "you won't need a prequel; by the time I am finished, you will know enough."[15] This essay concludes that the plots and subplots of each of the first six books have been resolved in different ways, the most "artistically satisfying" being

---

13 "The Leaky Cauldron and MN Interview with Joanne Kathleen Rowling". 16 July 2005. http://www.the-leaky-cauldron.org/#static:tlcinterviews/jkrhbp3. Accessed July 11, 2007.

14 Emily Bytheway, "Divination Made Easier: A Few Guidelines for Making Predictions for Book 7". http://www.the-leaky-cauldron.org/#static:bookseven/predictions. Accessed July 11, 2007.

15 http://www.jkrowling.com/textonly/en/news_view.cfm?id=80. Accessed July 11, 2007.

when plots and subplots are resolved "interrelatedly with perspective change or reversal" (as with the revelation that Sirius Black is innocent after all). Based on this, the plot of the series is expected to be resolved in similar ways. This would also mean that clues can be found in the first six books, also in terms of their plotting strategies, which is why, according to this third strategy, a focus on the books themselves and their narrative structures is a very relevant way of predicting what will happen in *Deathly Hallows*.[16]

All the essays in HarryPotterSeven.Com predict what will happen in *Deathly Hallows* and thus concern themselves with the end of the series and how it can be anticipated. But why is it so interesting for readers and fans to speculate about the end? The *Potter* series' reliance on the genres of fantasy and mystery is part of the reason, but these genre conventions can be put into perspective by considering why, in general, it matters so much to people how stories end. This issue has been discussed extensively by narrative theorists.

Reflections on the End

In general, narrative theory emphasises the need for endings. In his now-classic book published in 1966, Frank Kermode connects endings of fiction to more general needs and desires for endings.[17] Kermode's underlying assumption is that we use fictions to make sense of our lives. Fiction is particularly suitable for sense-making, because there is a human need for order, and literature offers form and order to a disordered world. Contrary to (our experience of) reality, fictions can provide order and form where beginning, middle, and end are consistent, that is, where past, present and future belong to the same order. In (our experience of) reality this is not the case, even though we have a "deep need for intelligible Ends. We project ourselves – a

---

16 The majority of the other essays in the guide concern specific hitherto unanswered questions: One essay analyses Snape's loyalties in the books published thus far, and other essays discuss the future of Hogwarts, the importance of the prophecy etc.

17 Frank Kermode, *The Sense of an Ending: Studies in the theory of fiction.* New Edition. Oxford and New York: Oxford University Press, 2000.

small, humble elect, perhaps – past the End, so as to see the structure whole, a thing we cannot do from our spot of time in the middle." (Kermode, 8) This means that fiction and their plots provide us with temporary models of consonance. To stress his underlying assumption, Kermode says, "Men in the middest make considerable imaginative investments in coherent patterns which, by the provision of an end, make possible a satisfying consonance with the origins and with the middle. This is why the image of the end can never be *permanently* falsified." (Kermode, 17) Kermode's argument is therefore existential in nature: we desire and need Ends for sense-making (for giving shape and meaning to our lives), and since we cannot experience our life from anywhere else than "the middle," fiction becomes a way of making sense of our lives.[18] In Kermode's view, then, fiction serves a very fundamental and existential role for people.

If we compare Kermode's existential discussion of the need for endings to genre-based discussions of endings, we have a framework both for discussing the expectations for the end of the *Potter* series and the way *Deathly Hallows* will actually end the series. In "Magic Abjured: Closure in Children's Fantasy Fiction," Sarah Gilead argues that many children's fantasy fictions are structured within a "return-to-reality closural frame," and she outlines three basic types. The first is where the fantasy narrative is an exposure of forbidden wishes and emotions, and where the protagonist at the return-to-reality is "a more fully formed social entity" Here the return-to-reality normalises fantasy as socializing therapy (as in *The Wonderful Wizard of Oz*), and there is a strong element of *Bildung* in this type. In the second type, fantasy is rejected or denied in the return-to-reality and there is no linear socialization plot (as in Lewis Carroll's *Alice* books). Here fantasy is seen as something that "fosters a neurotic avoidance of social and psychic realities." In the third type, the return-to-reality reveals both the "seductive force and the dangerous potentiality of fantasy," and it does so in a tragic mode (as in *Peter Pan*). (Gilead, 278) Gilead points to the ways in which particularly the third type of children's fan-

---

18 Kermode's argument includes very interesting aspects about time and the experience of time, but an examination of these would be beyond this discussion.

tasy fiction may disturb the hierarchies of realities (where the extraliterary reality is the highest level of reality and the fantasy narrative the lowest, and in between is the fictional reality, which potentially mediates between the other two):

> But this hierarchy is unstable: the fantasy may satirize the reality claims of ordinary modes of perception and experience, and the frame reality may be more consoling and escapist than the preceding fantasy narrative. The return frame may establish the hierarchy of realities by classifying the foregoing fantasy as dangerously-or safely-remote from extraliterary reality; or it may, ironically, reveal the equal or even deeper fictionality of both literary and extraliterary versions of reality (Gilead, 289).

Broadly speaking, the end thus has different functions in the three basic types, which gives a different (or supplementary) view on endings from Kermode's existential: the end as a return-to-reality in children's fantasy fiction can both been seen as *Bildung* or therapy from a socio-cultural point of view (as in the first type), as repression from a psychological point of view (as in the second type), or as fundamentally disturbing from either a socio-cultural, psychological or existential point of view (as in the third type).

Even if the *Potter* series as a whole does not have the explicit "return-to-reality" structure (it is highly unlikely that Harry Potter will abandon the magical world and go back to live in the Muggle world), the fantasy narrative of books 1-5 are framed by the fictional real world of the Dursleys, where Harry spends his summers away from Hogwarts. The hierarchy of the fictional reality and the fantasy narrative discussed by Gilead is central to the Potter series as a whole as well, exactly because it is challenged: The fictional real world is to a certain extent more alienating for readers than the magical world. (Harry Potter lives in a closet, his aunt and uncle hate him, his is constantly being treated in an unfair way, his cousin is cruel, he does not seem to know anybody outside the Dursley family, etc.) Even though Harry develops as a character in the magical world (this is where the *Bildung* aspect manifests itself), his relation to the Dursleys does not develop: *nothing* seems to change in the Dursleys' part of the fictional real world. Together with the ironic ways in which for example the Minister of Magic and The Office of Misinformation patiently try to help the Muggle world, and Mr Weasley's fascination of what are for a wizard low-tech Muggle inventions such as cars, this shows the supremacy in the fictional world of the magical world over the fictional real world. At the same time, however, the fantasy narrative mirrors the logics of not only the fictional reality of the series but the extra-literary reality (by means of "expanded realism"), which makes it an ironic version of that same reality rather than a kind of utopian reality. The very fact that there is something called The Office of Misinformation seems an ironic comment on bureaucratic institutions. As Barfield argues, there is no clear political or metaphysical framing (either in the fictional real world of the fantasy narrative), which again makes the fantasy narrative – as well as the fictional reality – ironic versions of aspects of our own world.

So, how do satirical fantasy fictions like the *Potter* series end? And what effect does the end of the story have for *Harry Potter* as a series of novels and cultural phenomenon? There is a need for narrative and thematic closure (see below), which would correspond to Kermode's discussion of endings as existential needs. At the same time, however, there may be no political or metaphysical framing of the Potter series to rely on, which creates a potential paradox: is it possible to tie all the loose ends (plot-wise and thematically) and still maintain the satirical aspect and the tangled hierarchies of extra-literary reality, fictional reality, and fantasy world? Obviously *Deathly Hallows* will end the series, but not necessarily the cultural phenomenon of *Harry Potter*, and not necessarily the tangled hierarchies of realities.

What Ends?

As shown so far in this chapter, the anticipation of the end in *Deathly Hallows* is framed by literary conventions, the author's and the publishers' hints and clues, and readers' and fans' prefigurations and "preconstructions" of the end in terms of theories, analyses, and general speculation about what will happen in the final novel. At this point, however, it is important to repeat the interconnection between author and publishers, fans and readers for the construction of Harry Potter as a cultural text "beyond" the series of seven books by Rowling. The existence of Harry Potter fan fiction is an example of this, as it represents the initiatives taken from official sides to postpone the end of the Potter phenomenon.

Potter fans do not only *discuss* the end of the series on the basis of the structure of the first six books, interviews with Rowling, and various hints and clues; they also *write* their own versions of Potter stories, in which they produce their own fictions about the Potter characters and their fictional world using the various genres on which the Potter series relies.[19] Fanfiction is a significant part of the Potter phenomenon on the Internet, and several ends to the Potter series have already been written, but by fans. At harrypotterfanfiction.com, according to its editors the oldest dedicated Harry Potter fanfiction site on the Internet (launched in February 2001), more than 41,000 Harry Potter stories are uploaded, many of which narrate Harry's seventh year at Hogwarts.[20] Without going into detail about all these fanfictions, it is clear from these texts that genres are a much-used means for writers to rely on when they write their own *Potter* narratives. Several generic categories are used to organise the website, among them drama, horror/dark, mystery, romance, action/adventure, young adult, humour, and crossover. Together with story format (one-shot, short story, novella, novel, short story collection and songfic) and popular character pairings (Harry/Ginny, Ron/Hermione, James/Lily, Draco/Hermione) the genres are used by both writers and readers to frame the stories.

In connection with the coming release of *Deathly Hallows,* A Writers Duel was set up for fans to write the best end to the story in three "challenges": "When Harry meets Ginny," "The Last Horcrux," and "It Ends with a Scar". The competition ran from May 4 to May 16, 2007.

---

19 In addition to the electronic fanfiction texts, at least two books of fan writing have been published: Bill Adler, *Kids' Letters to Harry Potter from around the World: an unauthorized edition.* New York: Carroll & Graff Publishers, 2001; and Sharon Moore, *We Love Harry Potter: We'll Tell You Why.* New York: St. Martin's Griffin, 1999.

20 www.harrypotterfanfiction.com. Accessed July 11, 2007.

The winning story was Lupa Manera's one-shot "We Cannot Lose."[21] It tells the end of the Potter series as seen and narrated from Ginny's point of view and in the first person. In this story, Tonks' soul is taken by a Dementor, and consequently the Order members must kill her to relieve her pain. The central characters are all there: Remus, McGonogall and Sirius of the Old Order, and Harry, Ron, Hermione, Fred and the twins, who have just become members of the New Order. The story ends with Ginny and Harry realising that they will have to fight on together, since — and this is put into the mouth of Ginny's father, Mr Weasley — they are not only fighting Death Eaters, dark creatures of Lord Voldemort, but despair in itself. "Succumbing to the despair that threatened each and every one of us would be the only defeat."

This story is revealing in terms of expectations for endings and the paradoxical need for the *Potter* stories to both end and continue: in this story, the end of something is the beginning of something else (like the symbol of the Phoenix, after which the Order is named). By introducing the *new* Order, the writer here shows a way in which a new series – with a new set of characters, including Ginny as the main character – could be initiated. By emphasising "despair" as the dark force against which they fight, the story moves beyond the actual quest of the Potter series, *internalising* the darkness, again setting the scene for new quests to appear. Internalising Voldemort and what he stands for in the form of "despair" means that there will always be dark forces to fight, and so this story uses one of the premises of the fantasy genre as a framework for ending the *Potter* story and for initiating the Ginny story and thus keeping the narrative moving on.[22]

The winning story from harrypotterfanfiction.com suggests that there is another opposing desire at work together with the need for narrative closure and endings, which Kermode emphasises in *The Sense of an Ending*. It is the desire to be suspended between disorder and order, which is one of the characteristics of both the fantasy genre and the mystery genre. This does not reduce the impact of the

---

21 http://www.harrypotterfanfiction.com/viewstory.php?chapterid=257809. Accessed July 11, 2007.
22 http://www.fanfictionworld.net/contestarchive/index.php. Accessed July 11, 2007.

ending on the entire narrative – the end is still a driving force in the dynamics of narrative – but the end itself, and the solutions it is supposed to reveal, is incompatible with the desire of suspense.

It is, of course, possible for fans to write their own "alternative endings" to the Potter series after July 21, 2007, but knowing then how the series will have ended, fan writers will be in a different position. Not only will they know how the plot ends (and who lives and who dies), but the context of the Potter books will be likely to have changed. On www.the-leaky-cauldron.org's HarryPotterSeven.Com, "the end of an era" is mentioned, and maybe the *"Harry Potter* era" *is* ending.

There are some signs that this is the case: HarryPotterSeven.Com collects money for Book Aid, but *only until* July 21 can Harry Potter fans donate money to it. This suggests that the editors of www.the-leaky-cauldron.org acknowledge that the world for Harry Potter and his fans will be changed after July 21, and that, possibly, the interest in Harry Potter, or this website at least, might diminish after that. Fans thus see July 21, 2007 not only as the day when *Deathly Hallows* is released (to end the *Potter* narrative and a decade of speculation) but *also* as the day after which the Potter phenomenon, at least at the unofficial websites, will have changed.

Official initiatives are taken, however, to extend the Potter era beyond July 21, 2007: Rowling will go on a reading tour in the United States in October 2007, and a *Harry Potter* theme park is planned to open at the Universal Orlando Resort in Florida in 2009, where it will be part of Orlando's Islands of Adventure that already houses Marvel Super Heroes and Dr. Seuss islands.[23] These planned "post-*Deathly Hallows*" events are, of course, also part of the future marketing of *Harry Potter*, but at the same time they also point to the wish to extend the *Potter* era beyond the publication of the final book and to keep fans interested in the *Potter* phenomenon even after they have read the final book.

Taken together, these *Harry Potter* constructions illustrate that *Harry Potter* has expanded beyond its status as a literary phenome-

---

23 "Harry Potter Theme Park Planned," BBC, May 31, 2007. http://news.bbc.co.uk/2/hi/entertainment/6706939.stm. Accessed July 11, 2007.

non and become a complex textual and cultural phenomenon, produced and reproduced by different agents.

Harry Potter and Secondary Worlds

As appears from the above, the Harry Potter phenomenon is not only a literary phenomenon but also very much an Internet phenomenon. Not only have the readers of the *Potter* books "grown up with" Harry (as critics have emphasised); the phenomenon of Harry Potter has also grown with the phenomenon of the Internet as a cultural framework or as a new way for cultural texts to be consumed, constructed, and reconstructed. Of course one could insist on treating the *Potter* series as six (soon seven) books, without paying attention to the aspects of the phenomenon that clearly exceeds the books themselves, but then one would not be able to account for the cultural (or literary, for that matter) impact of the series.

If we return to the discussion of genre use in *Harry Potter* and Byatt's claim that the secondary world of *Harry Potter* is a *secondary* secondary world, this radical contextualisation of the *Potter* books becomes significant. The emphasis in fantasy theory on the secondary world presupposes a primary world, a real world, from which the secondary world and its logic deviate. And of course, the magical world of *Harry Potter* does that, but what is more important is that the primary world may differ from "itself." All the hype around the release of *Deathly Hallows*, including Rowling's website, other official and unofficial websites, and fanfiction sites, is *part* of the real world, which means – as many postmodern thinkers have stressed – that our world is a mediated world and that reality has become hyperreality. To understand *Potter* as a (secondary) secondary world, we need to also focus our attention to the primary world – which may also be a "secondary" primary world, where clear distinctions between art and reality, high and low art, readers and writers, writers and publishers/producers are not so easily distinguished from each other. In his essay "Harry Potter's World: Magic, Technoculture and Becoming Human," Peter Appelbaum asks us not to ask what it is about the Potter books that have made them such a success, but rather "what it is about our culture that embraces the Harry Potter books and has turned Harry Potter into such a phenomenon?" (Appelbaum, 25). This is a way of describing the (contextual) primary world as the reason for the success of *Harry Potter*, rather than the secondary world of the series itself.

Appelbaum focuses on the issues of technology, magic, and the role of science as popular culture resources. He argues that "the books and associated fanware are key sites for the cultural construction of science and technology; in speaking to issues of magic and science, technology and culture, *Harry Potter* is emblematic of the kinds of cultural practices that lead to its popularity." (Appelbaum, 26) In other words, it is the primary world – to which *Harry Potter*'s secondary world should be related in certain ways according to traditional fantasy genre theory – that accounts for the success of *Harry Potter*, which again suggests that the analysis of *Harry Potter* is something more than an analysis of the books in the series.

One might then say that it is no longer a question of literary quality (Byatt) but of a literary-turned-into-cultural phenomenon reflecting a certain cultural context and participating in it. To say that the *Potter* books are "satirical fantasy" means that the secondary world of the *Potter* books is used to present a satire of the 'secondary' primary world. So maybe it is a secondary secondary world when measured against Tolkien's definition (and his writing), but only in so far as the secondary world should be significantly different from the primary world. If it is rather a satirical reflection of that world, there is nothing "secondary" about the *Potter* books. If the *Harry Potter* phenomenon is considered a cultural text, reaching beyond the books themselves, it does not make much sense to speak in terms of primary and secondary worlds in the first place, as the borders between what is *outside* the logics of the *Potter* world, and what is inside it become blurred – in particular if the *Potter* series is considered satirical fantasy.

So, how does this way of viewing the Potter phenomenon affect the expectations for *Deathly Hallows*? Both because of the genres the *Potter* books rely on (first and foremost fantasy and mystery) and Rowling's statements about the final book, thematic and narrative closure and ends are expected in *Deathly Hallows*. At the same time the above discussion of the *Potter* phenomenon shows a need for the suspension and something "beyond" the end of the series (whether in the form of a new series of fantasy books or an American theme park). After July 21, we will presumably know who will live and who will die; if Snape is good or evil; if Hogwarts will open; and where the last Horcruxes are. We may also begin to get a sense of what will happen to the *Potter* phenomenon on the Internet, and to see to what extent 2007 will turn out to be the end of the *Potter* era. Even though the *Potter* phenomenon is a complex cultural and mediated and remediated text, it is still one book that will present the thematic and narrative closure to ten years' speculation and guesswork. The futures of the other aspects (apart from the underlying plot) of the *Harry Potter* phenomenon are governed by other logics, which, as Appelbaum emphasises, require a cultural studies approach rather than a literary one.

Postscript: Harry Potter and the Narrative Order

He did not die. Or, he may have died momentarily, but lived after all. Voldemort, on the other hand, did die, along with several beloved characters such as Remus Lupin and Dobby. The final Horcrux was Harry himself. Hogwarts did reopen. Snape was loyal to Dumbledore – even when he killed him. Ron and Hermione married, and so did Harry and Ginny. These are the answers to some of the most frequently asked questions about the ending of the series as revealed in *Deathly Hallows*. It convincingly ties together all the loose ends and provides its readers with narrative as well as thematic closure. The underlying mystery is revealed (Voldemort unknowingly placed part of his soul in Harry when he tried to kill him as a young child, and Snape has guarded Harry all the years in love of Harry's mother), and the "return-to-reality" structure often found in children's fantasy is found here as well, but with a twist. Harry does not return to the Muggle world (the fictional reality), but the fantasy world returns to "normal." In the epilogue set sixteen years later, we find an echo of Harry setting off to Hogwarts for the first time, as we witness Ron and Hermione and Harry and Ginny sending their children to Hogwarts on the Hogwarts Express from Platform 9 ¾. Now a parent himself (with a son named after *both* Dumbledore and Snape), Harry is undoubtedly wiser and has learned from his experiences in the series (this is the *Bildung* aspect of the series), and the logic of the fantasy world is restored. The fact that the fantasy world remains an integrated part of the fictional reality and the sustained use of "expanded realism" places the *Potter* series as a whole within the genre of satirical fantasy.

The expanded realism is only set out of play in the significant epiphanic moment when Harry almost dies, or dies momentarily, and Dumbledore reappears. This moment of recognition is clearly set beyond time (Harry describes it as "a long time later, or maybe no time at all" (*Deathly Hallows,* 565) and space (it is a surreal version of King's Cross Station) and the logics of both the fictional real world and the fantasy narrative (relying on expanded realism). This passage (chapter 35, "King's Cross") reveals central elements of the plot (for example, the seventh Horcrux and the Hallows), and it cannot be explained by means of expanded realism. Dumbledore's final words places it into what Todorov would call the marvellous: Harry asks if this is real or only happening inside his head, and Dumbledore answers: "Of course it is happening inside your head, Harry, but why on earth should that mean that it is not real?" (*Deathly Hallows*, 579) This comment functions almost as a supplement to the use of realism in the series: "realism" depends on definitions of "reality," and that is a negotiable term in the fictional reality of the *Potter* books as well as in other kinds of realities.

In August Bloomsbury uploaded a web-chat with J.K. Rowling from July 30, 2007, when she answered readers' post-*Deathly Hallows* questions about the characters' future lives and the wizarding world in general. According to The Leaky Cauldron, Rowling received more than 120,000 questions.[24] Here she clarifies not only what happens in *Deathly Hallows,* but also "after" *Deathly Hallows.* For example, Rowlings tells us that Hermione has a career in the

---

24 "Web-chat with J.K. Rowling, July 30, 2007". http://www.bloomsbury.com/harrypotter/default.asp?sec=3 . Accessed August 8, 2007.

Ministry of Magic and that Ginny ends up as a Quidditch correspondent for the Daily Prophet; she also provides information not found in the books (such as a description of Hufflepuff common room and how it is accessed). All in all, her attitude to her own fictional world suggests that it still exists, even after the final book has been written, and that its characters will "live on" independently of her as their author. (She says, for example, that "[she's] got the feeling" that Harry did not give the Marauders Map to any of his children, but that James took it himself.)

www.the-leaky-cauldron.org has set up a new writing contest – this time not about the plot of the series but about how the series has affected its readers (ages 13 and older).[25] And at harrypotterfanfiction.com texts are still being written about the Hogwarts era, but also about the era preceding the Potter series and the one following it (which the website refers to as "the next generation" or "post-Hogwarts").[26] On August 5, a 16-year-old French Harry Potter fan was arrested for having posted an unofficial (but "semi-professional") French translation of *Deathly Hallows* on the Internet, apparently dissatisfied that non-English speaking readers will have to wait for months for translations of *Deathly Hallows*.[27] Taken together these official and unofficial initiatives suggest that the *Potter* era is not over yet. The final book has been published and mysteries have been resolved, but as a cultural text *Harry Potter* is still being consumed, constructed and reconstructed. Even though the books have been judged "very, very longterm – perennial classics" (by Jon Howells from Waterstone's), only time will tell if the books and the phenomenon of *Harry Potter* will last. J.K. Rowling puts it this way: "When all the hype and everything else dies down, they

---

25 "Tell a Tale of Harry Potter". http://www.the-leaky-cauldron.org/2007/8/6/tell-a-tale-of-harry-potter. Accessed August 8, 2007.

26 For example the text "Chapter 1: Dawn Over a New World" http://www.harrypotterfanfiction.com/viewstory.php?chapterid=264693 Accessed 8 August 2007.

27 "Harry Potter and the boy wizard translator". *Guardian Unlimited*, August 8, 2007. http://books.guardian.co.uk/harrypotter/story/0,,2144206,00.html Accessed August 8, 2007.

will have to float or sink on their own merits, won't they? So in 50 years time, if people are still reading them, they deserve to be read, and if they're not, then that's OK."[28]

---

[28] "JK Rowling already writing post-Potter novel". *Guardian Unlimited*, July 27, 2007. http://books.guardian.co.uk/harrypotter/story/0,,2136432,00.html#article_continue Accessed August 8, 2007.

References

Adler, Bill. *Kids' Letters to Harry Potter from Around the World : An Unauthorized Collection.* New York: Carroll & Graf Publishers, 2001.

Aethon. "Chapter 1: Dawn Over a New World" <http://www.harrypotterfanfiction.com/viewstory.php?chapterid=264693> Accessed August 8, 2007.

Akbar, Arifa. "Rowling ranked the second richest woman in global entertainment." *The Independent,* January 20, 2007. <http://news.independent.co.uk/uk/this_britain/article2169251.ece> Accessed July 11, 2007.

Alton, Anne Hiebert. "Generic Fusion and the Mosaic of Harry Potter." *Harry Potter's World: Multidisciplinary Critical Perspectives.* Edited by Elizabeth E. Heilman. New York: Routledge, 2003.

Appelbaum, Peter. "Harry Potter's World: Magic, Technoculture, and Becoming Human." In *Harry Potter's World: Multidisciplinary Critical Perspectives.* Edited by Elizabeth E. Heilman. New York: Routledge, 2003.

Barfield, Steven. "Fantasy and the Interpretation of Fantasy in Harry Potter." *Topic: The Washington and Jefferson College Review,* 54 (2004): 24-32. Bloomsbury Publishing website. <http://www.bloomsbury.com/harrypotter> Accessed July 11, 2007.

Brown, Stephen. *Consuming Books: The Marketing and Consumption of Literature.* London and New York: Routledge, 2006.

Bunker, Lisa and Deborah Skinner. "Hint, Hint: Jo Rowling Speaks about *Harry Potter and the Deathly Hallows.*" <http://www.the-leaky-cauldron.org/#static:bookseven/hinthint> Accessed July 11, 2007.

Byatt, A. S. "Harry Potter and the Childish Adult." *The New York Times,* July 7, 2003, A: 13.

Bytheway, Emily. "Divination made easier: A Few Guidelines for Making Predictions for Book 7." <http://www.the-leaky-cauldron.org/#static:bookseven/predictions>. Accessed July 11, 2007.

Chidel, Adam. "JK Rowling already writing post-Potter novel." *Guardian Unlimited,* July 27, 2007. http://books.guardian.co.uk/

harrypotter/story/0,,2136432,00.html#article_continue> Accessed August 8, 2007.

Eccleshare, Julia. *A Guide to the Harry Potter Novels*. New York: Continuum, 2002. "Harry Potter theme park planned." *BBC News*. May 31, 2007. <http://news.bbc.co.uk/2/hi/entertainment/6706939.stm> Accessed July 11, 2007.

Heilman, Elizabeth E. *Harry Potter's World: Multidisciplinary Critical Perspectives*. New York: Routledge Falmer, 2003.

Kermode, Frank. *The Sense of an Ending: Studies in the Theory of Fiction. With a New Epilogue*. New York: Oxford University Press, 2000.

Manera, Lupa. "We Cannot Lose" <www.harrypotterfanfiction.com> Accessed July 11, 2007.

Moore, Sharon. *We Love Harry Potter!: We'll Tell You Why*. New York: St. Martin's Griffin, 1999.

"Rich List Search" *Times Online*. <http://business.timesonline.co.uk/tol/business/specials/rich_list/rich_list_search/ > Accessed July 11, 2007.

Rowling, J. K. *Harry Potter and the Deathly Hallows*. London: Bloomsbury, 2005.

⎯⎯⎯⎯. *Harry Potter and the Half-Blood Prince*. London: Bloomsbury, 2005.

⎯⎯⎯⎯. Official website. <http://www.jkrowling.com> Accessed July 11, 2007

Scholastic, Inc. <http://www.scholastic.com/harrypotter/home.asp> Accessed July 11, 2007.

Schwartz, Daniel R. "The Consolation of Form: The Theoretical and Historical Significance of Frank Kermode's the Sense of an Ending." In *The Centennial Review* 28-29 (1984): 29-47.

Sectus 2007 (unofficial Harry Potter event) <http://www.sectus.org/index.php> Accessed July 11, 2007.

"Tell a Tale of Harry Potter". <http://www.the-leaky-cauldron.org/2007/8/6/tell-a-tale-of-harry-potter> Accessed August 8, 2007.

The Leaky Cauldron (unofficial fansite). <http://www.the-leaky-cauldron.org/> Accessed July 11, 2007.

The Leaky Cauldron and MN. Interview with Joanne Kathleen Rowling."

July 16, 2005. <http://www.the-leaky-cauldron.
org/#static:tlcinterviews/jkrhbp3> Accessed July 11, 2007.

Willsher, Kim. "Harry Potter and the boy wizard translator". *Guardian Unlimited*, August 8, 2007. <http://books.guardian.co.uk/harrypotter/story/0,,2144206,00.html > Accessed August 8, 2007.

"**Web-chat with J.K. Rowling**, July 30, 2007." <http://www.bloomsbury.com/harrypotter/default.asp?sec=3> Accessed August 8, 2007.

www.amazon.co.uk
<http://www.amazon.co.uk/Harry-Potter-Characters-Games/b/ref=sv_w_h__4/202-9396445-1104642?ie=UTF8&node=470448> Accessed July 11, 2007.

Jørgen Riber Christensen

Certain Regressive Tendencies in Rowling and Tolkien
Fantasy and Realism

This chapter discusses the relationship between fantasy and realism. With characters that can perform magic and settings that are often medieval and feudal, fantasy may be considered the opposite of realism, which concerns itself with present-day social problems in a contemporary setting. Fantasy can consequently be regarded as an escapist and regressive genre. However, this chapter examines the *Harry Potter* books and *The Lord of the Rings* trilogy in order to discuss whether fantasy is regressive and without connection to contemporary reality. Perhaps surprisingly, the chapter concludes that the theory of critical realism does share similarities with fantasy.

The Family Discourse in *Harry Potter*
One of the memorable scenes from Chris Columbus' adaptation of *Harry Potter and the Sorcerer's Stone* shows Harry standing spellbound in front of the Mirror of Erised. In it, his deceased parents, James and Lily, smile weakly at him, nodding slightly when Harry asks "Mum - Dad?" The book's description of the scene can show better than the film Harry's dawning realisation that he is looking at his parents:

> He looked in the mirror again. A woman standing right behind his reflection was smiling at him and waving. He reached out a hand and felt the air behind him. If she was really there, he'd

touch her, their reflections were so close together, but he felt only air – she and the others existed only in the mirror.

She was a very pretty woman. She had dark red hair and her eyes – *her eyes are just like mine*, Harry thought, edging a little closer to the glass. Bright green – exactly the same shape, but then he noticed that she was crying; smiling, but crying at the same time. The tall, thin, black-haired man standing next to her put his arms around her. He wore glasses, and his hair was untidy. It stuck up at the back, just as Harry's did.

Harry was so close to the mirror now that his nose was nearly touching that of his reflection.

"Mom?" he whispered. "Dad?"

They just looked at him smiling. (Rowling, 208-09)

The magical Mirror of Erised shows what one desires the most. (Erised is "desire" spelled backward, and the mirror carries the inscription: "erised stra ehru oyt ube cafru oyt on wohsi" — which reversed is "I show not your face but your heart's desire.") When Ron looks into the mirror, he sees himself as the head boy and a successful Quidditch player, and Dumbledore claims he sees a pair of socks: "One can never have enough socks." Harry's deepest desire, then, is to have a family.

One of the strongest discourses, perhaps the dominant one, running through all the *Harry Potter* books is about family. First of all, Harry is an orphan in the literary tradition of Oliver Twist and David Copperfield, and his main quest may be to win a family. He does not succeed in this until the end of the final volume, when he has a family of his own and is married with children. Significantly his family is first presented to the readers at the moment on Platform 9 ¾ at King's Cross when Harry and Ginny are sending their children away to their own boarding school. Even as the family celebrates, it is separated: "The train began to move, and Harry walked alongside it, watching his son's thin face, already ablaze with excitement. Harry kept smiling and waving, even though it was like a little bereavement, watching his son glide away from him…" (Rowling 2007, 607)

The family discourse in the books examines different constellations.

Harry's own nuclear family is tragically broken up by Voldemort. He is placed with his foster family, the Dursleys, at 4 Privet Drive. Vernon and Petunia Dursley and their ridiculously spoiled son, Dudley, form Rowling's devastating critique of the suburban nuclear family. This family only brings misery to the young Harry, and the sibling rivalry with Dudley has its parallel in Harry's much more serious and dangerous conflict with Draco Malfoy. The class aspect aggravates the conflict with Draco. His place in the magical realm can be seen as Rowling's critique of the value system of the upper classes. The Weasleys provide a positive contrast to the Dursleys. The Weasleys are a nuclear family, but an old-fashioned atmosphere surrounds them. The family has seven children; they live in a large rambling, seven-story house with a garden that in more than one sense is wild. The house is called The Burrow and is located in the village of Ottery St. Catchpole. The Dursley are Muggles, and the Weasleys belong to the magic world. Whereas Molly Weasley cannot hide her maternal feelings for Harry, who appreciates the warmth and concern, Harry has to go through an extensive catalogue of father figures across seven thick volumes in his quest for a father. Dumbledore is the obvious choice, but he also alienates Harry. Hagrid is not quite up to the job, though his size as such corresponds to a young child's conception of a father. Sirius Black is Harry's godfather, but just as is Harry's father, Sirius is lost to Harry through death. Negative father figures are present as well. Where Vernon Dursley is a parody, Voldemort may in a sense be regarded as the feared father figure from a classical Freudian Oedipal conflict.

Harry's quest for a family and a father is not successful. When J.K. Rowling was writing the first Harry Potter book, she was an unemployed single mother living on public assistance (Nel, 20). In the year 2000 alone, she donated £500,000 to Britain's National Council for One Parent Families and as an ambassador for the council she has remarked that a quarter of Britain's children are raised by single parents: "We may not be some people's preferred norm, but we are here." (Nel, 25-26). Positively, it may in other words be expected that the *Harry Potter* books are a plea for tolerance for different forms of family structures and lives, and negatively, that they are a critique of the nuclear family. Rowling has taken care to provide two alternatives to the nuclear family for Harry – and for the readers. One is the boarding school Hogwarts, where the teachers and staff bring up the children *in loco parentis*. The methods used are strict and authoritarian and include severe forms of punishment. The other alternative is the peer group consisting of Harry, Hermione, and Ron. This is where Harry's emotional needs are fulfilled.

The family discourse in the Harry Potter books is tied firmly to the changes in the family institution during the last decades in which society has taken over many of the functions that earlier belonged to the family. The upbringing and education of children take place outside the family in institutions, and society cares for the old and the disabled. Family members live active lives outside the home, and only few functions remain in the family such as rest and perhaps meals. Extra weight has been added to the emotional and sexual functions of the family, and family members may find it difficult to cope, especially because work outside the home is demanding. Just as the family has been emptied of functions, the home itself is empty most of the day. It has already been noted how many children are being raised by a single parent. If a father is in the home, he is not a patriarchal authority, and the mother must both cope with a job and the home. The German sociologist Thomas Ziehe described how the changes of the family institution together with other changes in society (Ziehe, 1975) have resulted in a new character formation, the narcissist. The narcissist has a super-ego that is not as domineering and strong as the super-ego resulting from the traditional, patriarchal Oedipus conflict; the father figure internalised at the end of the conflict is a reflection of the weakened father role in modern families. All in all, the mind of a narcissist is not as strong as the mind produced by an Oedipal conflict of a more patriarchal society, and the narcissist compensates for this by joining a peer group, friends of a similar disposition. In the *Harry Potter* universe Hermione, Ron, and Harry form such a peer-group, which serves two functions. The reader is attracted to them: the peer group may reflect the reader's own social and mental needs, and it offers an alternative and supplement to family life.

Where the peer group seems a contemporary answer to what may be termed the crisis of family, Rowling's other alternative, Hogswarts, seems to reflect a more regressive character. Hogwarts has a decidedly medieval or feudal atmosphere with all the trimmings of a castle. This public school can only be attended by the social class of magicians. There is no admittance for Muggles. In the hierarchical system of the school, the teachers exercise patriarchal authority, and they distribute punishment or affection at will. A patriarch of a kind that has not been walking the earth for decades has here substituted the father figure that may be more or less absent in modern families. One of the reasons for the powerful appeal of the *Potter* books may be found here. The longing for a father figure is fulfilled magically at Hogwarts, the School of Witchcraft and Wizardry. The *Harry Potter* books as fantasy illustrate the function of therapy such as Bruno Bettelheim has described it in the case of fairy tales in *The Uses of Enchantment: The Meaning and Importance of Fairy Tales*. It is in the magical world of Hogwarts that children, and perhaps adults as well, can meet the great father that is no longer viable in the real (Muggle) world, but who nevertheless is part of the Oedipal conflict. Though Hogwarts in this way may fulfil a contemporary social or psychological need, this school as an answer to the dissolution of the traditional nuclear family cannot help looking back to earlier societal formations.

Among the intertextual ancestors to Hogwarts are public school novels such as Kipling's *Stalky & Co.* from 1899 and Thomas Hughes *Tom Brown's Schooldays* from 1857. Draco Malfoy harkens back to Flashman, and Tom Brown's football and cricket are comparable to Harry Potter's Quidditch. These schoolboy novels may be termed regressive today as they reflect Victorian notions of class and discipline. E.M. Forster was less enthusiastic than Hughes and Kipling about the character-building qualities of public schools and their influence on British society at large when he wrote about them in "Notes on the English Character" in 1921: "With its boarding houses, its compulsory games, its system of prefects and fagging, its insistence on good form, and on *esprit de corps*, it produces a type whose weight is out of all proportion to its numbers." (Forster 1964, 4) When they leave school,

Forster wrote, the pupils go into the world with "with well-developed bodies, fairly developed minds and undeveloped hearts." (ibid., 5) The family discourse is dominant in the *Harry Potter* books. The series is also a story of coming-of-age and a kind of *Bildungsroman*, exhibiting the genre's strong emphasis on separation from the parents and thoughts on finding substitutes. It is this discourse that has fascinated readers, and not just the books' magical universe. Or rather, it is the merging of a magical discourse with a discourse about family that is quite real that provides the fascinating effect of the books. They are not silent about contemporary problems, and though part of the answer to these problems may seem of a regressive nature, an even more severe critique in fantasy form of modernity can be seen in Tolkien's *Lord of the Rings*.

The Industrialisation of the Shire

The Shire in the final volume of *The Lord of the Rings*: *The Return of the King* is greatly changed from the rural and pastoral place of *The Fellowship of the Ring*, the first volume of the trilogy. This change is foreshadowed in the "Prologue Concerning Hobbits, and other matters" with its pseudo-folklore or ethnography at the start of the first volume:

> Hobbits are an unobtrusive but very ancient people, more numerous formerly than they are today; for they love peace and quiet and good tilled earth: a well-ordered and well-farmed countryside was their favourite haunt. They do not and they did not understand or like machines more complicated than a forge-bellows, a water-mill, or a handloom, though they were skilful with tools. Even in ancient days they were, as a rule, shy of "the Big Folk," as they call us, and now they avoid us with dismay and are becoming hard to find. (*The Fellowship of the Ring*, 13)

This passage with its slight but significant confusion of grammatical tenses is reminiscent of John Aubrey's description of the disappearance of the fairies (see p. 207). There is the same looking back at something that has disappeared and a longing for it. And with good reason, for this Shire has turned into a kind of black satanic mill with social housing estates in *The Return of the King* as seen in the chapter "The Scouring of the Shire":

> The pleasant row of old hobbit-holes in the bank on the north side of the Pool were deserted, and their little gardens that used to run down bright to the water's edge were rank with weeds. Worse, there was a whole line of the ugly new houses all along Pool Side, where the Hobbiton Road ran close to the bank. An avenue of trees had stood there. They were all gone. And looking with dismay up the road towards Bag End they saw a tall chimney of brick in the distance. It was pouring out black smoke into the evening air. (*The Return of the King*, 249)

Until the returning party of Hobbits sets matters right with force and magic elven powder from Sam's box, the Shire is polluted with noise and stench from mills. Behind it all there is Sharkey, or rather the wizard Saruman, who had already felled the trees, industrialised Isengard, and turned it into a huge underground arms factory.

Though Sam replants the Shire, *The Lord of the Rings* is a heroic elegy for the end of the age of magic and the coming of the Age of Men. Yet the sense of tragedy and loss that runs through *The Lord of the Rings* is also a celebration of a mode of life that is gone. In this respect *The Lord of the Rings* can be written into a long tradition of literature and cultural critique that combine the passing of country life with a critique of modernity. To judge from the quotation above, the change in the Shire -- with its black smoke pouring out of chimneys — is the move from one mode of production, artisan and farm-based — into industrialisation, similar to the one Britain went through in the Victorian Period and even before. The Victorian cultural critic Thomas Carlyle may to some extent be seen as a parallel to Tolkien in his 1829 *Signs of the Times* about industrialisation and its effects. The mode of production is combined with the spirit of the age and the passing of heroical aspects:

> Were we required to characterise this age of ours by any single epithet, we should be tempted to call it, not an Heroical, Devotional, Philosophical, or Moral Age, but, above all others, the Mechanical Age. It is the Age of Machinery, in every outward and inward sense of that word... Our old modes of exertion are all discredited, and thrown aside. On every hand, the living artisan is driven from his workshop, to make room for a speedier, inanimate one. The shuttle drops from the fingers of the weaver, and falls into iron fingers that ply it faster. The sailor furls his sail, and lays down his oar; and bids a strong, unwearied servant, on vaporous wings, bear him through the waters...There is no end to machinery. Even the horse is stripped of his harness, and finds a fleet fire-horse yoked in his stead. (Carlyle, 268-69)

However, there is more to this observation – and others similar to it -- than merely an invective against industrialism. In *The Country and the City* Raymond Williams has created a brief, but persuasive survey of the ancient tradition of lamenting the present in his chapter "A Problem of Perspective." "'The organic community' of 'Old England' has disappeared" (Williams 1975, 18) is a sentiment that runs through not only works of the twentieth century, but as Williams documents, goes far back until the lost rural and pastoral world becomes the mythical Garden of Eden. This longing for the past seems to be pervasive in the chivalric romances, grail legends, gothic romances, etc., which all in turn have influenced Tolkien to some degree. It is not only in fiction, e.g., Thomas Hardy's novels, that the changes of rural life are recorded. Also in sociological writings and in cultural critiques the theme of the vanished and vanishing rural world has been persistent. Matthew Arnold is in line with Carlyle's view of the spiritual and cultural consequences of the changes of the mode of production. In *Culture and Anarchy* from 1869, Arnold opposes the Utilitarian attitude, based on industrialism, that education is meant to train men to carry out specific tasks instead of taking part in a general and more organic culture. Arnold criticised his society for being "mechanical and external" (Arnold, 37), and Carlyle's "There is no end to machinery" is spelled out by Arnold:

> Faith in machinery is, I said, our besetting danger; often in machinery most absurdly disproportioned to the end which this machinery, if it is to do any good at all, is to serve; but always in machinery, as if it had a value in and for itself. What is freedom but machinery? what is population but machinery? what is coal but machinery? what are railroads but machinery? what is wealth but machinery? what are religious organisations but machinery? (Arnold, 37-38)

The cultural consequences of the fetishism of production, machinery, and wealth are that the middle classes have become Philistines, i.e., "The people who believe most that our greatness and welfare are proved by our being very rich, and who most give their lives and thoughts to becoming rich, are just the very people whom we call the Philistines." (Arnold, 39). The working classes are just waiting to take over this status and attitude of cultural impoverishment (ibid., 48). Arnold's bid to counteract this development is general education based on "the best which has been thought and said in the world." (ibid., 5)

> Though Tolkien's *The Lord of the Rings* in a sense may be read as a critique of modernity in the tradition of Carlyle and Arnold, he does not offer any solution to the loss of the old world of Middle-earth and the coming of the Age of Men, insofar as escape to the immortal West is just an escape, and only for the Ring-bearers. The World of Men has no longer any place for the magical and fantastical. Technology and industry for better or worse seem to have replaced innocence, the fantastical, and qualities such as honour and chivalry. Tragedy and loss are the outcome of the quest, and at the end of the book, not to mention the prolonged end of Peter Jackson's adaptation, it is sorrow and sadness that fill the characters: Then Elrond and Galadriel rode on, for the Third Age was over, and the Days of the Rings were passed, and an end was come of the story and song of those times. With them went many Elves of the High Kindred who would no longer stay in Middle-earth; and among them filled with a sadness that was

> yet blessed and without bitterness, rode Sam, and Frodo, and Bilbo (Tolkien, 274)

Yet, it seems that the sadness is not only caused by the end of the Third Age, but also that there is a sadness that the characters as well as readers have come to the end of the story or the long novel ("an end was come of the story and song of those times"). It is significant that Tolkien stresses the textual nature of the story and its outcome. Tolkien may not have offered a solution or attempt at a solution to passing of the times and of a way of life; however, he has written a story that has become a classical discourse about this type of loss alongside a critique of modernity.

Fantasy vs. Realism?

The relationship between fantasy and the imagined, on the one hand, and realism in an Aristotelian mimetical sense, on the other, forms the foundation of the definition of the genre fantasy as found in Tolkien's primary and secondary worlds. In the *Harry Potter* books, Rowling's division of the universe into a Muggle-world, which corresponds to the readers' world, and the world of magic, which is the secondary world, exemplifies this duality. It is the dialogue between the two worlds that creates much of the significance of fantasy. Here we now examine the potential for social critique in fantasy by applying Georg Lukács' theory about critical realism to fantasy, and in the context of a genre discussion of fantasy, we also compare aspects of Lukács' theory to Louis Marin's concept of the endlessly receding horizon.

Georg Lukács' critical realism has as one of its cornerstones that mimetical rendition of reality is only one of the preconditions for a work of art to be called realist. Other conditions must be fulfilled as well. Here it may be noted that the theory of critical realism is prescriptive as well as descriptive. Georg Lukács developed it as a response to two movements of his time: the ideological, political authoritarian tendencies (Fascism and Stalinism) and the modernist movement within art. Basically, Lukács found modernism an inadequate response to the anti-democratic movements. He looked back in cultural history to the great realist novels of the nineteenth century with their humanist elements to define the traits a literary work must have in order to counteract reactionary political ideologies. Lukács demands that a real work of art has an organic unity of objectivity and subjectivity. By objectivity, Lukács means a realist aesthetic reproduction of objective reality, and by subjectivity he means the subject's partisanship or taking part in society and being a member of a community. The literary subject is at the core of Lukács' theory: "The central aesthetic problem of realism is the adequate presentation of the complete human personality." (Lukács 1972, 7). The type or the literary character, which is always found in a social and historical context, Lukács writes, solves this problem. As an experiment one may bear Harry Potter and his family discourse in mind while heeding Lukács' demand that realism must dissolve the distinction between the particular and the general when creating a literary character:

> "Realism is the recognition of the fact that a work of literature can rest neither on a lifeless average, as the naturalists suppose, nor on an individual principle which dissolves its own self into nothingness. The central category and criterion of realist literature is the type, a peculiar synthesis that organically binds together the general and the particular both in character and in situations." (Lukács 1972, 6)

Though Lukács' main point in his literary theory is that art must have an ideological function, he takes care to point out that propagandist novels ("the well-intentioned and honest propagandist novels") are not the solution. (Lukács 1972, 10) The realist novel must not provide its readers with ready-made solutions to topical problems.
Critical realism has a cathartic function. The literary types or characters embody stages in the development and struggle of mankind, and the readers must be brought to realise that his or her own life is an integral part of this development. Some parts of the critical realist work must be recognised by the reader as his or her own experience in order that the reader accept the rest of the work and suspend his or her disbelief.

CERTAIN REGRESSIVE TENDENCIES IN ROWLING AND TOLKIEN

The critical realist work does not provide a solution or an answer to social and historical problems. Lukács writes in his 1936 essay "Tolstoy und die Probleme des Realismus" (1964, 177-261) that the solution to a problem and the right way to ask a question are two different things, and that only the latter is essential for the artist. This is one of the main points that distinguish critical realism from propaganda, and it is an essential tool in the process of catharsis that belongs to critical realism. The critical realist work of art must ask the question in the right way.

Both Tolkien and Rowling have created literary characters (Frodo and Harry Potter, respectively) that to a great degree could compare with Lukács' literary types. Although living in Middle-earth Frodo also faces situations that are the consequences of modernity and industrialism. There certainly are no valid answers in *The Lord of the Rings,* with its overall sense of tragedy and loss, to the problems of modernity, but one could well ask whether this fantasy novel does not pose questions that are important to the current topical problems of modernity? In the case of Harry Potter the issue is more specific than *The Lord of the Rings*' general concern with modernity. The *Harry Potter* books have as their most central theme the position of children and young people in the contemporary transition of family life. Harry's question in front of the mirror of Erised -- "Mum - Dad?" -- though not quite on par with Oliver Twist's "Please Sir, can I have some more?" is, with the rest of the books, the right way to ask questions about contemporary family problems. As discussed earlier, Rowling's answers are not necessarily as valid as her questions, but the readers of her novels will be able to achieve catharsis with regard to their own family lives, or at least come to realise that their own lives cannot be as miserable as living with the Dursleys. They will be able to see their individual development as a link in the chain of a more general historical development.

Are *The Lord of the Rings* and the Harry Potter books realism, or critical realism? No, they are fantasy; but this chapter has sought to show that there is a connection between fantasy and realism and that fantasy is not a mere escapist response to contemporary social life and historical issues. Not only with regard to character and thematics are there similarities between realism and fantasy. Where critical realism asks the question in the right way and does not provide the reader with a ready-made answer, there may be the same ontological mechanism in fantasy. Louis Marin's article "Frontiers of Utopia: Past and Present", which is also discussed in the first chapter of this book, defines fantasy using the concept of the endlessly receding horizon. This spatial concept is turned into a cognitive one in the reception process of the work of fantasy. The whole point is to be on the way and never reach the destination of the otherworld, but still being able to glimpse its frontier. Critical realism's unwillingness to provide answers and fantasy's unwillingness to let destinations be accessible are ontologically related. Both invite the reader to consider present-day problems and issues.

References

Arnold, Matthew. *Culture and Anarchy*. 1869. Reprint, Oxford: Oxford University Press, 2006.
Bettelheim, Bruno. *The Uses of Enchantment – The Meaning and Importance of Fairy Tales*. 1976. Reprint, Harmondsworth: Penguin, 1987.
Carlyle, Thomas. *Critical and Miscellaneous Essays*. 1839-1869. Vol. 2. Reprint, London: ElecBook, 2001. (http://site.ebrary.com/lib/aalborguniv/Doc?id=2001752&ppg=2)
Christensen, Jørgen Riber. *Psycho Analysis and Texts*. Copenhagen: Gyldendal, 1987.
Forster, E.M. "Notes on the English Character." 1921. Reprinted in *Abinger Harvest*. New York: Harcourt Brace Jovanovich, 1964.
Lukács, Georg. *Werke Probleme des Realismus II*. Berlin: Luchterland, 1964 .
―――――――. *Studies in European Realism*. 1950. Reprint, London: Merlin Press, 1972 .
―――――――. *The Meaning of Contemporary Realism*. 1957. Reprint, London: Merlin Press, 1972.
Nel, Philip. *J.K. Rowling's Harry Potter Novels*. New York: Continuum, 2001.
Rowling, J.K. *Harry Potter and the Sorcerer's Stone*. 1997. Reprint, New York: Scholastic, Inc., 1999.
―――――――. *Harry Potter and the Deathly Hallows*. London: Bloomsbury, 2007.
Tolkien, J.R.R. *The Lord of the Rings*: *The Fellowship of the Ring*. 1955. Reprint, London: Unwin Books, 1974.
―――――――. *The Lord of the Rings*: *The Two Towers*. 1955. Reprint, London: Unwin Books, 1974.
―――――――. *The Lord of the Rings*: *The Return of the King*. 1955. Reprint, London: Unwin Books, 1974.
Williams, Raymond. *Culture and Society 1780-1950*. 1958. Reprint, Harmondsworth: Penguin, 1976.
―――――――. *The Country and the City*. 1973. Reprint, Harmondsworth: Penguin, 1975.

Ziehe, Thomas, *Pubertät und Narzissmus*. Frankfurt am Main: Europäisches Verlagsanstalt, 1975.

Dorthe Andersen

L-space
Transtextuality and Its Functions in Terry Pratchett's Discworld

Terry Pratchett is a renowned writer of fantasy. The year 2008 marked the twenty-fifth anniversary of *Discworld*, and at the time of the anniversary Pratchett's books number thirty-eight. They have been published in thirty-five languages and more than forty-five million copies are in print around the world. (Smythe 2006) His popularity, then, is hard to deny, and this chapter certainly would not want to do so. What we *will* do here is examine some of the elements that make *Discworld* so well loved[1].

While Pratchett's books have enjoyable storylines, they are, in and of themselves, not the key to *Discworld's* popularity. It is to a much larger degree the humour and wit, not to mention parody and satire, underlying the stories, that account for the number of readers and fans. Pratchett acknowledges his wish to use and reinvent clichés: "Now, how did I start out? It was to have fun with some of the clichés. It was as simple as that." (Pratchett in Young 2005) However, beyond mere clichés, his interest has spread and now includes more issues and cultural products than any one person can readily imagine.

"It's terribly tempting to say: Yes, I made it up. But given what human beings have done, practised and believed in the last ten thousand

---

1 This chapter is based on the work that resulted in my master's degree thesis "Bewitching Writing," Aalborg University 2006. See my thesis for a more detailed analysis and theoretical outline.

years, it's quite hard to make up anything new, and it's a shame to see the old stuff lost ..." (Pratchett 2008, 28) The challenge for any reader is the effort to recognise upon which clichés, or other material, Pratchett has drawn.

This chapter employs a wide definition of what constitutes a text; language and cultural products such as film or media also fall into this category. This web of connections among elements is what Pratchett terms L-space:

> All books are tenuously connected through L-space and, therefore, the content of any book ever written *or yet to be written* may, in the right circumstances, be deduced from a sufficiently close study of books already in existence. (Pratchett 1998b, 23)

My field of investigation lies in the dialogue between two texts. As long as there have been stories, or texts in the broadest definition, there has been interaction between them. This interaction is what occurs in Pratchett's L-space. It has had many names; one of the more well-known is intertextuality. In his outline of a terminology to describe this interaction, Genette uses the term transtextuality to define "... the textual transcendence of the text, which I have already roughly defined as 'all that sets the text in a relationship, whether obvious or concealed, with other texts.'" (Genette 1997, 1) In this chapter I employ Genette's terms, and so transtextuality is the term for the broadest definition of the relationships between texts.

Genette defines five types of transtextual relationships. The hypertextual relationship is the one most relevant for an exploration of Pratchett's work. In Genette's words:

> By hypertextuality I mean any relationship uniting a text B (which I shall call the *hypertext*) to an earlier text A (I shall, of course, call it the *hypotext*) upon which it is grafted in a manner that is not that of commentary. (Genette 1997, 5)

The word "grafted" is important, as the hypertextual relationship involves transformation of the text. It is precisely the manner in which the hypertextuality is grafted, which is interesting when we use it to look at Pratchett's work. This chapter will examine what kinds of hypotexts Pratchett uses when he creates transtextuality, and for what purpose.

What effects does he achieve through transtextuality? Transtextuality, once it is used in a text, can take many forms. In Pratchett's work, parody is predominant. For the purpose of this chapter parody is imitation of another text, with a distance. It differs from pastiche in that it does not intend flattery but commentary or critique, though not necessarily comedy. It is different from satire because it takes its point of departure from texts or other cultural expressions, whereas satire focuses on human follies or elements of society with intent to ridicule or scorn.

I find it necessary to further illuminate the function of allusion in relation to the other terms. The key is the difference inherent in, and intended by, parody. In comparison, allusion has a "… 'free', that is, un-predetermined, nature …" (Perri 1978, 299) Allusion is not necessarily preconceived to create either satiric ridicule or the flattery inherent in pastiche, nor to create the distance needed for parody. What is more, allusion is an aspect of transtextuality, yet as the only form of transtextuality it can refer to something not itself textual. This is a useful distinction in working with Pratchett's work, which employs references to many practices and expressions, not all of which are necessarily textual.

Types of Hypotexts

My investigation of transtextuality in Pratchett's work has been centred on the witch sequence; Equal Rites, Wyrd Sisters, Witches Abroad, Lords and Ladies, Maskerade, and Carpe Jugulum. I have found that we may set up four categories which encompass different kinds of hypotexts: texts, the formulaic, human folly, and grand narratives.

Texts

How can texts be a subset, a category of its own, when everything can be regarded as a text? It is not an easy distinction. This category embodies what most people would probably associate with transtextuality; references to other literary works as Genette applies the term. Beyond literature as such, however, I have chosen to include plays, music, and art.

These hypotexts are canonical works as well as mundane. One example is the dedication in *Equal Rites*, which mentions "[...] the *Liber Paginarum Fulvarum*..." (Pratchett 1987:7) A translation reveals that we are talking of the *Yellow Pages*, a phonebook. However, the hypotexts more often belong to what is recognised as literature or art. *Maskerade* relates to *The Phantom of the Opera*. It is not one single edition of the story, though: "The only book squarely based on something else was *Maskerade*, which was based not just on the book AND the musical AND the movie but also on people's *perceptions* of them." (Pratchett in Metherell-Smith and Andrews 1999) In fact, Pratchett wanted a different version of the ghost than portrayed by Andrew Lloyd Webber's musical, with more emphasis on the effects of his actions. (Pratchett in Robinson 2000) This is a case of specific parody, as it is directed at a specific text, in different versions.

Of the six books examined here, the literary hypertextuality lies the thickest in *Witches Abroad*. This novel deals thematically with the power of stories, and many instances of well-known ones poke out their heads at the reader. One is Tolkien's *The Lord of the Rings*. When at the entrance to the mines of Moria, Gandalf has to speak the dwarfish version of "friend" in order for the portal to open. (Tolkien 1991, 325) The three witches also find themselves in a situation where they have to seek entrance to a dwarven mine: "Then she stood back, hit the rock sharply with her broomstick, and spake thusly: 'Open up, you little suds!'" (Pratchett 1991, 49) The reader recognises the reference to Tolkien's book, yet Pratchett's use of bathos renders the scene parodic. *The Lord of the Rings* is often regarded as a seminal work within fantasy. When Pratchett parodies it, he is showing his awareness of the genre itself. Baum's *The Wonderful Wizard of Oz* has also left tracks on the storyline, such as:

> "What some people need," said Magrat, to the world in general, 'is a bit more heart."

IN TERRY PRATCHETT'S DISCWORLD

"What some people need," said Granny Weatherwax, to the stormy sky, "is a lot more brain."

...

"What *I* need," thought Nanny Ogg fervently, "is a drink." Three minutes later a farmhouse dropped on her head. (Pratchett 1991, 139)

This refers to the wishes that Oz fulfils for the Tin Woodman, the Scarecrow, and the Lion (Baum in Wolstenholme 1997, 196-98), and the falling farmhouse is of course based on Dorothy's arrival after the tornado or "twister" transports the farmhouse from Kansas and to the world of Oz. (Baum in Wolstenholme 1997, 12-18) Apart from these types, the entire witch sequence is full of references to Shakespeare's plays. *Hamlet* and *Macbeth* are there, as is *A Midsummer Night's Dream* and others. These hypotexts are often referred to though allusion or parody invoking laughter.

The Formulaic

Another type of hypotext is what I call the formulaic. This encompasses the use of elements that have become stagnant or formulaic. For instance, in his use of textual forms and formats, Pratchett employs footnotes and punctuation in entirely new fashions.

My term the formulaic also applies to those expressions and myths that have become standard. They are known to most of us, and used so often that we no longer consider them metaphors or images, but merely expressions with a specific meaning. They are what Abrams calls dead metaphors. (Abrams 1993, 68) Another element in this category is the use of language in many forms. Pratchett's choice of words is often inventive and surprising, sometimes constructing entirely new lines of association and imagery. In the following example, a known word is used in a new way: "Henry Slugg frisbeed the plate into the wings ..." (Pratchett 1985, 366) Using an unexpected word as allusion marker arrests the reader's attention and functions as a spotlight on the action described. The image is, if possible, stronger yet when one realises that the contents of the plate were spaghetti, possibly bolognaise. Such vivid visual description is, I would argue, part of the trademark of Pratchett's use of language.

The dead metaphors are also revitalised. This example employs a well-known American phrase -- the self-made man:

> "I've been through the mill, I have," Bucket began, "and I made myself what I am today."
> "Self-raising flour?" thought Salzella. (Pratchett 1985, 31)

Bucket has launched into a somewhat pompous autobiography, and Salzella's irreverent comment punctures the balloon and allows the reader to have a good laugh at Bucket's expense. So Bucket is betrayed to the reader, as his, undoubtedly serious, speech is undermined. Pratchett has taken the phrase and interpreted it literally. How does one make oneself? The reintroduction or reawakening of dead metaphors mostly takes place through allusion. However, I find that in this case the transtextuality is directed at neither another text nor the characters. Rather, Pratchett achieves awareness within the reader of his or her own conceptions and predisposed use of language. In this way it is a parody of language use, directed at the reader. Certainly a metatextual effort, yet also immensely effective.

Pratchett also uses what might be termed common knowledge, or accepted myths as hypotexts:

> Elves are wonderful. They provoke wonder.
> Elves are marvellous. They cause marvels.
> Elves are fantastic. They create fantasies.
> Elves are glamorous. They project glamour.
> Elves are enchanting. They weave enchantment.
> Elves are terrific. They beget terror. (Pratchett 1992, 169)

This builds on the general notion, the sum of general knowledge and myths we share in a culture, of elves as creatures of fantasy and beauty. These commonly acknowledged traits are recognised, yet put to us in entirely new and unexpected ways, opening a whole new field of meaning. The same kind of common knowledge is referred to in *Carpe Jugulum*, here dealing with vampires. This field of knowledge is comprised of both folklore and knowledge gained from literature and film, that which Umberto Eco terms our "intertextual encyclopedia." (Eco 1997, 23) That is something which we all share and draw upon as common knowledge.

The use of this kind of hypotext shows new avenues of possibility and meaning in the smallest or most mundane elements of what we use every day: our language and general knowledge.

Human Folly

This category deals with those traits of human behaviour that Pratchett mirrors in his writing. An example is opera, which Salzella, the musical director, describes:

> Opera happens because a large number of things amazingly fail to go wrong, Mr Bucket. It works because of hatred and love and nerves. All the time. (Pratchett 1985, 79)

I think it is safe to say, based on this quote, that both Pratchett and Salzella are amazed that such a thing as opera can actually exist and function in reality. Salzella, of course, is himself subject to the love-hate relationship he describes since he cannot live without opera, and yet finds himself unable to live with it. This oxymoron presents an unsolvable contradiction, and thus Salzella dies a most operatic death. (Pratchett 1985, 356-58) Pratchett treats opera to satire; where comedy has laughter as its goal, satire evokes laughter as a weapon, pointed against something outside of the work itself. (Abrams 1993, 187) While satire uses texts as references, it can point to something outside the texts. In this way it is in Hutcheon's term, extramural, whereas parody is intramural, focusing on the text itself. (Hutcheon 2000, 43) Here opera as a theme is treated through the use of *The Phantom of the Opera* as hypotext. Yet the issue at stake, the focus which the satire ridicules, is outside the text, namely the audience's relationship to, and treatment of, opera.

However, satiric ridicule is not the purpose behind the transtextual use of all instances of human behaviour. In *Carpe Jugulum* Pratchett creates an image of the contract between humans and vampires, as seen from the vampire's perspective. I am thinking here of the visit to Escrow, where the citizens have made a pact with the vampires who come only when announced and otherwise leave the people alone. Agnes is horrified to see people lining up in queues for the bloodletting:

> Agnes thought about Escrow, and the queues, and the children playing while they waited, and how evil might come animal sharp in the night, or greyly by day on a list... (Pratchett 1998a, 406)

Pratchett has commented on this illustration of evil: "In the last century we came up with a very good name for people who inflicted terror by numbers, by lists." (Pratchett in Robinson 2000) This is an allusion to the Nazis, of course, and their systematic extermination of Jews. I find that this is a case of general parody, where parody does not have a playful purpose. Rather, it is a case of imitation with difference. The underlying message is not to make fun of or to ridicule but to reexamine the effects of actions, and how the results affect people. Thus, Pratchett takes one of the most evil human actions of our history, and parodies its thematic content in his text.

Grand Narratives

The hypotexts encompassed in this category are stories that are not written down by any one at any time, yet which permeate our culture and society. They are underlying themes of life or culture. Religion is an example. For lack of a better term I have named them grand narratives; as they influence our lives on a grand scale. This category of hypotexts contains those stories; they are the backbone of society, the underlying stories of our lives. Pratchett draws on them, even as he utilises stories and themes from literature and art, in his work.

In my sense of the concept, the creation of identity is a grand narrative and one treated in some detail in *Maskerade* through the element of masks. One example of this is the character Walter Plinge, who is revealed as the Ghost once he puts on a mask:

> "I don't know what you are when you're behind the mask," said Granny, "but 'ghost' is just another word for 'spirit' and 'spirit' is just another word for 'soul.' Off you go, Walter Plinge."
> (Pratchett 1985, 348)

The seemingly helpless figure of Walter Plinge is revealed as the suave, self-reliant Ghost once he puts on his mask. He is, in fact, granted leave for an entirely different personality, the realisation of a different identity. However, once it is revealed that he is the one who transforms into the Ghost, the duplicity is compromised and no longer possible. The reality within the opera house cannot bear the existence of Walter Plinge and the Ghost as the same person. Therefore, a choice must be made. Hence, Granny gives Walter an invisible mask which he needs never take off, and behind which his Ghost-persona can forever live in the light. (Pratchett 1985, 354)

Pratchett has worked with the elements of *The Phantom of the Opera* as a hypotext, which he openly recognises. This use constitutes parody rather than allusion because Pratchett seeks to create a difference. Even though there are funny elements along the way, the difference in the ghost's role is not, and hence the parody is used to show us other aspects of the hypotext. Pratchett has highlighted certain aspects of the story and twisted them to allow for a reworking of their thematic value. Here the theme of identity can be seen as the hypotext, that which lies behind, or in the background. Foregrounded, as part of the hypertext, is the narrative of Walter Plinge's quest for identity and a place in the world. This use of parody is akin to what Dentith names the parodic paradox, which is to say that parody inevitably preserves that which it attacks. (Dentith 2000:36) That which is in the background is both attacked and preserved; identity as a theme is both taken apart and presented to us in a new light. The creation of identity is preserved and legitimised through the renewed use of it.

Thus, this type of hypotext is used in connection with a more local, surface- level narrative. In that way it serves as a background, informing the local narrative with meaning beyond what is apparent from the local situation. What is more, though, the hypertextuality also reflects back upon the hypotext, drawing it into our time.

As has become clear, transtextuality in Pratchett's work is at once deceivingly simple and deeply intricate. Transtextuality exists both at the surface of the text, playfully subjecting language to new interpretation, and deep within the thematic contents. It is safe to say that, much as there can be no text without a reader; there would be no *Discworld* without transtextuality.

Transtextual Functions

So far we have seen the different categories of hypotexts upon which Pratchett draws to create transtextuality in his novels. But how does transtextuality function in his texts? The relationship can take many forms. I have identified many instances of parody, yet no pastiche. Pratchett has not set out to create a pastiche in order to flatter and pay homage to a certain author or text. This might have been the case had he created a complete transformation of a single text with, for example, formal parody. While *The Phantom of the Opera* in its entirety is used as hypotext, the novel *Maskerade* is not built solely upon *Phantom*, nor does it take the form of a complete transformation. The parodic element, then, has another function. I find that the hypertextual categories function on different levels. Texts and the formulaic are evident on the first level, or surface, of the text. But there is a second, deeper level. The category grand narratives only functions on this second level, whereas human folly alone may function on both levels.

The First Transtextual Level

The first transtextual, or surface, level is the most readily accessible. The purpose of the first level is to provoke an immediate reaction through humour or satire. The hypertextual references here provide an extra set of implications for the reader to decode, sometimes without the characters being aware of it; such is the case with the witches and Oz, as mentioned earlier. These instances of hypertextuality are compliments to the reader. In decoding them the reader feels gratified to have – inherently -- a level of knowledge not readily apparent in the text.

This level is realised in many ways. One is the parodic rejuvenation of dead metaphors. Pratchett has employed this technique on a much broader canvas than used hitherto. He has chosen the most evocative metaphors, proverbs, and figures of speech on which to ply his trade.

Both verbal and structural irony function in this way, as well as allusions and parody when it is used to evoke laughter. Pratchett's use of language functions on this, the first transtextual level. The playful reinvention of the words we use every day alerts the reader to the fact that something beyond the storyline itself is happening in the text. Pratchett uses both allusion and irony to open the reader's eye to language in new ways. In this manner, he reawakens the reader to all the nuances and levels of transtextuality in language, and fights back against the deadening use of fixed images.

Satire is not used as prolifically as parody. However, one of its uses functions on the first transtextual level. The instances of satire are directed not at specific people or places. Rather, they describe the actions of a certain group of people, exemplified by Pratchett's dealings with the world of opera. It is ridiculed and made ripe for laughter: operatic customs are ridiculed in scenes such as Salzella's three-page-long death on stage. Here, Pratchett's approach is firmly rooted in the first level. However, the satirical treatment of *The Phantom of the Opera* as hypotext is complex. Although, on the first level, the reader sees an amusing illustration of the operatic world, Pratchett also provides a commentary on other themes. These belong to the second transtextual level.

The hypertextual relationships which we identify here on the first transtextual level, therefore, are eye openers, preparing the reader for some of the more complex issues dealt with elsewhere in the text.

The Second Transtextual Level

This level might also be called the thematic level; it deals with deeper, broader issues. Whereas the transtextuality of the first level often leads to humour, the second level is concerned with parodic distance: the difference achieved when the hypertext uses the hypotext, yet changes it. In this way, the reader's expectations are thwarted, but reflection is engendered.

The satiric focus on human action in relation to opera is of the first level, yet the treatment of evil in relation to the vampires exemplifies the second level. Here the parodic difference is not humourous at all; instead, it invites reflection. The thematic treatment of identity, as exemplified through Walter Plinge and his mask, was categorised as a grand narrative, and the way it is used to engender reflection is typical of the second level of transtextuality. Through the many references made to *The Phantom of the Opera,* the reader is invited to consider not only the similarities between the two works, but also the differences. The role of the ghost provides the medium for Pratchett to comment on the story and to criticise the way Andrew Lloyd Webber interpreted it. Pratchett has taken apart the role of the ghost, making it possible to highlight the discordant elements of the character that underlie his actions. Here, the parodic distance enables the reader to focus on the creation of self and identity, and on the rights of the individual to be who we are, regardless of our surroundings and the expectations of others.

Pratchett uses parody to disconcert his reader, in so far as he forces us to reconsider facts and certainties. Parody allows for a reconsideration of deeper, thematic issues. Pratchett uses what Hutcheon terms ironic representation: namely, that parody simultaneously legitimises and subverts or deconstructs that which it parodies. (Hutcheon 1991, 230) This happens on both transtextual levels, as parody permeates both. Yet this feature is most relevant to the second level since it deals with extramural themes. Those, in turn, are subverted through Pratchett's use of them, and they are presented to the reader in a new light.

The various categories and levels may, in a simplified version, be illustrated by this figure:

Categories of Hypotexts	Encompassing	First transtextual level	Second transtextual level
Texts	Literature Music Art	Allusion and parody evoking laughter directed at the hypertext itself	
The Formulaic	Accepted myths and forms Language use		
Human Folly	Human actions	Satiric ridicule directed at something outside of the hypertext itself	Re-examination of human actions and their consequences in history
Grand Narratives	Unwritten stories permeating our culture and society		Through dialogue with a local narrative the grand narratives are re-introduced and reconsidered

The first transtextual level evokes an immediate humourous or parodic reaction. The two first categories -- texts and the formulaic – are intramural or internal as far as the reader's reaction is directed to the hypertext itself. Human folly, through the use of satire, is the only category that enables a function on both levels: either the humourous ridicule of the first level, or the more thematic considerations of human actions which exist on the second level. The hypotexts used dictate that grand narratives will be of the second level, where greater issues are reconsidered and rethought. The genius of Pratchett's use of transtextuality is that he is able to serve both humour and reflection at the same time, through the same means. Jackson claims that fantasy interrogates the real through the unreal (Jackson

1981, 4), which is true of Pratchett's writing. This effort to make us consider things anew, to bring us to a new awareness of them, is what Tolkien coined "recovery." It is the regaining of a clear view of things through fantasy. (Tolkien 1947, 19) Pratchett reaches the same goal through his own means, as has been outlined.

Subversion

This chapter has investigated the use and function of transtextuality in Terry Pratchett's *Discworld* novels. Transtextual relationships not only employ a number of different hypotexts; they are also constructed for various purposes and with different functions in mind. What remains to be seen are the implications for the categorisation of Pratchett's fiction.

According to Rose, two elements are necessary in order for parody to be post-modern. One is that it must have a comic effect. As already mentioned, parody is not delineated by its ability to evoke laughter. However, this does not prevent it from doing so, as the analysis has shown. There are instances of comic parody in Pratchett's work. However, Rose argues that there must be one additional element present in order for parody to be post-modern: meta-fiction. (Rose 1993, 271) This meta-fictional element consists of an awareness of, and reference to, the media through which the parody is presented. The extensive transtextuality in Pratchett's work shows meta-textual awareness not only in acknowledging other texts, but also in the use of language and forms, and even footnotes. There is no doubt that parts of Pratchett's use of parody can be termed post-modern according to Rose. What are the implications of this? Arguably, Pratchett's work can be characterised as post-modern not only because of his use of parody, but through his focus on transtextual relationships.

Subversion is an important function of fantasy, according to Jackson. (Jackson 1981, 14) In terms of Pratchett's work one can say that the use of transtextuality in itself leads to subversion. According to Eco, the interaction between reader and text necessary for transtextuality can also allow the reader to reflect on the genre itself. When a reference is created, the reader has in mind the hypotext and all that it implies. However, in the creation of parodic distance, a change occurs in the transformation from hypo- to hypertext. This difference exploits the readers' expectations. According to Eco, the reader can create an ironic distance from the text itself (Eco 1997, 22), inducing yet another level of metatextuality into the field. One might say that through transtextuality it is possible to subvert the reader's expectation of what will happen in the text. The change Pratchett constructs through parody -- especially on the second transtextual level -- leads to something the reader did not expect. Thus, the reader's expectations are subverted.

Subversion can also be found in the way in which Pratchett handles the trappings of genre. I find that he is eminently aware of where he is placed: the genre of fantasy. As has become evident, he uses parody to pay homage to earlier masters of the genre, such as Shakespeare, Baum, and Tolkien. In particular, Tolkien is recognised as one of the most prominent practitioners of fantasy. In parodying him, Pratchett also constructs a parody of the fantasy genre. What we have then, is a writer of fantasy who, in a work of fantasy, parodies the genre in which he expresses himself. This serves to illustrate that Pratchett has not sought to create "consolation," to use Tolkien's term. Rather, Pratchett makes fun of the established genre and conventions. He achieves this in numerous ways; parody is one of them. Thus, Pratchett firmly establishes himself as an exponent of postmodernism, within the genre of fantasy.

The presence of L-space cannot be ignored in any consideration of Pratchett's work. It has become clear that in the *Discworld* novels analysed here, Pratchett not only refers to other texts, but also seizes on the link between author, text and reader. He forges a reverse effect; the reader is drawn into the text and led to a reconsideration of her own preconceived notions of language and themes.

References

Abrams, M.H. *A Glossary of Literary Terms*. sixth edition. Fort Worth: Harcourt Brace College Publishers, 1993.
Andersen, Dorthe. *Bewitching Writing, An Analysis of Intertextual Resonance in the Witch-sequence of Terry Pratchett's* Discworld. Master's thesis, Aalborg University, 2006.
Dentith, Simon. *Parody*. London: Routledge, 2000.
Eco, Umberto. "Innovation and Repetition: Between Modern and Post-Modern Aesthetics." In *Reading Eco*. Edited by Rocco Capozzi. Bloomington: Indiana University Press, 1997.
Genette, Gérard. *Palimpsests, Literature in the Second Degree*. Lincoln: University of Nebraska Press, 1997.
Hutcheon, Linda. "The Politics of Postmodern Parody." In *Intertextuality*. Edited by H. Plett. New York: Walter de Gruyter, 1991.
Hutcheon, Linda. *A Theory of Parody*. Urbana: University of Illinois Press, 2000.
Jackson, Rosemary. *Fantasy, The Literature of Subversion*. London: Routledge, 1981.
Metherell-Smith, Stephen J., and Donna Andrews. "Terry Pratchett: Carpe Discworld *Crescent Blues"* September 1999 edition. Available online at http://www.lspace.org/about- terry/interviews/crescentblues.html. Accessed 23 May 2006.
Perri, Carmella. "On Alluding." *Poetics* 7: 289-307.
Pratchett, Terry. *Equal Rites*. Reading: Corgi Books, 1987.
_____. *Wyrd Sisters*. Reading: Corgi Books, 1988.
_____. *Guards! Guards!*. Reading: Corgi Books, 1989.
_____. *Witches Abroad*. Reading: Corgi Books, 1991.
_____. *Lords and Ladies*. Reading: Corgi Books, 1992.
_____. *Maskerade*. Reading: Corgi Books, 1995.
_____. *Carpe Jugulum*. Reading: Corgi Books, 1998.
_____. *The Last Continent*. Reading: Corgi Books, 1998.
_____. "Imaginary Worlds, Real Stories."' In *Discworld Convention 2008 Programme Book*, London: Star Turtle Limited.

Robinson, Tasha. "On the business – or busyness – of being Terry Pratchett." In *Science Fiction Weekly* 156 (17 April 2000). Online at: http://www.scifi.com/sfw/issue156/interview.html. Accessed 23 May 2006.

Rose, Margaret A. *Parody: ancient, modern and post-modern*. Cambridge: Cambridge University Press, 1993.

Smythe, Colin. "Terry Pratchett" Online at: http://www.colinsmythe.co.uk/terrypages/tpindex.htm. Accessed 5 October 2008.

Tolkien, J.R.R. "On Fairy-Stories." Online at: http://brainstorm-servivces.com/wcu-2004/fairystories-tolkien.pdf. Accessed 3 November 2006.

Tolkien, J.R.R. *The Lord of the Rings*. London: HarperCollins Publishers, 1991.

L. Frank Baum. *The Wonderful Wizard of Oz*. Edited by S. Wolstenholme. Oxford World Classics. Oxford: Oxford University Press, 2000.

Young, Jim. "Terry Pratchett on the origins of *Discworld*, his Order of the British Empire and everything in between." In *Science Fiction Weekly* 449 (November 28, 2005). Online at: http://www.scifi.com/sfw/issue449/interview.html. Accessed 7 February 2006.

Torben Rølmer Bille

Sword & Sorcery
The Barbarian Archetype and the Conan Tales of Robert E. Howard

Introduction

The subgenre of Sword & Sorcery (or heroic fantasy) has prevented the fantasy genre as a whole from becoming a subject of serious academic consideration.

As seen in numerous books and articles on the fantasy genre, academics do not ignore the importance of Tolkien, Lewis, or Rowling. They have artistic merit, certainly, but have also enjoyed great success and have, in turn, influenced popular fiction in general. But when considering fantasy, one must not forget the dark underbelly of fantasy fiction – the genre that most vividly appeals to the adolescent bad boy – Sword & Sorcery.

In this essay, I will give a brief overview of this subgenre of fantasy and focus specifically on its most famous hero, Robert E. Howard's Conan the Cimerian. Critical opinion coupled with Howard's fiction and his personal correspondence will help to illustrate the characteristics of the Sword & Sorcery subgenre. I will also present avenues one could explore to place these texts for study on a more academic plane. In short, my goal is to point up the ways in which a cultural and critical reading of the *Conan* tales could benefit not just only understanding of the stories themselves, but also draw critical attention to Howard's oeuvre. I am both an avid fan of Howard's writing and a proponent of academic practice. I believe, and hope to show here, that literary theory may be applied to the *Conan* stories while remaining faithful to the spirit of the narratives.

The Origins and Definitions of Sword & Sorcery

As with many other types of fantasy writing (or fiction in general), it is impossible to trace the origin of the genre to one particular source, but some precursors seem most probable.

Some critics claim that Robert E. Howard's contemporary, author Fritz Leiber coined the term "Sword & Sorcery" in 1961. It was used to describe the type of fantasy stories that Robert E. Howard produced. More precisely, George Knight claims that it was Howard's 1929 short story "The Shadow Kingdom" that should be considered the first true Sword & Sorcery work. (Knight 2004)

Sword & Sorcery is a subgenre of fantasy that mixes horror, fantasy, historical fact, adventure, and barbarism and is often used interchangeably with the term "heroic fantasy." However, there *is* a difference between the two subgenres. Heroic fantasy is a much broader category (Pringle 2002), as it also includes stories with more than one protagonist; therefore, it could include works Tolkien's Ring trilogy, David Edding's *Belgariad* series, and Stephen Donaldson's *Chronicles of Thomas Covenant*. Since the *Conan* tales are centered on one protagonist, as will be discussed below, the term Sword & Sorcery will be used exclusively here.

A formalist approach could be applied to the texts that inspired the writers of Sword & Sorcery stories, but the traits that characterise the subgenre are not clear, defining markers, but rather general guidelines one can use to separate Sword &

Having said that, we can safely say that Sword & Sorcery is characterised by one or more of the following: an action-oriented protagonist, a setting and narrative heavily influenced by Gothic literature, a clearly defined antagonistic opponent. Finally, the genre deals with all things taboo.

THE BARBARIAN ARCHETYPE AND THE CONAN TALES

The Action-oriented Protagonist

The fictional barbarian hero, like other protagonists in the fantasy genre, is often a man who is very similar to the heroes of late Victorian adventure novels. (Sword & Sorcery only rarely employs female leads.), In addition to the influence of Classic mythological characters such as Achilles, Odysseus, and Hercules, the action-oriented protagonists of Sword & Sorcery owe much to writers such as Alexander Dumas, H. Rider Haggard, Edgar Rice Burroughs, and Jack London.

Many critics find that stories about Tarzan and Alan Quatermain seem to have influenced Howard's writing greatly, not only the nature of the protagonist, but also Howard's choice of exotic and fantastic settings. But whereas Quatermain and Tarzan were of noble birth and behaved courteously, the heroes of Sword & Sorcery are often more closely related to what Michael Moorcock terms the hero-villain. (Moorcock 2004) He is a protagonist willing to deal out violence in excessive and even sadistic ways, at times in order to help others, but primarily to help himself. This egocentricity also allows critics to see the characters as childlike, as I will discuss below.

The protagonists of Sword & Sorcery are often imbued with many of the virtues that characterised their predecessors: strong physical power, a (somewhat primitive but) sly intellect, and -- most importantly -- an instinct for survival.

This survival skill is not only the way in which the protagonist narrowly escapes his doom, but also refers to the protagonist's ability to survive the harsh and untamed lands on the outskirts of civilisation. As Moorcock states:

> If the form of Howard's stories was borrowed at third and fourth hand from Scott and Fennimore Cooper, the supernatural element from Poe and others, the barbarian Hero of the *Conan* stories owed a great deal to Tarzan and other Burroughs natives. Given to impulsive violent action, sudden rough affection and bouts of melancholy, Conan was a pint-sized King Kong. Conan mistrusted civilisation. (83)

In the *Conan* tales, the division between civilisation and culture is distinct. As Conan says in the short story "Beyond the Black River" (Howard 2001, i): "Barbarism is the natural state of mankind. Civilisation is unnatural. It is a whim of circumstance. And Barbarism must ultimately triumph." Herron writes in his essay *The Dark Barbarian* (1984):

> The Howardian mood and philosophy is not simply barbaric, it is a *dark* barbarism, a pessimistic view that holds the accomplishments of society of little account in the face of mankind's darker nature ... Howard's barbarians are not the Noble Savages one associates with Rousseau, nor yet are the superhuman qualities one identifies with Conan truly realistic in terms of the way history records barbarians. (150-51)

In short, Herron argues that pessimism is at the core of the tales, but I would claim that the tales and philosophy of Conan are more than just pessimistic and nihilistic. Conan's chief trait might be his brooding, but he is also imbued with a dark sense of humour and a great lust for life. In many *Conan* tales he openly praises women and drink, but most stories also have some form of grotesque comic relief.

As to barbarism, Howard was not naïve about his fiction, as he demonstrates in a letter to his colleague H.P. Lovecraft: ..."civilisation even in its decaying form, is undoubtedly better for people as a whole. I have no idyllic view of barbarism ...it's a grim, bloody, ferocious and loveless condition." (Herron 2004, 105)

This mistrust and critique of civilisation is an essential part of Conan's philosophy, and points toward yet another source of inspiration, the Gothic. This is perhaps most visible when we examine the settings of the stories.

Narratives and Settings Influenced by the Gothic

The setting in traditional high fantasy typically combines or recasts existing mythology, pastoral landscapes, and pseudo-historical fact. However, Sword & Sorcery differs from high fantasy in its use of strong Gothic elements. The Hyborean Age of Conan and King Kull is a dark and dangerous time; the land is filled with gloomy castles, deadly traps, brooding towers, deep chasms, dark caves, and vast underground tunnel systems. Fred Botting says about the Gothic genre:

> Gothic excesses and transgressions repeatedly return to particular images and particular loci. Familial and sexual relations, power and suppression ... In villains, masculine sovereignty is staged and scrutinised. Old castles, houses and ruins, as in wild landscapes and labyrinthine cities, situate heroines and readers at the limits of normal worlds and mores. Historical events or imagined pasts, also, delineate the boundaries of the normalised present in a movement, an interplay, that leaves neither where they were. (Botting, 20)

In Sword & Sorcery the stock villains and heroes, as well as the setting, all have one thing in common: the Gothic. With respect to the somewhat cliché (Gothic) trademarks found in Howard's writing, Fritz Leiber states:

> He [Howard] knew the words and phrases of power and sought to use them as often as possible, the words and phrases that the writer of literary aspirations usually avoids (sometimes quite mechanically) because they are clichés or near-clichés, words or phrases like (I select from the Solomon Kane story "The Moon of Skulls") *black, dark, death, volcanic, ghost, great black shadow, symbol of death and horror, menace brooding and terrible, ... black spires of wizard's castles, ju-ju city, grim black crags of the fetish hills, henchmen of death, the tower of death, the black altar.* (3-4)

Howard's settings -- filled with a sense of death, darkness and fear – are similar to those of many Gothic writers. Botting (1996) continues:

> Shadows, indeed, were amongst the foremost characteristics of Gothic works. They marked the limits necessary to the con-

stitution of an enlightened world and delineated the limitations of neoclassical perceptions. Darkness, metaphorically, threatened the light of reason with what it did not know. (32)

In the *Conan* tales, the darkness and all the metaphors of death, decay and necromancy help to create settings that are vast in contrast to the romanticised versions of untamed nature found in many other adventure and fantasy stories of the time. Howard's settings are even further away from those we find in high fantasy.

Perhaps this emphasis on death and darkness helps to maintain the continual appeal of Sword & Sorcery fiction. In other words, it is a subgenre that appeals to those writers and readers who prefer the more transgressive forms of literature. Sword & Sorcery has, in this way, the same allure as hard-boiled crime fiction, splatter-punk horror, cyberpunk, or even pornographic fiction.

The landscapes of heroic fantasy often are symbolic reflections of the inner states of the protagonists. (cf. Moorcock 2004) Characters such as Conan, King Kull, Fritz Leiber's Grey Mouser, Moorcock's Elric, and many others have a much gloomier outlook on life and a darker, more brutal nature than their high fantasy counterparts.

As to the setting in Howard's *Conan* stories, the Hyborean Age is a collage of ages and styles. Moorcock writes:

> If Scott could make errors involving a few years or a couple hundred miles, Howard's hero spanned several thousand years of history and thousands of miles. It is as if Conan is trapped in a movie studio, or movie library of old clips, shifting from seventeenth-century Russia, to Rome in the first century B.C., to nineteenth-century Afghanistan, to the Spanish Main of the eighteenth-century, to the court of Lorenzo the Magnificent, all the way back to the Stone Age. (Moorcock, 83)

Fritz Leiber adds:

> We soon realise that Howard's Vendhya, Iranistan, Afghulistan, the Zhaibar Pass and the Himelians are Hyborian-Age vari-

THE BARBARIAN ARCHETYPE AND THE CONAN TALES

ants of Mogul India, Persia, Afghanistan, the Khyber Pass and the Himalayas, but they are stepper-up versions, painted with simpler, darker, lusher, more vibrant colours than reality. (8)

In this way Howard presents us with an alternate linguistic universe. Not only is the fantasy world a distortion of what we know, but the names of the locales are slightly warped, thus emphasising a familiar unfamiliarity. Another example can be found in the short story "The Frost-Giant's Daughter" albeit on a smaller scale. In that story Howard's mixes words such as Niord, Valhalla, Æsir, Vanaheim, Ymir – which are places, gods, and names from Norse mythology -- with Cimeria, Conan, "the dark gods of my own race," and Atali. All of the latter are Howard's own creations.

While Tolkien worked for at least two decades to create Middle Earth, the Hyborean Age was created in the span of just four years, making the internal logic and workings of this fictional world much more brittle, but allowing that world to be much more colourful and illogical. Perhaps most important is the fact that Howard created his world roughly six years prior to Tolkien's first publication of *The Hobbit*.

The notion of suspension of disbelief, I would argue, should be turned on its head when discussing Sword & Sorcery. I would suggest that the reader give in to "constant willing disbelief." This is one of the main attractions of the subgenre: the fantastic elements are emphasised to follow the dictionary definition "fantasy." According to Webster's, fantasy is "1. imagination, esp. when extravagant and unrestrained. 2. the forming of grotesque mental images." (1994) Grotesque imagery and unrestrained imagination are called into play when one reads stories about Conan.

Such a distortion of our known history and landscapes is not only found in Howard's writing, but applies to many Sword & Sorcery tales, as well as to many other texts in the broader fantasy category. Even though the landscape seems independent from normal temporal-spatial relations, it has a direct impact and influence on the characters living in it. Like Tarzan, Conan is a child of nature and is thus more attuned to survival in this wilderness than his travelling companions, who are often civilised, or at least used to city life.

Nevertheless, the collage of setting, culture, and historical "fact" is also visible in the works of writers who have been influenced by Howard, perhaps most notably in Moorcock. His hero Elric even had a brief encounter with Nazis in *The Dreamthief's Daughter*. This collage-like structure of time and place could, on the surface, seem to bear many similarities to postmodernist fiction, where setting often is a similar cacophony of styles and timeframes. However, in the fantasy world, the setting is not meant to break or destabilise the ontological status of the fiction. Quite the contrary. The fantasy world of Sword & Sorcery is not meant to collapse onto itself; the collage is meant to strengthen the structure of the setting. While protagonists in postmodern fiction are often unstable and unreliable, the protagonist in fantasy is (almost) always to be trusted. (Moorcock 2004) The reader of Sword & Sorcery trusts the observations and musings of the main characters and this helps to affirm the "reality" of these fictional worlds. It has even been postulated that fantasy exhibits a type of realism and grim comedy. Moorcock writes:

> To keep a form vital you must draw your inspiration not from other books in that form but from life itself, from experience, from knowledge of men and women, and, where fantasy fiction is concerned, from an enthusiasm for the epic, the myth, the noble metaphor which speaks to us on hundred levels. And to make such things speak to their fellows in as many voices as possible, writers must employ comedy to remind readers that no matter how intense the images, how grand the themes, how awe aspiring the terrors, one is still writing about *reality*. (121; italics mine)

In several letters, Howard has noted that his fantasy world had ties to some form of reality, or at least a forgotten past, central to his writing. More on this later.

A Clearly Defined Antagonistic Opposite

As with much fantasy writing, Sword & Sorcery employs clearly defined antagonistic forces. But much like the protagonist, the antagonists of Sword & Sorcery are often more brutal, sadistic, and sexually oppressive than the archetypical villains of high fantasy or children's fantasy. In Howard's writing the antagonists are almost always evil sorcerers, necromancers, or corrupt lords. This shows the strong contrast between the brutally honest barbarian, and, on the other hand, culture and civilisation as a means of degeneration and corruption. The sexually driven, power-mad perverse characters in Howard's stories seem to echo the many menacing antagonistic male figures found in Gothic literature. In Sword & Sorcery, these antagonistic forces are also represented by the gods of good and evil, (or in Moorcock's writing, the eternal battle between the personified deities of Law and Chaos) who interfere and interact with other characters.

The villains in Howard's fantasy writing are heavily influenced by Lovecraft's *Weird Tales*. Lovecraft is perhaps best known for the creation of what August Derleth (1988) later called "the Cthulhu Mythos" – the idea that ancient gods from beyond the cosmos have influence on and can wield power over human life. Howard, who had a very lively correspondence with Lovecraft, admired the latter greatly. Perhaps Lovecraft's influence can be seen most strikingly in the story "Worms of the Earth" (Howard 2001, iii), a straightforward horror story placed in a fantasy setting. Howard also wrote a number of pure horror stories, often imitating Lovecraft's distinct style.

But Howard's Sword & Sorcery tales also incorporate horrific elements and monsters, such as the ancient golems in "The Devil in Iron", the frog-like creature in "Tower of the Elephant,", or the giant snake with a human head in "The God in the Bowl," to name but a few. The most dominant of monsters, however, is as Lieber (1984) says: "The Giant Ape which appears so often as a stock menace in Howard's subsequent tales." We could speculate that this threat is so often repeated because it is as wild, strong, and ferocious as Howard's protagonists – making the ape an uncanny, albeit more hairy – doppelganger of Conan or King Kull.

All Themes Taboo

What really sets Sword & Sorcery apart from other types of fantasy is the treatment of taboo- ridden subject matter. Sexuality as well as extreme, gory violence and cannibalism are very rarely found in high fantasy.

Even though such themes may be most predominant in the pulp fiction of the 1930s, these narrative ingredients still prevail in modern Sword & Sorcery tales. Much fantasy, as do its related sister-genres of horror and science fiction, relies on extremes in order to satisfy readers. More important, these extremes set the genre apart from the standard literary canon, which tends to deal with the taboo in much less explicit ways.

Reading the tales of Conan, one is struck at how bloody the narratives often are. Howard was aware that his tales were gruesome; the sheer number of decapitations, guts spilled, and limbs sliced off could be one of the reasons for his continual success. Pulp magazines were defined by their transgression of "good taste," and, as everyone knows, sex and violence sell. And they sell especially well to youngsters.

Matthews (2002) offers the following explanation for the excessive violence in Howard's tales:

> The emphasis on violence ... seems partly a reaction against the blandness of nineteenth-century life, in England presented by the bourgeois Victorians, in the United States by the quiet agrarians or middle-class tradesmen after the taming of the Wild West and the collapse of authentic frontier experience. ... in Howard's more often more elaborate use of force and violence, we are graphically reminded of our bodies, of our vulnerable flesh and blood – and the moral decisiveness of life-and-death choices. (124)

Yet violence is not the only taboo subject that Howard tackles. His barbaric hero is also a blatant representation of male oppressive sexuality. Often, Howard satisfies the (adolescent) readers' lust for ravaging young, scantily clad, beautiful women. In "The Frost-Giant's Daughter,"

THE BARBARIAN ARCHETYPE AND THE CONAN TALES

Conan is tracking a nearly naked woman -- clad only in a gossamer veil -- across an icy plain. It seems as though his sex drive is even stronger than his instinctual urge to do battle. Howard (2001, i) writes:

> He had forgotten the fight, forgotten the mailed warriors who lay in their blood, forgotten Niord and the reavers who had failed to reach the fight. He had thought only for the slender white shape which seemed to float rather than run before him. (108)

And when he catches up with the woman, the ensuing scene is described almost like a rape:

> She writhed her golden head aside, striving to avoid the fierce kisses that bruised her red lips. "You are cold as the snows," he mumbled dazedly, "I will warm you with the fire of my own blood." (110)

Howard has not only limited the sexual exploits of his characters to heterosexual encounters. He has also touched upon sadomasochism. As he put it to his editor about the story "Red Nails", he would "… like to know if you like my handling of the subject of lesbianism." (Lieber 1984) Here, Howard refers to a scene where one woman strips down, ties up, and whips another. I, for one, would argue that Howard's portrayal is perhaps not how feminists, lesbians, or women in general would like the subject to be handled, but let us leave that discussion for another time and place.

Howard has also flirted with cannibalism. In the story "Shadows in Zamboula" (Howard 2001, i), a group of cannibals terrorise a town and the owner of the local inn drugs and sells his guests to them in return for gold. The outcome is, naturally, that Conan sells the proprietor to the cannibals and listens to the death cries of the unfortunate man as he rides out of town.

Tied closely to this grotesque content of Sword & Sorcery fiction is the media form in which these tales first appeared. The so-called pulp magazines had a great impact on what was allowed to be published.

Pulps and Publication

Until recently, pulp magazines have been disregarded by academia. This could be one of the reasons that fans of Howard and other pulp fiction authors have had an ongoing dislike of academe, even though a few critical texts about Howard's works have been published, predominantly by his fans. I hope this essay will open the door to further critical investigation.

Pulp fiction is an all-American genre. These magazines were collections of stories published monthly or weekly on very cheap paper. Richard Matthews (2002) elaborates:

> A different American contribution evolved as an outgrowth of successful capitalism giving birth to a thriving circulation for pulp magazines, and an extension of the fantasy territory suggested by the work of H. Rider Haggard. Edgar Rice Burroughs and Robert E. Howard each made substantial contributions to the genre ...both creating heroes who have assumed, like Sherlock Holmes, an enduring life beyond the pages of a book or the hand of a single author. Their influence was possible to a large extent because of the capitalistic innovation of American publisher Frank A. Munsey, whose *Argosy* magazine ... suffered financially. In 1896 Munsey came up with the idea of printing *Argosy* on cheap wood-pulp paper and cutting the cover price to 10 cents, so it could compete with the popular dime novels. *Argosy's* fortunes quickly reversed; Munsey became a millionaire.... Munsey set an example other publishers could follow. ... (28-29)

In 1923 the first issue of *Weird Tales* magazine was published and it was this magazine which introduced authors such as Howard, Lovecraft, Robert Bloch, and August Derleth.

These magazines were often extremely genre specific, dealing with either crime, horror, gangsters, science fiction, Westerns, boxing, sex, adventure stories, and, of course, fantasy, each in their separate pulps. Such subject matters coincided with the growing demand for entertainment and (for a lack of better word) "escapism" in the United

States during the Great Depression. (Matthews, 2002) *Weird Tales* and other serialised pulps like *The Shadow* or *Doc Savage* sold more than 300,000 issues monthly or bimonthly during this period. Lovecraft wrote to Howard that *Weird Tales* was "the only magazine in the world, as far as I know, in which the writer can give full sway to his imagination." (Herron 2004) That censorship was not an issue with regard to these magazines could also explain why some of the barbaric stories are so extreme.

Conan Mythology

Robert Ervin Howard said, " I took up writing simply because it seemed to promise an easier mode of work, more money, and more freedom than any job I've tried." But it was also hard work: "It seems to me that many writers, by virtue of their environments of culture, art, and education, slip into writing because of [them]. I became a writer in spite of my environments." (Lord 1984) Howard also stated that he was not a writer aspiring to any literary acknowledgement or broad critical acclaim. He simply wrote because he got paid. (Jones 2001)

There is no denying that Howard wrote at an astounding pace. All of his Conan stories were written from 1932-1935; at this time, he was also writing other stories, from boxing tales and crime fighting stories to Westerns. It is, therefore, safe to assume that Howard wrote for a living. (cf. Lord 1984) The various pulp magazines paid their authors per word if the stories were accepted at all.

One of the most popular stories about the origins of the Conan character is presented in the film *Conan Unchained*. (2000) Here it is said that Howard imagined a fierce barbarian in his living room commanding him to write his biography or be killed. Therefore, Howard wrote in a frenzy, collapsing in the morning and discovering that the barbaric entity had gone.

The idea that the barbarian came into existence during the dangerous hallucination of a madman does not coincide with Howard's own version. In several letters and on other occasions he has mentioned the "birth" of Conan in somewhat different terms. In a letter dated January 1931, he writes;

> I believe my dreams are the result of ancestral memories, handed down through the ages. I have lived in the Southwest all my life yet most of my dreams are laid in cold, giant lands of icy wastes and gloomy skies ... With the exception of one dream I described to you, I am never, in these dreams of ancient times, a civilised man. Always I am the barbarian, the skin-clad, tousle-haired, light-eyed wild man, with rude axe or sword, fighting the elements and wild beasts, or grappling with armoured hosts marching with the tread of civilised discipline, from fallow fruitful lands and walled cities. (Waterman, 43)

One of the possible reasons for the misunderstanding presented by John Milius in *Conan Unchained* may be found in a letter Howard wrote in 1933 to the editor of *Weird Tales*:

> While I don't go so far as to believe that stories are inspired by actual existent spirits or powers ... I have sometimes wondered if it were possible that unrecognized forces of the past or present – or even the future – work through the thoughts and actions of living men. This occurred to me when I was writing the first stories of the Conan series especially. I know that for months I had been absolutely barren of ideas, completely unable to work up anything sellable. Then the man Conan seemed suddenly to grow up in my mind without much labour on my part and immediately a stream of stories flowed off my pen – or rather, off my typewriter – almost without any effort on my part. I did not seem to be creating, but rather relating events that had occurred. Episode crowded episode so fast I could scarcely keep up with them. For weeks I did nothing but write of the adventures of Conan. The character took complete possession of my mind and crowded out anything else in the way of story writing. When I deliberately tried to write something else, I couldn't do it. I do not attempt to explain this by esoteric or occult means, but the facts remain. I still write of Conan more powerfully and with more understanding than of

> any of my other characters. But the time will probably come when I will suddenly find myself unable to write convincingly of him at all. That has happened in the past with nearly all of my numerous characters; suddenly I will find myself out of contact with the conception as if the man had been standing at my shoulder directing my efforts, and had suddenly turned and gone away, leaving me to search for other characters. (Waterman, 43-44)

One could interpret this passage to mean that Howard was stalked by a real entity, but students of literature will not misunderstand the quote in that way. In less melodramatic terms, in 1935 Howard told the readers of *Fantasy Magazine* that

> Conan simply grew up in my mind a few years ago when I was stopping in a little border town on the lower Rio Grande. I did not create him by any conscious process. He simply stalked full grown out of oblivion and set me at work recording the saga of his adventures. (Jones, 547)

It was never Howard's intention to follow a linear chronology or progression in his tales. In that respect they should be seen as individual tales, having only the setting and protagonist as common denominators. (Herron 1984) Nevertheless, it is possible to track developments in style, setting, and character by reading Howard's tales chronologically, which can be done in the Gollancz collections. (Howard 2001, i, ii)

A Conan "Critique"

When investigating the literature on Sword & Sorcery, particularly Howard's tales, it soon becomes clear that "criticism" is hardly the word to describe the process. In fact, when reading the Don Herron's two anthologies, *The Dark Barbarian* and *The Barbaric Triumph*, it is striking how often the words "genius" and "unique" are used to describe Howard's writing. Additionally, critics in Herron's anthologies attack academe for misunderstanding their favourite author.

Most of Herron's collection is based on close readings of Howard's texts, comparative readings of other fantasy works, and, most importantly, the available biographical data on Howard. Roland Barthes' (1977) observation that the author should (or could) be considered dead, and that one should examine the text on its own merit has not yet reached the contributors to Herron's anthologies. It would be fair to say that this chapter has also been influenced by biographical material, but I still claim that the analysis of Howard's works suffers from an author-oriented perspective.

Much of the critique in *The Dark Barbarian* focuses on writers who, after the death of Howard, continued to work with the Conan character and create new stories. These, it is claimed, are vastly inferior to Howard's original, "genial" vision. Most notably L. Sprague De Camp (a fellow writer for *Weird Tales*) is attacked. This discussion may possibly be of importance to people interested in distinguishing between Howard's Conan and the way the character is treated by other authors. But in my opinion, the discussion contributes very little to an overall critique and analytical stance on Howard.

Lastly, the reverence for Howard as a prolific author seems to overwhelm the Herron's contributors so that they only hint at the more controversial sides of Howard's work. Examples are issues such as fascism, racism, or misogyny, issues that might seem to permeate the works. Perhaps these considerations have led to a dismissal of further investigation by academics. It could also be postulated that Herron's contributors deliberately avoid these issues because they do not want to be narrowly identified as academics.

In 1950 John D. Clark wrote in the introduction in the first collection of Conan tales, "Don't look for hidden philosophical meanings or intellectual puzzles in the yarns – they aren't there" (Herron 1984), and it seems as if some of the texts in Herron's two collections try to heed this warning. The narratives should of course be read as entertainment at face value. But there are ways to discuss the texts in more academic terms and gain a greater understanding of them without simultaneously deconstructing the narratives completely.

I have chosen to apply a cultural critical approach to the works, and by so doing, some of the most dominant prejudices, especially the supposed fascist elements, seem to diminish as our understanding of the texts increases. Others issues such as frontier mythology and the notion of the American Dream could be brought into play in order to look for answers as to why Howard's fiction is still as popular today as it was in the 1930s.

Cultural Critique

The solitary, male heroic figure in Sword & Sorcery, and the fact that the pulps were an all-American medium, might conjure up images of frontier mythology and the archetypical lonesome cowboy western hero. This frontier mythology seems to be a natural part of some of Howard's writing, both because of his Texan background, and his use of the frontier setting. As mentioned above, the boundary between civilisation and nature is an integral part of the Conan tales. Mathews writes:

> ...Howard moved decisively beyond mere Gothic tribalism and northern European sagas, setting his stories in a wild, unexplored ancient world. In this world the African continent is still joined with Europe, the area of the Mediterranean sea is dry lowlands, and what is today modern Africa is framed by the river Styx (Dante's river of Hell); the land Stygia is roughly parallel to an enlarged Egypt, and Zimbabwe, and the Black Kingdoms lie to the south. This is an oddly familiar, yet unfamiliar and untamed geography appropriate for bringing an American frontier mentality into fantasy. (119)

In his study on the American western, *Regeneration Through Violence: The Mythology of the American Frontier, 1600-1860*, Richard Slotkin (1971) writes:

> The [frontier] myth recounts the regeneration of the soul and the attainment of salvation through a complex experience of violent confrontation with the powers of nature, equated with the forces of darkness; the hero is either a captive or an aveng-

> ing destroyer – or some combination of both. Men are victims, avengers or devils. The cosmos consists of a world and an anti-world. The former is the common-day world of pastoral peace, as world which retains the memory and some of the attributes of a Golden Age, an Eden or Acadia. – but the landscape is dimmed by a nameless malaise, a fear of dark forces both inside and outside the world. (60)

Howard was also aware of this myth being incorporated in his tales. He writes: "Why shouldn't I look back on the frontier with envy? For a man who loved untamed liberty more than he did ease and security, the frontier was an ideal place." (Trout, 59).

Another idea can as easily be seen in Howard's works, the idea of the American Dream. In *The Hyborean Age*, a text that describes the world and history of the fantasy stories, Howard tells the reader about the barbarian King, Gorm, who through the aid of an educated priest has risen to govern most of the lands.

> He who had been born in a mud-walled, wattle roofed hut, in his old age sat on golden thrones, and gnawed joints of beef presented to him on golden dishes by naked slave-girls who were the daughters of kings. (20)

Perhaps this is the ultimate (albeit exaggerated) description of the American Dream. If we combine the rise to power with the violence of the frontier, this reading becomes even more interesting. Yet this does not apply to only one text. Regardless of the internal chronology of the *Conan* tales, the character starts out as a lowly thief in "Tower of the Elephant", becomes a barbarous/Middle Eastern warlord at the head of a huge nomadic tribe in "The Devil in Iron & People of the Black Circle", to finally become King of Aquilonia in the novel *Hour of the Dragon*. The progression from simple-minded, thieving barbarian to occupier -- or rather *usurper?* – of the king's throne could also echo a clichéd version of the American Dream: the paperboy becoming president! As Mathews notes:

THE BARBARIAN ARCHETYPE AND THE CONAN TALES

> The very idea of a Barbaric King is, particularly in the context of modern history, oxymoronic: Conan is a paradoxically "uncivilized" head of a civil society. There is no doubt an implicit American rejection of the European model of monarchy, particularly all traditions of rarefied, dandified, inherited courtly royalty that is so strongly associated in cultural terms with monarchy. (122)

By insisting that only the strong survive the wilderness, Sword & Sorcery stands apart from European fantasy fiction, most notably the works of the Inklings (amongst them writers such as Tolkien, C.S. Lewis, Charles Williams, and others. (See Carpenter 1997 for more information).

This leads us to the next possible way in which to view Howard's fantasy: a fictionalised version of Social Darwinism. This approach states that -- just as competition between individual organisms drives biological evolutionary change (speciation) -- competition between individuals or groups in human societies society drives social evolution. Some of the more radical versions of Social Darwinism were the precursors of scientific racism, and theories of racial hygiene and fascism. It would be possible to view some of Howard's texts in this light, as many – especially French critics -- have done. But prior to jumping to conclusions it would be proper to examine Howard's stories in the context of *when* they were written.

It has been claimed that Howard is a bigot and that he is promoting pseudo-fascist ideas through his fiction, but others, such as Connors (2004), claim that:

> Unlike his friend, H.P. Lovecraft, Howard does not appear to have held anti-Semitic beliefs, although his views on blacks and other minorities are not atypical (indeed they are in some ways lenient) for a rural white southerner of the period. (105)

Even though it is hard to ignore the stylistic markers usually related to fascism, Howard abhorred the idea of it. This might be obscured by Howard's focus on Nordic themes, Nietzschean supermen, the constant mentioning of the Aryan race, blue-eyed barbarians, and the aforementioned Social Darwinism. Even though the worst facets of fascism had yet to be uncovered almost a decade after his death, Howard opposed Lovecraft's fascination with fascism. In a letter dated December 1934, he writes to Lovecraft:

> I do not condemn the reforms you say would be possible under Fascism. I simply do not believe they would exist under a fascist government. Of course you can draw glowing pictures of a fascist Utopia. But you cannot prove that Fascism is anything but a sordid, retrogressive despotism, which crushes the individual liberty and strangles the intellectual life of every country it inflicts with its slimy presence... I know that the fad now is to sneer at Democracy; but Democracy is not to blame for the troubles of the world. The men who are most to blame are the very men who now would "save" the country under the new name of Nazis or Fascists... . (Herron 2004, 174)

This is not to dismiss the fact that some of Howard's tales can be seen as racist or fascist by today's standards, but this is perhaps also what makes the texts so interesting. Reading them is an ambiguous undertaking, and there is not one single way to interpret the stories. A disclaimer that opens the collection of Howard's horror fiction seems to address this: "The stories herein are complete and unexpurgated. Some contain racist stereotypes and references. Readers can judge them for themselves." (Howard 2001, iii)

Conan might also be viewed as the power fantasy of an egoist child. It is not hard to imagine a thirteen-year-old boy being attracted to blood, swords, barbarians, and perhaps especially, scantily clad maidens ready for the taking. This childlike machismo permeates Howard's fiction. This is not to say that the writing is childlike or totally naïve, but sometimes the main protagonist is.

Moorcock (2004) writes: "The pretend-adults like Conan might claim adult motives – simple greed, sexual lust, calculated vengeance – but emotionally they are prepubescent. "And this is even further substantiated when looking at Howard's own writing, as for example in 'Queen of the Black Coast.'":

> He was a valiant trencherman, and strong drink was a passion, a weakness with him. Naïve as a child in many ways, unfamiliar with the sophistry of civilisation, he was naturally intelligent, jealous of his rights and dangerous as a hungry tiger. (118)

It is not a new idea that the protagonists of fantasy can be compared to children. Just think of hobbits or the more recent young protagonists of Rowling, Colfer, Delaney, Eddings, or Pullman. But in Sword & Sorcery, the child (and Howard's Conan) is caught in the body of a grown, powerful, sexual man – and this ambiguity between mind and body could also be one of the reasons that the figure of the barbarian remains so fascinating.

Howard's stories are not completely free of social or political undertones. Even though they present themselves as (as has been interpreted) tales about fascism or the superiority of man over woman, they can also be thoroughly enjoyed as exaggerated, violent fantasy stories. These are stories that should not be subjected to closer (Freudian) analysis.

To condemn fiction as having a bad influence on children or readers in general, would be similar to Frederic Wertham's condemnation of comic books in *Seduction of the Innocent*. This reaction, however, misstates the sheer entertainment value of these stories and underestimates the critical judgment of readers. How to interpret Howard's stories can perhaps never be answered completely, but it is clear that his tales have had, and continue to have, an impact on our current cultural landscape.

New Guises of the Barbarian

It would be fair to say that the population at large knows of the barbarian, or Conan, from sources other than Howard's stories. Perhaps some have seen the documentaries on the Barbarians of history. Perhaps we know about Conan from comics, or have seen a barbarian on a poster. Others may have encountered barbarians when role playing or examining heavy metal covers. The following section examines other media forms where the iconoclastic barbarian is encountered.

Film

One of the first images that might come to mind when hearing the word "Conan" is Arnold Schwarzenegger. He portrayed the character in the two Conan films; readers might also have seen him in the role of the barbarian Kalidor in the spin-off *Red Sonia,* who, incidentally is also a Howard creation. Even though Howard afficionados often criticise the Conan films for being far removed from Howard's original, some scenes are lifted directly from the stories. In John Milius' *Conan the Barbarian* (1981), the crucifixion scene is taken from the story "A Witch Shall be Born", and the scene where Conan and his thief companions climb and enter the tower to capture a sacred emerald is lifted almost verbatim from "Tower of the Elephant."

In the first Conan film, the protagonist often prays to his god Crom, and curses him if he does not ensure his victory. It is not uncommon in Howard's stories for Conan to address his god, and he almost always does so in a defiant tone. But the gods in both the films and Howard's fiction are non-existent. They are man-made fantasies or (in the case of antagonist Thulsa Doom) are self-proclaimed deities. The casting of James Earl Jones in the role of Doom also has fuelled the idea of the barbarian as a vehicle for racist ideas. Milius has been nicknamed "Hollywood's resident fascist" according to Scott Connors. (Herron 1984) *Conan the Barbarian* opens with a voiceover of the infamous Nietzsche quote: "What does not kill you, makes you stronger" from his 1888 work *Twilight of the Idols [Götzen dämmerung]* and seems only to reaffirm that the Conan narratives have political and ideological subtexts.

The absence of deities in the film could also point to the pervasive nihilistic undercurrents of Howard's stories. However, we may also interpret it the other way around: Crom *does* in fact, via Conan's sword, intervene, and help Conan to prevail against overwhelming odds.

The hugely successful *Conan* films spawned quite a few imitations. In retrospect, age has not treated Ruggero Deodato's fantasy comedy

THE BARBARIAN ARCHETYPE AND THE CONAN TALES

The Barbarians well. The film can be seen today as both a spoof, as a misunderstood and even a "light" form of barbarism. The film revolves around a set of identical barbarian twins, separated at birth and later reunited to do battle, first between themselves and then against evil forces. The film is, admittedly, a bit of a joke, and it relies much more on physical comedy and slapstick than the traits of the Sword & Sorcery subgenre. But even though the film may fail miserably as a genre piece or as art, many reviews on the Internet movie database show that fans revere the film. It is every little boy's fantasy, in that it seems to address the insatiable craving of seven-to-thirteen year old boys for violence, gore, topless women, and shows of strength. Furthermore, the film promotes the idea that the Sword & Sorcery subgenre is primarily aimed at this age group.

Even though the general popularity of *The Barbarians* can be questioned, it would seem that some television series that are part of the Sword & Sorcery subgenre, such as *Hercules* or *Xena: Warrior Princess*, try to reach this demographic by imitating Deodato. Even though *The Barbarians* may seem ludicrous, it is still far from being nearly as horrifyingly bad as *The New Barbarians*. This film has only very few links to the Sword & Sorcery subgenre, since it is, in fact, a low-budget science fiction film, made in the wake of such blockbusters as John Carpenter's *Escape from New York* and the first two *Mad Max* films. I mention *The New Barbarians*, however, for good reason: it shows that barbarians and the savage value system embodied in Howard's tales can even be placed in a futuristic setting and still make sense. The moral of the story: when civilisation is absent or has been destroyed, man reverts to barbarism.

Videogames

When the first home computers were introduced in the 1980s, games featuring barbarians were quick to follow. A good example is Datasoft's *Conan* for the Apple II. Barbarians were also featured in the ZX-Spectrum game *Barbarian*. Even though the graphics are appalling by today's standards, these were the first encounters many youngsters had with the character of the barbarian in media other than film or books and magazines. *Barbarian* was a basic one-on-one battle game, where two barbarians were placed in a pit to fight to the death, similar to some films. Datasoft's game was a very early version of martial arts games such as *Mortal Kombat* or *Tekken*. Datasoft included the visual feature of decapitation, if one got that far.

In recent years an official *Conan* game has been released. The game, a third-person adventure/action offering, was created in co-operation with the Robert E. Howard trust and uses music from Milius' film. The basic storyline is faithful to Howard's fiction and, by using music, the game remediates the two different media. The latest development is a big-budgeted, impressive Massive Multiplayer Role Playing Game (MMORPG) aptly named *Age of Conan - Hyborean Adventures*. It was released to mixed reviews in summer 2008, and it still remains to be seen if the manufacturers can succeed in appealing to the cyber-barbarians in all of us. Or will it be just another game unable to compete the most successful MMORPG game: *World of Warcraft* - where barbarians are also allowed to roam?

Other Media

Apart from barbarians cropping up on CD covers for bands such as Manowar, posters by Frank Fazetta and other fantasy artists, and even in role-playing games – some devoted solely to Conan – the barbarian character has also appeared in the world of comic books.

Conan was serialised originally in the 1970s by Marvel Comics, starting with "Conan the Barbarian", "The Savage Sword of Conan" (1974) and "King Conan" from 1980. Some of the original Conan comics have recently been reprinted and collected in hardback format complete with new colouration, appealing to new fans and adding to the frustration of collectors who have to invest in that version as well.

Now published by Dark Horse Comics, Conan is still enjoying new adventures. Dark Horse initiated their series in 2003 with many of the best comic writers and artists working on the character.

In a much lighter vein, *MAD Magazine* cartoonist, Sergio Aragones created a barbarian character called Groo the Wanderer around 1981. Perhaps inspired by the first Conan film, Groo was also a spoof of the barbarian and of Sword & Sorcery in general. It must be noted, however, that even though Aragones' comic books poke fun at the genre, the success of the series, as with video games and comics, introduced a new generation of readers to fantasy literature in general and to Robert E. Howard in particular.

Finally, I turn to television shows such as *Xena: Warrior Princess*, *Hercules,* and, possibly in a slightly altered form, professional wrestling. All of these utilise the heroes and villains of Sword & Sorcery, albeit in a more politically correct and anaemic version. Conan's character has also been seen in both a live action and an animated series called *Conan the Adventurer*. The animated Conan was itself a spin-off of the popular character He-man, who could be seen as a futuristic Sword & Sorcery version of Howard's original.

The latest animated barbarian adventurer is seen in the pilot for *Korgoth of Barbaria,* an animated series from 2006. The pilot is a blatant satire and pastiche of the barbaric character and Howard's writing. But even though Korgoth pokes fun at the many clichés and formulaic Sword & Sorcery characteristics, *Korgoth* also seems to synthesise what the thirteen-year-old boy inside all of us really wants from Sword & Sorcery: scantily-clad maidens, blood, excessive violence, dark castles, guts and gore, fantastic beasts, alcohol, excitement, mad necromancers, hidden traps, monsters, and a huge, silent, muscular protagonist waving a gigantic sword at the centre of the action.

References

Books and Magazines

Barthes, Roland. *Image, Music, Text*. Glasgow: Fontana Press, 1997.

Botting, Fred. *Gothic*. London: Routledge, 1996.

Carpenter, Humphrey. *The Inklings* London: HarperCollins, 1997

Colfer, Eoin. *Artemis Fowl*. London: Puffin Books, 2002.

Connors, Scott. "Twilight of the Gods: Howard and the Völksturmbevegung." In *The Barbaric Triumph*. Edited by Don Herron. New Jersey: Wildside Press, 2004.

Delaney, Joseph. *The Spook*. London: Random House, 2004.

Donaldson, Stephen. *The Chronicles of Thomas Covenant the Unbeliever.* London: Ballantine Books, 1977.

Eddings, David. *The Belgariad series*. London: Corgi Books, 1983-1985

Howard, Robert E. *The Conan Chronicles.* Vol. 1, *The People of the Black Coast*. London: Golancz, 2001.

_____. *The Conan Chronicles.* Vol. 2. *The Hour of the Dragon* London: Golancz, 2001.

_____. *Nameless Cults. The Cthulhu Mythos Fiction of Robert E. Howard.* Vol. 3. Oakland: Chaosium, 2001.

Jones, Stephen. "Robert E. Howard and Conan: The Early Years" in Howard Vol. 1, 2001.

Knight, George. "Robert E Howard: Hard Boiled Fantasist." In *The Dark Barbarian – The ritings of Robert E. Howard: A Critical Anthology.* Edited by Don Herron. New Jersey: Wildside Press, 1984.

Leiber, Fitz. "Howard's Fantasy." In Herron, ibid.

Lord, Glenn. "Robert E. Howard: Professional Writer." In Herron, ibid.

Mathews, Richard. *Fantasy – The Liberation of Imagination*. New York: Routledge, 2002.

Moorcock, Michael. *Elric*. London: Golancz, 2001.

_____. *The Dreamthief's Daughter*. London: Simon Schuster/ Earthlight, 2001.

_____. *Wizardry & Wild Romance – a Study of Epic Fantasy*. Austin, Texas: Monkey Brain Inc., 2004.

Pringle, David. *Fantasy – The Definitive Illustrated Guide.* London: Carlton Books, 2002.
Pullmann, Phillip. *His Dark Materials.* 3 Vols. London: Scholastic Books, 1998-2001.
Rowling, J.K. *The Harry Potter - series.* London: Bloomsbury, 1998-2007.
Slotkin, Richard. "Regeneration Through Violence: The Mythology of the American Frontier, 1600-1860." In *The Barbaric Triumph.* Edited by Don Herron. New Jersey: Wildside Press, 2004.
Tales of the Cthulhu Mythos. Edited by August Dereleth. London: Grafton, 1988.
The Barbaric Triumph. Edited by Don Herron. New Jersey: Wildside Press, 2004.
The Dark Barbarian – The Writings of Robert E. Howard: A Critical Anthology. Edited by Don Herron. New Jersey: Wildside Press, 1984.
Tolkien, J. R.R. *The Lord of The Rings.* 3 Vols. London: Harper Collins, 1991.
Trout, Steven R. "Heritage of Steel: Howard and the Frontier Myth." In *The Barbaric Triumph.* Edited by Don Herron. New Jersey: Wildside Press, 2004.
Webster's *Encyclopaedic Unabridged Dictionary of the English Language.* New Jersey: Random House, 1994.
Waterman, Edward A. "The Shadow from a Soul on Fire: Robert E. Howard and Irrationalism." In *The Barbaric Triumph.* Edited by Don Herron. New Jersey: Wildside Press, 2004.

Film

Castellari, Enzo G. *The New Barbarians.* Deaf International, 1982.
Carpenter, John. *Escape from New York.* AVCO Embassy Pictures, 1981.
Deodato, Ruggero. *The Barbarians.* Canon Films, 1987.
Fleischer, Richard. *Conan the Destroyer.* Universal Pictures, 1984.
_____. *Red Sonia.* Universal Pictures, 1985.
Milius, John. *Conan the Barbarian.* Universal Pictures, 1984.
Miller, George. *Mad Max.* Warner Brothers, 1979.

Miller, George. *The Road Warrior.* Warner Brothers, 1981.

Television Programs

Bail, Charles, and Martin Denning. "Conan the Adventurer." Keller Entertainment Group, 1997.

Bozereau, Laurent. "Conan Unchained: The Making of Conan." Universal TV, 2000.

Friedman, Ed, et al. *He-Man and the Masters of the Universe,* Filmation Associates, 1983-85.

Lawrence, Katherine. *Conan the Adventurer.* Animated series. Jetlag Productions, 1992-94.

Schulian, John. *Xena: Warrior Princess.* MCA Television / Renaissance Pictures, 1995-2001.

Springer, Aaron. "Korgoth of Barbaria." Comedy Central, 2006.

Williams, Christian. *Hercules – The Legendary Journeys*, MCA Television / Renaissance Pictures, 1995-2001.

Comics

Aragones, Sergio. *Groo the Wanderer.* Marvel /Dark Horse Comics, 1981-current.

Conan the Barbarian. Marvel Comics, 1970-93.

Savage Sword of Conan, Marvel Comics, 1974-95.

King Conan. Marvel Comics, 1980-89.

Conan. Dark Horse Comics, 2004-

Videogames

Blizzard. "World of Warcraft." For PC Windows, 2004.

Datasoft. "Conan - Hall of Volta." For Apple II & Commodore 64, 1984.

Funcom. "Age of Conan - Hyborean Adventures." For PC Windows - Vista, 2007.

Namco. "Tekken." For Playstation, 1995.

Palace Software. "Barbarian." For ZX Spectrum 48k & Commodore 64, 1987.

Sega. "Mortal Kombat." For Sega Megadrive & Genesis, 1993.

TDK Interactive. "Conan." For PC Windows & various consoles, 2004.

Steen Christiansen

The "Rat" in Fraternity
China Mieville's King Rat

Discussions of radical politics and socialist dogma are rarely found in fantasy novels, yet they are not unusual in China Miéville's works. As an academic with a Ph.D. in international law, Miéville is no stranger to such discussions, even if he denies any direct connection between his academic and literary careers. It is obvious that Miéville exhibits a high degree of social consciousness; he is a professed socialist and a member of the British Socialist Workers Party.

In the following chapter, I will examine the way in which Miéville's work explores social issues in narrative form, and how the fantasy genre's conventions are used but also turned upside-down in the process. I will focus on his novel *King Rat,* where Miéville's narratives stage critical inquiries into social issues. These narratives take fantastic forms primarily as a means of challenging political and socio-economic borders in radical ways. Fantasy, as a particular form of narrative construction, is suitable for such challenges in the way it enables writer and reader to question our relationship with reality, in Lucie Armitt's words. (Armitt 2005) She goes on to argue that fantasy exists within a space where the real and the speculative "come adrift," encouraging us to lose, question, and reorientate ourselves to the real. (121-22)

It is therefore possible to view fantasy as a subversive literature at times, even if subversion is not an inherent feature of the genre. This argument is not unique to Armitt, so now I turn to clarify how fantasy may function as subversive literature, and how I will interpret Miéville's work as a cultural critique in narrative form. First, we need to establish two things:

1. how fantasy can function as subversive writing, and what that means, and
2. how narrative form can function as cultural critique.

As to the first point, fantasy is, in fact, more often viewed as an inherently conservative genre, which Miéville himself has pointed out with considerable disgust:

> Tolkien's clichés - elves 'n' dwarfs 'n' magic rings - have spread like viruses. He wrote that the function of fantasy was "consolation," thereby making it an article of policy that a fantasy writer should mollycoddle the reader. (BoingBoing 2003)

How does such a conservative ideological reassertion come about if fantasy functions as a discursive space where we may examine our relation to reality? The answer comes from the function of closure inherent in any narrative text; it is a common ending for most fantasy fictions to re-establish order and harmony. As Lucie Armitt states when talking about fairy tales:

> The political dangers of this [accepting the "happily ever after" of fairy tales] are that if we are seduced into believing the fairy-tale world to be one of order and harmony, we may end up following the rules of these stories ourselves. (1996, 28)

This passage shows how — even in the case of fantasy fictions other than simple fairy tales — the return to order may be seen as distinctly reactionary in the way the narrative resists change. Novels as different as C.S. Lewis' *The Lion, the Witch and the Wardrobe*, Robin Hobb's *The Farseer Trilogy* and Terry Brooks' *The Sword of Shannara* (not to mention Brooks' countless sequels and prequels), all take as their starting point the assumption that equilibrium must be restored to the fictional world. Indeed, Rosemary Jackson in her book *Fantasy: The*

Literature of Subversion argues that "Fantasies... frequently serve... to reconfirm institutional order by supplying a vicarious fulfilment of desire and neutralising an urge towards transgression." (Jackson cited in Armitt 1996, 35)

Jackson's point – and by extension Armitt's, who agrees with her – is that while fantastic literature reveals the limits of the dominant cultural order, often by introducing disorder and illegality, that same cultural order is reaffirmed when order and harmony are (re-)established at the end of the text. The transgression of this cultural order is typically cast as the villain of the fiction, furthermore emphasised by the transgressive and unnatural powers and abilities: making the dead walk again, casting the land into eternal winter, or otherwise disturbing the natural order. By extension, the ideological aspects of the fictions are naturalised in precisely the same way: the rule of the king is as natural as the seasons, etc. Miéville himself is fully aware of this convention of fantasy, arguing that

> The usual charge that fantasy is escapist, incoherent and nostalgic (if not downright reactionary), though perhaps true for great swathes of the literature, is contingent on *content*. Fantasy is a mode that, in constructing an internally coherent but actually impossible totality – constructed on the basis that the impossible is, for this work, *true* – mimics the 'absurdity' of capitalist modernity. (2002, 42)

This last bit of Miéville's quote needs a bit of elaboration, but it certainly shows that Miéville is a socialist and schooled in Marxist thought. Miéville's argument comes from the Marxist axiom of commodity fetishism, defined as "the definite social relation between men themselves... assume here, for them, the fantastic form of a relation between things" (Marx cited in Miéville 2002, 41), a statement that Miéville extends to this:

> Under capitalism, the social relations of the everyday – that "fantastic form" - are the dreams, the "grotesque ideas," of the commodities they rule. (42)

Capitalist modernity, Miéville argues, is just as absurd as fantastic fiction, in the way that they both construct a totality from something which is actually impossible but still stated as true. Capitalism and the fantastic therefore share a similar grotesque structure, which makes the fantastic well suited to deal with capitalist modernity. This same notion can be found in Jack Zipes' work, where he argues that reading fantasy separates the reader from the restrictions of reality, and so reveals what Armitt refers to as the oppressive forces (Zipes cited in Armitt 1996, 27). Fantasy can thus be used to threaten the dominant order; in the way it employs textual strategies of openness that challenge the literary reproduction of the real. As Armitt writes:

> This endlessly open and thus non-containable text must therefore pose a dangerous threat to established notions of fixity and conformity, a characteristic that obviously makes the fantastic a particularly appealing form for the exploration of socio-political marginality and ex-centricity. (33)

The point can thus be made that while fantasy might at times function as reactionary and conservative, it also has the potential to radically reexamine the boundaries of the real – ideological, economic, cultural, and others – by employing transgressive narratives that do not depend on a return to harmony and order at the end of the story. Armitt goes on to state that

> Jackson has, as we have seen, categorically argued that it is via strategies of narrative and not simply of content that fantasy fictions can "disturb" the rules in a way that is analogous to, if not to be equated with, "anarchic or revolutionary politics." (34)

Through the construction of narratives, fantasy fiction may therefore challenge the dominant cultural order by creating connections between disparate elements and reflecting on the relation between specific details and the broader social structure. Freed from the constraints of reality or realism, fantasy is able to enact possibilities that have been negated or neutralised in hegemonic discourses, thus representing alternatives to hegemonic thought and ideology. Here we should keep in mind that even conservative fantasy represents an alternative to the capitalistic hegemony, in the way that feudal society is represented as an ordered, structured, and attractive society. Kings are benevolent, serfs are content, and only encroaching evil can disturb the peace. Viewed this way, all fantasy becomes subversive in its representation of alternatives, and Miéville's argument that the reader is being mollycoddled seems to be a polemical overstatement.

At the same time, there is a very different thrust to Miéville's writing than, for example, in Tolkien's, and clearly Miéville is advocating radical politics. Such fantasy narratives can provide a different logical system as the means to make society cohere. As Miéville himself said about the relation of the fantastic to real concerns:

> the realism of concern and the weird of expression are each their own end, but through metaphor, that magic dialectical glue, they are also, in a critical fantasy, functions of each other. (Miéville 2005)

Metaphor is therefore the obvious place to go when examining Miéville's novel. With that in mind, let us investigate the following metaphors in *King Rat* and analyse their critical potential: 1) the rats, King Rat and Saul; 2) urban London, the homeless and the conspiracy of architecture; and 3) the jungle metaphor of drum 'n' bass music.

The plot of *King Rat* is straightforward enough: Saul Garamond arrives at his father's home, but goes straight to bed without saying hello since he and his father do not have a particularly good relationship. He is awoken by the police and discovers that his father has been killed, and that the police suspect him. In jail, a strange person calling himself King Rat frees Saul and tells him that he is half rat, half human. Meeting the king of the birds, Loplop, and the king of the spiders, Anansi, Saul learns of a strange world that exists between the cracks of the London he thought he knew. It turns out that the Pied Piper of Hamelin has returned, intent on killing not just the animal kings but Saul, too.

THE "RAT" IN FRATERNITY

A second narrative strand concerns Saul's friends, primarily Natasha, the Jungle DJ who begins to make music with a strange flutist called Pete. Obviously, Pete is the Pied Piper, wanting to learn how to layer music so that he can control more than one species at a time. True to convention, the book ends with a massive showdown between Saul, the Pied Piper, and the three animal kings, where Saul has to fight to free his friends and defend the rats to which he is related.

However, it is after this showdown that the novel diverges most distinctly from convention: Saul refuses to ascend to the title of King Rat as the rats desire. Instead, he abolishes the feudal rule, stating that the rats are free and that he is simply one of them: "I'm Citizen Rat." (Miéville 1998, 420) Here we see how the novel does not return to the equilibrium destroyed by the Piper's first appearance (in 1284, according to legend), but instead not only rejects that convention, but breaks down even further the typical *faux* feudalism of so much fantasy fiction. This is a pattern that is maintained in Miéville's next three novels: *Perdido Street Station*, *The Scar*, and *Iron Council*; each concludes with a social revolution, overthrowing the old social order (though not always clearly for the better). Even from this quick examination, we can see how Miéville's novels are engaged with social change, revolution, and political struggle.

Let us now focus on the motif and metaphor of the rats of London, the creatures that are supposedly led by King Rat. I say supposedly, because -- since the Pied Piper tragically drowned all the rats of Hamelin -- King Rat has been a king without subjects. Although still supernaturally connected to the rats and with powers derived from them (immunity to poison and spoiled food, the ability to squeeze through the tiniest cracks, heightened sense of smell), King Rat would not be followed by his subjects. They blame him for the catastrophe and see Saul as the logical successor.

The rats of *King Rat* are actual rodents; there is nothing supernatural about them. This is left to King Rat and Saul. However, the metaphor of the rat comes to the fore through the hybrid state of being rat and human – Saul lives, thinks and acts more and more like a rat and his latent powers are awakened by acting like a rat. Shortly after meeting King Rat for the first time, Saul is invited to eat from a dumpster:

> He willed himself to feel ill. He strove for nausea. He took a bite. He wriggled his tongue into the meat, pushed apart the fibres. He probed, tasting the dirt and decay. Lumps of gristle and fat split open in his mouth, mixed with his saliva. The burger was delicious. Saul swallowed and did not fall ill. His hunger, piqued, demanded more. He took another bite, and another, eating faster and faster all the time. He felt something slipping away from him. He drew his strength from the old cold meat, food that had surrendered to people and decay, and now to him. His world changed. (59-60)

This rather detailed quote clearly attempts to gross out the reader, to show through the image of spoiled food how much Saul is, in fact, changing. No one reading this passage can help but feel the nausea that Saul cannot conjure, and even Saul realises how he is changing, transgressing the cultural (and biological) boundaries that stop us from eating spoiled food. However, when we consider the structure of the passage and what it means for the narrative, we realise that this is Saul's equivalent of tumbling down the rabbit hole, walking through the wardrobe cupboard, or being carried away by a funnel cloud. This is the paragraph that marks the transition from the ordinary world into the fantastic "secondary" world – from London to rat-London, so to speak. As Lucie Armitt points out, it is precisely in this introduction of a secondary world that fantasy questions our relationship with reality. (2005, 52) The rats are thus an image of what we do not wish to be confronted with in our society; after the transition, Saul begins to live in sewers, eating food scavenged from dumpsters, encountering homeless people. In general, he begins to interact with the urban environment in a completely different way.

The rats – and by extension King Rat and Saul, who live like human rats – represent something with which we cannot empathise. Living in sewers, never showering, eating spoiled food are all revolting actions that we cannot imagine, and, just as significantly, they are not actions that hold any form of the fulfilment of desire. Saul's frustration at being dragged into this world is clear, even as he begins to feel more and more at home in it. It seems unlikely that any reader should feel the desire to live as Saul does, as his life is far from romanticised.

Instead, the fantastic world of rats and London between the cracks serve as a contrast to our own reality. We see our world reflected through it, reversed and unpleasant at times. The clearest instance of this is the reversal of the story that informs Miéville's novel: *The Pied Piper of Hamelin*, the fairy tale collected by the Brothers Grimm and retold in verse by Robert Browning. This well-known tale of the Piper who rids the town of Hamelin from a plague of rats, and when the citizens refuse to pay, leads their children away, remains at first unchanged when told from the perspective of King Rat. But eventually the perspective does change, and so does the moral of the story.

For King Rat, the tragedy is not that the children are led away, but instead that the rats are drowned, purged in what he refers to explicitly as a holocaust. (Miéville 1998, 163) Even we as readers cannot help but evoke some remorse from this description:

> The third note sounds, and apocalypse begins ... As I troop ravenous onwards, I suddenly feel queer horror in my gut. I was using my nose?, and I saw there wasn't no food where we were going. "Stop," I shrieks, and *no one listens* ... we're trotting in time, all four legs stately and sharpish to that... *abominable* piping, tails swaying like metronomes ... I can see them getting ready and I'm screaming at them to stop, but I'm pissing in the wind, it's a done deal. They step off the stone walls of the bridge and into the water ... There was a frantic mass of us kicking up froth, an isle of rat bodies, fighting and killing to climb atop, the foundations dying and disappearing below ... Screams and choking are everywhere; stiff little bodies bob past me like buoys in hell's harbour. This is the end of the world, I think, and the stinking water fills my lungs, and I sink. Everywhere are corpses. (159-63; italics original)

This reversal of the Pied Piper tale shows the importance of perspective in such narratives, and even if we cannot fully empathise with the rats, we certainly feel that the story suddenly has a different resonance. Our steady assumptions are playfully challenged by this reversal, and the Piper is definitely cast in the role of the villain.

But the most clear reversal and contrast that the new rat-life of Saul shows us is how immediately he becomes as invisible as a homeless person London. Saul is completely ignored by pedestrians when he walks through the streets; they hardly even look at him. Saul is at first frustrated with this, but learns that the "rules of the city no longer concerned him. The prohibition against pedestrians on the Westway did not apply to rats." (130-31) The distance between Saul as rat and ordinary humans is much more than what one should at first expect. "Again he thought: these things take place so close to the real city, and no one else can see them. They take place ten feet away, somewhere in another world." (213)

However, even as Saul becomes dissociated from the rules of the city, it takes on a new meaning for him. "With King Rat by his side, Saul had seen a new city. The map of London had been ripped up and redrawn according to King Rat's criteria." (126) London becomes a primary part of the novel, particularly the way in which it offers an alternative view of the city, just as the revised Pied Piper tale creates an alternative view of the original. The geography of London and the way it changes become an image of Saul's transition from human to rat. As the city alters its meaning for Saul, we gain a different perspective – the underground London becomes the structuring metaphor of the entire novel, and to decode the city is to decode much of political struggle taking place. It is the fantastic reflection of the underground London which serves as a contrast to our own reality, and it is through the image of the city that we are confronted with the critical function of Miéville's narrative.

Saul's ascension to the position of Prince Rat is hardly a glorious move into an enchanted kingdom of wonder. Instead, Saul is presented with the downside to modern London. His return from the Suffolk coast, before becoming a rat, foreshadows some of the city's gloom:

> The train was now below the houses. It wound through a deep groove in the city, as if the years of passage had worn down

> the concrete under the tracks ... Outside, the gash through which the tracks passed had widened as the station approached. The walls on either side were punctuated by dark alcoves, small caves full of rubbish a few feet from the track ... He wound through the cold until his father's house rose before him. Terragon Mansions was an ugly Victorian block, squat and mean-looking for all its size. (8-11)

The sombre, rubble-filled description feels much like the process of going underground and Saul feels appropriately oppressed by the buildings. The point seems clear enough; the buildings are oppressive in themselves and living among them – returning to London – does not please Saul. The physical architecture seems to bear down on Saul and the picture of London is grim.

All this changes once Saul becomes a rat. The city does not become any more pleasant, but Saul's relationship to it changes. The first thing we notice is that Saul can crawl up straight walls, even if it takes time to learn this skill. He can find his way through the sewers more instinctively than when above ground, using what is referred to as his "I Suppose" (56), a supernatural sense which is inexplicable but always gets him to the right place. In the end, Saul discovers the significant fact that the urban space no longer has the same hold on him:

> He realised that he had defeated the city. He crouched on the roof (of what building he did not know) and looked out over London at an angle from which the city was never meant to be seen. He had defeated the conspiracy of architecture, the tyranny by which the buildings that women and men had built had taken control of them, circumscribed their relations, confined their movements. These monolithic products of human hands had turned on their creators, and defeated them with common sense, quietly installed themselves as rulers. They were as insubordinate as Frankenstein's monster, but they had waged a more subtle campaign, a war of position more effective by far. (288)

The conspiracy of architecture is a reference to an article by Miéville himself, published in *Historical Materialism* (Miéville, 1998b), where he argues that architecture and especially its representations are "an aesthetic response to the peculiar alienated relation between humanity and architecture under capitalism" and that (2) this meaning is invested in buildings by humans, as part of our lived experience. The result of this, according to Miéville, is that in

> thinking about society through buildings, we turn to the cultural *conception* of architecture, "architecture once removed." In being reflected upon, the culture that is embedded in the architecture is brought to the forefront of social consciousness, made malleable. (Miéville 1998b, 17; italics original)

Miéville's argument is that built environment has an effect on inhabitants, much like we saw in the opening with Saul entering London. However, Miéville rejects a mechanistic view of this effect. While the effect is real enough, it is never simple or one-sided; there is no direct relationship between architecture and the effect it has on people. While built environment may exert totalitarian force and undermine people's power, this power represents a relationship that is open to interaction and negotiation. What is being negotiated is, of course, social power, and so the representation of London and its underground counterpart become a space for negotiating such social power.

This is why, I argue, we are confronted with the unusual spaces of sewers, abandoned tube stations, and garbage-filled alleyways. These spaces are liminal, ignored by the greater society as detritus and irrelevant, yet in *King Rat* they are alive with fantastic events. It is also why we hear about the lives of the homeless. These are people who have fallen through the cracks of what in Miéville's mind would be capitalist architecture, and now need to negotiate the urban space in a different way. Normal people are far removed from this shadowy, underground world and will never see it, just as Saul can never fully see the "normal" London he has left behind.

These liminal spaces are important because they are transgressive; they are places where the laws of society are suspended, simply because the conspiracy of architecture has closed the eyes of most people, making them blind to what goes on in the cracks. The map of London is redrawn because it is transgressed; Saul realises that there is not simply a map of London above and the London below, with its sewers and the tube; these two maps blend together for him. Just as he becomes part human, part rat, he lives partly in London above and London below. This notion of a London above and a London below is nothing new. In fact, the term "London below" stems from Neil Gaiman's *Neverwhere*, a novel that shares many affinities with Miéville's – both imagine a world apart from the everyday in the cracks of London, and both employ the motif of rats. However, there are also many differences in tone between the two novels, Miéville's being the darker.

   This transgression of the urban space as an image of social transgression (or perhaps even rebellion) is emphasised by the animals that the three animal kings command: rats, spiders, and birds. These are not only seen as pests (consider the pigeons of Trafalgar Square), but they also have a completely different way of interacting with urban space: they can move in three dimensions, ignoring the division between ground level, lower level, and upper level. Saul develops this characteristic when he becomes a rat, moving from sewer to rooftop with no problem. Consider the line in the quotation above of Saul defeating the conspiracy of architecture. He "looked out over London at an angle from which the city was never meant to be seen," indicating that this is more than simple newness. It is a breach of what is permissible.

   Saul moves beyond the permissible by negotiating the urban space differently, a negotiation which is at least somewhat similar to the alternate negotiation done by the homeless. It is important to stress here that Miéville does not romanticise the lives of the homeless; they are not presented as fascinating or positive in any way. What is stressed, however, is the different way of dealing with the city and the way that it exposes the failings of capitalist society. Much like the rats, the homeless do not truly fit into society, and have learned to navigate the marginal spaces of London, existing at the edges of society and only rarely coming into contact with established norms. As we see from Saul's encounter with the homeless woman Deborah, homelessness is one way of dealing with the conspiracy of architecture, but it is not a pleasant one. Deborah is mentally disturbed, something Saul attributes to the alienation she has experienced at the hands of the city. (Miéville 1998a, 224) The city can thus exert unpleasant control over people if they do not have a proper way to negotiate its architecture.

It is here that we can see how the final metaphor I will investigate becomes significant: the subculture of drum 'n' bass or Jungle music provides another way of negotiating the city. Using the explicit imagery of the city as wilderness (jungle), the musical subculture is inherently urban in its expression, but in a way that refuses to accept the city as built environment. Rather, the city is portrayed as animate, beyond the control of most but traversable by the rudeboys and rudegirls, who cast themselves as urban savages. In an attempt to convince one of his professors that Jungle is a worthy subject for painting, Fabian, one of Saul's friends, explains that there is no place for individualism in a Jungle club. He succeeds, as the professor "would rather have died than admit there were any gaps in [his] knowledge of *youth*." (Miéville 1998a, 265, italics original) Far from wanting to make the same mistake, I will not deal extensively with the drum 'n bass musical culture, but simply emphasise two images.

First, while Fabian argues that individualism has no place on the dance floor, the music itself is clearly unique and, at the same time, hybrid. Made from samplings of earlier music tracks, jungle does not have an originary moment, and only exists as the relation between these widely disparate pieces of music. A description of Natasha, Saul's DJ friend, gives an idea of the process involved:

> She scrolled through the selection and plucked a favourite bassline from her digital killing jar. She had snatched it from a forgotten Reggae track, sampled it, preserved it, and now she pulled it out and looped it and gave it another life. The zombie sound travelled the innards of the machine... Her eyes were wide as she scanned her kills, her pickled sounds, and

> she found what she wanted: a snatch of trumpet from Linton Kwesi Johnson, a wail from Tony Rebel, a cry of invitation from Al Green... This was Jungle. The child of House, the child of Raggamuffin, the child of Dancehall, the apotheosis of black music, the Drum and Bass soundtrack for a London of council estates and dirty walls. (Miéville 1998a, 66-67)

The significance of the music comes not so much from unity as it comes from hybridity; Natasha can hear each piece of music and where it comes from, zombie sounds that are individual in their own right. The painting that Fabian creates as a visual representation of Jungle is much the same:

> It was very large, contained in a box, and surrounded by ganja leaves and sound-system speakers and modern serfs, rudebwoys [sic] and gyals, an intricate parody, the expressionless zombies of monastic art executed by Keith Haring or one of the New York Subway Artists. The rest of the writing was mostly dark, but not matte?-black, shot through with neon strips and encased in gaudy integuments. In the corner below the writing lurked the police, like devils: The Man. But these days the sloganeering had to be ironic. Fabian knew the rules and couldn't be bothered to disobey them, so the devils coming up from the pit were ridiculous, the worst nightmares of St. Anthony and Sweet Sweetback combined. (264)

The bricolage style is the same, including the reference to "zombie" as the image of re-cycled cultural products. Also, the emphasis on the city is the same, regarding the work as existing in a distinct relation to the urban space (soundtrack for London, the visual style of New York Subway Artists). Blending all manner of references together, the music and the painting valorise the hybrid.

Second, Saul experiences the dance floor at the Junglist Terror event -- the final showdown between him and the Piper. The description strikes a middle ground between Fabian's comment and the hybridity of the music:

> The dancefloor was tight-packed, thronging with bodies, decadent and vibrant, thrilling, communal and brutal... He was struck by the multiplicity of expressions on the faces below. (Miéville 1998a, 371-372)

While the dance floor might be a communal place because people attain a shared identity there, they all do so in unique ways. Each expression is individualised; only the appreciation of the music is the same for all participants. As such, this image is a contrast to the dance performed when the Piper uses his flute:

> The dancers moved as one. They moved in time, dancing again, an incredible piece of choreography, every right foot raised together, coming down, then every left, a strange languorous hardstep, arms swinging, legs rigid, up and down in time to the beat, obeying the Piper's flute. (Miéville 1998a: 382-383)

Here, individuality is lost, and we can imagine that there is no longer a multiplicity of expressions. The Piper's music, although now borrowing the jungle technique of layering sounds, is a singular music. It is not based on hybridity but is intent on repressing people. It is as totalitarian as the conspiracy of architecture. The jungle music's hybridity becomes a strategy for navigating the urban space, and that is perverted by the Piper's layered, monolithic sound.

However, there is one person who is less affected that the others by the Piper's music. That is Saul, because he himself is a hybrid: both rat and human. However, Saul is not an integrated whole but rather something monstrous, even transgressive. Saul becomes like a jungle track, existing only as a link between rat and human, and because of that the Piper cannot use a combined rat and human song, as he had expected. Saul is something different, something new. His origins mean less than the combination of the two.

King Rat thus celebrates hybridity on several levels: Saul as rat plus man; Jungle as a zombification of sounds; London as both real and fantastic, its spaces opening up to transgressive uses. It is a hybrid-

THE "RAT" IN FRATERNITY

ity that is greater than its component parts, not reducible to the individual elements. Even on a meta-level, hybridity is primary: the real concerns of urban space and capitalist domination are expressed through the metaphors of the fantastic.

Miéville's novel *King Rat* thus functions in two interrelated ways. The first is a movement inward, where the fantasy genre conventions and the readers' expectations of it are questioned and subverted. On another level, is the movement outward, where the cultural dominant is challenged. Yet, as noted, the two movements are interrelated; the subversion of the genre conventions tie into the ideological aspect of the text; the overthrowing of feudal society so typical in most fantasy literature enables the deconstruction of a cultural dominant. However, even though the feudal society of the rats and their king is broken by Saul, the situation is more complex.

First, Saul abdicates as the successor to King Rat, who has fled in disgrace. And he does so with a nod to his dead father, a confirmed socialist. However, even as the feudal society is broken down, it happens with the proclamation:

> I declare this Year One of the Rat Republic... All equal, all working together, respect going to those who *deserve* it, not just those who claim it... Liberty, Equality... and let's put the "rat" back into "Fraternity." (Miéville 1998a, 420)

This is a distinctly bourgeois revolution, echoing the French Revolution more than any other. It is not clearly evident, however, that such a revolution is necessary to pass through before a true socialist revolution is possible. Furthermore, although he fled in disgrace, King Rat concludes the novel by telling us that he will be back. In other words, the novel's conclusion is not exactly a utopian revolution that frees the rats from oppression, nor are we as readers consoled that Saul will live "happily ever after."

Obviously, with Miéville's rejection of fantasy as a genre that could "mollycoddle" the reader, this ending is hardly surprising. Indeed, we can say that it is precisely the refusal to provide certain and satisfying closure that allows the reader to reflect on the events described.

Most, if not all, of our expectations of fantasy have *not* been met, and so we need to wonder why. Miéville's rhetoric has been quite clear, and it is evident that moralistically simple tales are not what he desires. In addition to that, we can also see how the narrative strategy of contrasting a realistic London with a fantastic one has made it possible for readers to generate an aesthetic space in which to reflect on the very issues Miéville raises.. The novel does not offer an easy resolution, since its whole thrust is to emphasise that there are no easy answers. Instead, we are presented with a distinct challenge to dominant cultural narratives and a call to transgress them, both in political terms and in the broader sense of turning from staid conventions. These must be seen as double-bound: dominant narratives employ specific conventions and only by resisting and transgressing these conventions can we hope to challenge the dominant narratives. As Miéville has argued, ideology is embedded in narratives and must not be left unchallenged.

References

Armitt, Lucie. *Theorising the Fantastic.* London: Arnold, 1996.
_____. *Fantasy Fiction: An Introduction.* New York & London: Continuum Books 2005.
Boingboing. "Miéville on Tolkien." 2003. Online at: http://www.boingboing.net/2003/11/02/mieville_on_tolkien.html Accessed July 27, 2007.
Miéville, China. *King Rat,* London: Pan Books, 1998.
_____. "The Conspiracy of Architecture: Notes on a Modern Anxiety." In *Historical Materialism.* 2, no.1: 1-32.
_____. "Editorial Introduction." In *Historical Materialism.* 10, no. 4: 39-49.
_____. "With One Bound We are Free: Pulp, Fantasy and Revolution." 2005. Online at: http://crookedtimber.org/2005/01/11/with-one-bound-we-are-free-pulp-fantasy-and-revolution. Accessed July 27, 2007.

Camelia Elias

There is a text in 'The Balloon'
Donald Barthelme's Allegorical Flights

> *Ideas of "bloat" and "float" were introduced, as well as concepts of dream and responsibilities.*
> – Donald Barthelme

Fantasy is all that which is counterfactual, contradictory, and counterintuitive. In general terms, and covering more levels of manifestation – from real life to aesthetic representations of it – this is a simple way of defining the notion. Fantasy is also all that which falls outside of our real world. A fantasy world is composed of creatures that are not necessarily human. In a fantasy world we often encounter magicians, witches, dragons, and the like. In terms of genre, fantasy is also characterised by resisting categorization. There is no such genre that is called fantasy. In this sense, when one talks about fantasy, one talks about a cultural practice that allows itself to put anything and everything into a text. The only rule is that the more unlikely the story gets, in terms of its entering a mimetic relation with reality or rather refusal to do so, the better.

In critical discourse about the fantastic, we have such seminal works as Tzvetan Todorov's *The Fantastic: A Structural Approach to a Literary Genre* (1975) in which he claims the following:

> In a world which is indeed our world, the one we know [...] there occurs an event which cannot be explained by the laws

> of this same familiar world. The person who experiences the event must opt for one of two possible solutions: either he is the victim of an illusion of the senses, of a product of the imagination – and the laws of the world then remain what they are; or else the event has indeed taken place, it is an integral part of reality – but then this reality is controlled by laws unknown to us. (25)

What Todorov suggests here is that the fantastic is context based. However, this context is dependent on the play between knowledge and non-knowledge, or else it can be contended that it takes place in the realm of the uncertain. Todorov makes this point even more clearly a little further on: "The fantastic occupies the duration of this uncertainty [...] The fantastic is that hesitation experienced by a person who knows only the laws of nature, confronting an apparently supernatural event." (25) As Todorov's writing, however, stems mainly from a structuralist tradition that has in focus the interplay between signs, or the way in which a sign relates to other signs, he does not give any attention to the notion of fantasy. Nor does he acknowledge the fact that when he talks about hesitation, what he really wants to talk about is not so much the underlying structure of a text in terms of its grammar or poetics, but reader response. If Todorov were to consider an element of fantasy in a text, it would have to be explained by way of making recourse to phenomenology. For instance, if a character, or reader, for that matter, hesitates when encountering a ghost in a text, based on the laws of logic, the character does so because he fears the unknown. On the other hand, if the character acknowledges that something supernatural occurs, then he can either ascribe it to a figment of his imagination, construe it as such linguistically, or else dismiss it as nonsensical.

There is thus a basic distinction that one can make between fantasy and the fantastic: whereas fantasy in critical discourse can be aligned with allegory, in which a supernatural world stands for a figurative representation of our real world, the fantastic has the potential to occur within the world that we know. In other words, the fantastic does not need a fantasy setting in order for it to happen, or to be experienced. In this sense, and from a genre perspective, it makes more sense to pair realism and the fantasy genre, rather than fantasy and the fantastic. In this essay, however, I intend to view these two concepts as closely interrelated, especially in the ways in which each one deals with epistemological questions.

In more general terms, the way of perceiving the fantastic is thus linked not so much to what we know, but to what we don't know. Conversely, in a fantasy setting, an *a priori* knowledge is given to the characters of what they don't know that they already are shown to know. The reader then takes this non-knowledge at face value, but in the context of the fantasy, he or she perceives it non-problematically as knowledge. In disciplines other than the production of fiction, e.g., studies in epistemology, there are many modes of knowing, with some bordering on fantasy or intersecting with "woowoo realism." (Kevin T. Kelly in Hendricks and Pritchard 2008, 192)

Viewed also through this prism, one can then advance the hypothesis that fantasy is allied with knowledge that manifests itself in non-traditional ways, in ways that do not follow normative thinking schemes, and in ways that do not register reality according to set conventions. In everyday language, we encounter phrases such as: "There is more between heaven and earth ..."; "there is more out there"; and "give up the ghost." (By the same token, these or similar idiomatic expressions can also be encountered in the fantastic.) Such phrases have been formulated eloquently at least since Shakespeare's time; Hamlet's encounter with the ghost of his father is all about Hamlet coming to terms with what he is told to "sense" rather than observe as fact. These terms now populate all aesthetic media, from films to books to computer games. (In academic circles, however, the study of fantasy is often linked to the study of the mysterious in paranormal phenomena, and we find them particularly in neuroscience and psychology. In these disciplines "fantasy" plays an important role.[1])

---

[1] See Newberg, Andrew and Eugene D'Aquili, *Why God Won't Go Away: Brain Science and the Biology of Belief.* New York, Ballentine Books, 2001.

THERE IS A TEXT IN 'THE BALLOON'

If we return to the close, if problematic relation between fantasy and the fantastic – or that which supersedes normative modes of perception – and knowledge that resists us, we can make the inference that non-knowledge – as a kind of knowledge à la Socrates's famous dictum: "All I know is that I know nothing" – is a type of knowledge that puts us in a state of perceiving ourselves quite besides ourselves, as it were. But whereas in a fantasy setting this awareness is accepted *as is,* insofar as it is part of the supernatural world, in a fantastic mode this awareness is merely disturbing, as it does not fall outside of the real, or normal, world. In any event, however, being besides ourselves induces an interesting ontological crisis on all levels of representation, whether supernaturally normal, or naturally abnormal, as the question: "who am I?" is reformulated along the lines of "what am I?" The assumption here is that the material body as we see it in the mirror and feel it if we pinch ourselves is also "in touch" with a higher, or perhaps, "unknown" form of being. This might be the non-material form of a soul or the idea of the divine.

In religious and occult contexts, the material body is often seen as a mere container of the immaterial or the intangible. The container can be thought of as being full, filled, fulfilled, emptied, possessed, or repossessed. If something mysterious or inexplicable happens between the body and what it contains (in medical terms), some form of manipulation has taken place. Thus the grounds for a belief in the fantastic are laid. Fantasy, on the other hand, can be said to arise from manipulations of facts that displace what is otherwise already perceived as a-rational or a-logical thinking. If there is anything that rules in either case, it is a constant repositioning of facts in schemes, or containers that are incongruous with general beliefs about what is normal. Where fantasy operates with the abnormal as normal, the fantastic operates with the abnormal as *ab*normal; the latter can thus be deemed a process of not only constant but endless manipulation and displacement of what are known to be facts, and of logical, or axiomatic, thinking.

Both fantasy and the fantastic share — in terms of engaging with knowledge — the fact that they are mediated by, and then operate within, at least three stages of knowledge:

1. The knowledge that the material body contains the immaterial (the mind itself can be considered as such; for example, imagination is intangible, but we know it exists.)
2. The knowledge that the mind loves the unknown; for example, when surrealist painter René Magritte says that: "The mind loves the unknown. It loves images whose meaning is unknown, since the meaning of the mind itself is unknown" he suggests that there is a relationship between the mental images that our imagination is able to conjure in our heads and our desire to decode, or interpret, what and how we ourselves produce as thought in relation to our environment; and
3) The knowledge that not-knowing produces silence. In the face of realizing that we sometimes stand in awe of that which we do not understand, not-knowing is not the result of ignorance. Instead, it is the result of what one can perceive as the ineffable, or that which cannot be expressed in words.

Socrates's statement then becomes quite mysterious as it suggests that silence has a performative quality. The immediate consequence of the statement "All I know is that I know nothing" has the effect of silencing us, because we are forced to confront the vast unknown in the form of acknowledging our limitations. But there are also reversals of this state, namely when we make recourse to the fantastic as a mode of reworking or working through our ignorance. When the Danish architect, epistemologist, and versatile thinker Piet Hein pronounces that "Knowing what thou knowest not, is in a sense omniscience," he suggests that there is a relation of symmetry between knowing and knowing nothing, and that this relation, if it is not mediated by a higher authority such as an omniscient God, is haunted by the Socratic ghost which, through proper reasoning, enables us to see ourselves as gods.

What are fantasy and the fantastic, then, in this scheme of mediated knowledge? They are modes of knowing, where knowledge is of two kinds: inadequate (which invites us to seek more of it) and instrumental (which invites us to use however much of it we have). Thus the fact that we can never 'know' knowledge, nor can we ever be certain, produces what one can call a fantastic atmosphere where beings, material or otherwise, engage in a dance with uncertainty. Where fantasy is concerned, in literary studies and away from the meta-discourse on the distinction between fantasy and the fantastic from an epistemological point of view, we can say that there is only one thing that sets fantasy – and the fantastic — apart from realism: in a fantasy setting, mediated uncertainty is embedded in certainty.

I am thinking about the novels of Jane Austen, which, while unambiguously deemed by critics to fall into the realist genre, can be seen as fantasies. While the women in Austen's novels may not fly on broomsticks, what they do, say, or think, may be seen as outrageous as in the most magical science fiction novel. Where imagination is concerned, what the mind produces, even in the case of mimetic representation, is, by definition, always fantasy. In other words, if there is an ultimate difference between works of fiction, it is because the props change. While this may be applied to all works of fiction – if one accepts that, insofar as all creative works stem from fantasy and so genre categories become pointless — there is something beyond generalization that is worth mentioning.

In terms of shared ground, both fantasy and imagination share synonyms that rely on the currency/efficacy of the same concepts: fancy, creation, fiction, figment, invention, bubble, castle-in-the-air, chimera, dream, pipe dream, daydream. Fantasy is thus none other than imagination that is unrestrained, extravagant, over the top, visionary, and able to conjure a mental image that recalls or resembles the occurrence of unnatural events. For the more etymologically oriented, we can cite the archaic, yet still used, meaning of fantasy as "making visible" (at least since 1275, according to the Random House unabridged dictionary).

This desire to "make visible" is something that both fantasy and the fantastic use, albeit on different levels. In general terms, making things visible is intertwined with the desire of a person to know things beyond the factual, or the explicable, and has been the subject of many myths. The best known is perhaps the Biblical story that narrates the creation of civilization and the fall from God's grace due to Adam's eating from the fruit of the tree of knowledge at Eve's insistence. The fact that Eve is Adam's tempter, seducer, and ensnarer is not insignificant. Other representations of the Fall – since the inception of the story — focus on the fact that giving in to knowledge, succumbing to the desire for it, has powerful consequences, especially for women. Here, the stage has been set for a primeval battle between man and woman.

Implicit in the Biblical story is the assumption that, while man acquires factual knowledge, woman must know something that man doesn't, including her discourse with the serpent. Supposedly, then, woman has access to the fantastic, insofar as Adam fell because he was bedazzled. Perpetuated throughout the ages is the notion that woman always has the potential to know more, but does not tell what she knows. This magical potential has been postulated as a marker that divides the sexes: man is rational because he takes what is given him on a concrete basis; woman is emotional – and potentially rational — yet in a supernatural way, insofar as she lets herself be lured by the "unknown."

That a woman might know more than a man has often intrigued men to the point that male beliefs in a woman's mystical powers went from fairly sound grounding to the utterly fantastic. One need only think about the seventeenth-century witchcraft trials, the culmination of decades of them. Based on discourses about women's fantastic powers these trials had fatal outcomes, as many women paid with their lives for their so-called secret knowledge. In his important monograph *Thinking with Demons: The Idea of Witchcraft in Early Modern Europe* (1997), Stuart Clark looks at how the historical treatments of witchcraft have been mediated by beliefs in constructions of strongly obscure meaning. This meaning, which has demonology at its heart, is often related to the enunciating position of woman as a subject vis-à-vis what she supposedly possesses: dark knowledge, in this case. The epigraph to the chapter "Women and Witchcraft," a quote from Alexander Niccholes's *A Discourse of Marriage and Wiving* (1615) is particularly telling: "There is a Text in women." (106) Indeed, even as a female academic in 2009, I am tempted to say that there is a "Text in women," and this text has kept men busy with interpreting.

THERE IS A TEXT IN 'THE BALLOON'

As a counterpart to real life events that raised the fantastic to legitimizing crusades against mysticism, fantasy, and ultimately good old imagination in the name of God, we find the myth of Faust and Mephistopheles. In this story, more fully and interestingly articulated by Goethe as a two-part drama in 1806 and revised in 1828 (the first known Faust story dates back to Johann Spies's version of 1587), Faust sells his soul to Mephistopheles in order to gain knowledge. As with the Romantics, the very idea of possessing knowledge is all about experiencing the sublime in the grandeur of thought about the divine. Thus, unlike the deglamorised, if fascinating, witches, Faust is depicted as the philosophically inclined young man who wants to know things for their own sake, rather than for the sake of harming others. However, as he prefers human to divine knowledge, he is punished in the end.

The fantastic, in whatever form it appears, will always be mediated first by the desire to know the unknown, to be certain about the uncertain, and then by language. In this relationship, however, between desire and the words needed to express it, language occupies the primary position. Language, as it conjures thought, whether rational or based on fantasy, is produced by an enunciating subject who speaks from the position that is available to him or her. In this sense it is always interesting to consider the position of the enunciating subject vis-à-vis the dominant discourses that produce it. In other words, if something fantastic occurs, what happens if the registering, rather than the experiencing, subject of such a phenomenon is a woman?

As suggested earlier, the fantastic mode is more likely produced by a fantasizing female subject than a male. In the seventeenth century, as Clark's study painfully shows, the issue of men viewing some women as witches who cast spells in real life, rather than in fantasy stories, was not the problem. In light of the aggressive witch hunts that swept through early modern Europe, it is hard to imagine the same rational men, often intellectuals, posing a question similar to Freud's: "What does woman want?" This question might be useful in discovering what constitutes the element of the unknown in the known. One is inclined to believe that throughout history, if men assumed anything about women, it must have been this: that women *want* to keep quiet.

As a counterpart to the production of fantasy stories, and considering the silence forced upon women by men, Lynn Hejinian, the contemporary American poet, critic, and essayist, says this in her essay "La Faustienne," published in the 2000 collection *The Language of Inquiry*:

> In the Faust legend, Faust is able, with Mephistopheles' help, to take nocturnal voyages, flying through the air to other times and places and summoning scenes and personages from them to his study. He is permitted to gaze on them – to have them as sights – but other interaction is impossible, including, explicitly, speech. In the face of knowledge, Faust is silenced. Scheherazade's position is the reverse of this. "Be silent then, for danger is in words" (5.1.27), says Marlowe's Faust to some companions before whom he is exhibiting Helen of Troy. But for Scheherazade danger lies in silence, death hovers at the edge of dawn on the horizon of light when all stories come to an end, inscribing her as well. Where Faust sells his soul for knowledge, Scheherazade saves her life by offering it. (260)

Given the proper rules of rationality and information, one could infer that the business of language is to follow reality, but as we see in the era of post-structuralism, language itself constitutes reality rather than following it. In Hejinian's essay, we note two competing speakers: the rational male, who knows things by making inferences and deductions (though he pays for this knowledge with his immaterial soul), and the emotional female, who fears for her life, talks all the time, and thus constitutes her reality by constantly shifting her position vis-à-vis the Sultan, who is represented as the higher authority. If her strategy doesn't work, she will lose only her head.

In *1001 Nights*, this unpredictable displacement of the final "truth," i.e., the end of the story, offers sufficient cause for uncertainty where the Sultan and his rational world are concerned. This uncertainty is something that is ultimately used against Scheherazade. One cannot predict by inference what she has in mind. Moreover, the fact that Scheherazade leaves her stories open-ended gives the rationally and teleologically oriented men an opportunity to deem her stories nonsensical, as the question, "what is the point of this story?" is therefore forever eluded, or rendered only in elliptical terms. Thus, while Scheherazade may succeed in postponing her death, in the rational world, in which pronouncements as to the effect of the end result are issued, the outcome will be the same, with the Sultan putting Scheherazade to death. In this sense, the rational discourse legitimizes its priority over nonsense by pointing out that unpredictability goes hand-in-hand with contrariety and ultimately with the counterfactual. Within this scheme, then, when Scheherazade talks, her words are bound to fall outside the "normative" linguistic order. Her speech becomes fantastic and fulfills what Todorov identifies as its three main characteristics:

> The fantastic requires the fulfillment of three conditions. First, the text must oblige the reader to consider the world of the characters as a world of living persons and to hesitate between a natural or supernatural explanation of the events described. Second, this hesitation may also be experienced by a character; thus the reader's role is so to speak entrusted to a character, and at the same time the hesitation is represented, it becomes one of the themes of the work – in the case of naive reading, the actual reader identifies himself with the character. Third, the reader must adopt a certain attitude with regard to the text: he will reject allegorical as well as "poetic" interpretations. (Todorov 1975: 33)

I do not intend to further analyse how Scheherazade unmasks the ways in which language constitutes the fantastic. (John Barth has already done a very good job in his playful *Chimera*, a postmodern take on the *Arabian Nights* from 1972.) I would, however, like to pursue two points. First, the fantastic genre is bound up with epistemological uncertainty at the level of the narrator herself. This is especially the case when the narrator seems unreliable, because she never lets us know what she has in mind. In her essay on narratology, "Unreliable Narration and the Historical Variability of Values and Norms,"

Vera Nünning makes the following statement pertaining to a reader's expectations to genre. The reader's anticipation, or rather *a priori* knowledge of the fact that he or she approaches or reads either a realist of a fantastic novel influences, says Nünning, "the type of values and norms that readers are willing to accept in a text – even when they do not correspond to their own worldview" (Nünning, 2004: 247). Her example is of a narrator who sees ghosts and is thus considered a "reliable storyteller" within the framework of a horror or ghost story. (247) Therefore, the fantastic is conjured by a reader's horizon of expectation when assessing the work's formal properties. In other words, if the narrator talks nonsense, I, as the reader, believe her if she is placed in an equally nonsensical or fantasy setting. So the law of congruence rules, even if the law of rationality doesn't.

My second point is that Todorov and other structuralist theorists emphasize the phenomenological aspect in the genre of the fantastic, rather than asserting that the fantastic is produced by a specific dominant cultural discourse. The fantastic is something that is experienced either as a case of a marvelous thing, which astonishes, or an uncanny thing, which is disturbing, shocking, or unexpected, but does not necessarily exceed the laws of physics. Things are merely odd or weird, and it is this feeling that guides our "experience of limits." (46) There is thus less focus on how language creates a sense of weirdness beyond what a narrator, or a protagonist says, does, or feels. There is also less concern with other types of epistemology that take into account not only the shifting and displacing ground of uncertainty, but also examine how this shifting uncertainty creates sets of oppositions that go against normative knowledge, or the very idea of knowledge.

In conclusion, I turn to the 1968 short story "The Balloon" by postmodern author Donald Barthelme. In this story, the concrete information presented to the reader is inextricably linked with the sense of experiencing limits; the fantastic can be said to occur through the mechanism of constructing meaning, which requires a heightened call for a catachrestic interpretation. At the level of plot, not much happens; the reader sees a balloon, out of the blue, landing on top of, yet still also hovering over, what seems to be New York. The balloon is huge, and covers most of Manhattan, hiding the sky and the tops of skyscrapers. At the level of discourse, an unnamed narrator, who is both active agent and passive observer, tells the reader how people react to his putting a balloon over the city. This act borders on fantasy, as the balloon is seen by the citizens as something supernatural. The significance of the balloon seems to preoccupy everybody, and questions range from 'what exactly is it?' to 'who put it there and for what purpose?' and 'what does it all mean?'

In contrast, the narrator — even when he acknowledges that the balloon means different things to different people — sees it as an unambiguous allegory of love. While love is introduced as a universal feeling that two people may share, only at the very end of the story are readers told who loves whom, and why. It is almost impossible not to notice that the narrator takes great pains to describe the crowd mesmerized by the balloon as de-sexualized. Within this framework it is thus harder to pass judgment on who keeps whom silent. The crowd is quite literally thought of as a round, uniform mass — like the balloon — in spite of the narrator's descriptions of the features of the crowd and the balloon. The balloon is gray and brown, has a rough surface, is of singular beauty; the crowd consists of critics, children, skeptics, and other stupid people. The function of Barthelme's allegory, then, is to place on equal footing the balloon's potential to convey allegorical or figurative meaning (ultimately a question of nuance and difference) along with its potential to stand in a metonymical relation to love (ultimately a question of undifferentiated affect).

Through an odd use of deixis (especially the use of demonstrative pronouns), the narrator transposes the reader into the realm of the uncanny. We are meant to experience the same feeling of anxiety as the questioning crowd. On the other hand, as the questioning crowd is also described as naïve, and downright stupid, we end up laughing at the parody of these incredulous people and their beliefs. The story thus begins with mostly concrete information, e.g., topography and the size of the balloon, yet the reader does not know to what the demonstrative pronouns and adverbials, such as "this," "that," and "then" refer. Here is an example from the first paragraph: "The balloon then covered forty-five blocks north-south and an irregular area east-west, as many as six cross-town blocks on either side of the Avenue. That was the situation then." (Barthelme 1989, 53)

At this point in the story, the reader is arrested by the desire to know how the narrator makes sense of his own actions. Towards the end of the story, however, and in spite of the fact that as the recounting of how the onto-epistemological concerns with the balloon's existence increase proportionally with the story's progression, the narrator – who contributes to a heightening of the fantastic in his otherwise logical argumentation – is disclosed to be less than the omniscient magician he wants us to believe he is. He is much more of a "regular guy." As the story proper ends with the deflation of the balloon, there is also a linguistic counter-performative deflation of the narrator; he is found to be an unhappy lover, albeit one with a vivid imagination, launching a balloon over New York City as a sign of his devotion for his temporarily absent, female lover.

While Barthelme's story parodies the reader's expectations for a love story and simultaneous mental fantasy, it also parodies the criticism of both, love story and fantasy. The ultimate joke is on the reader, as we are shown to embody the same cultural expectations to things such as a balloon and what it stands for. As meaning is deconstructed through people's reactions to the balloon – they think it looks like a symbol of something, but they sense that it is not really a balloon, they consequently resist the normative and primary indexical value of the balloon as something that represents joy, flight, or love. The meaning of the balloon thus split between its symbolic and literal manifestation (a coerced split) becomes obscure, both literally and symbolically, precisely because it becomes a question about meaning itself. The fact that the narrator implies that things are not ambiguous, as he points out that the balloon is just that, and very concretely a balloon, enhances what Todorov claims characterises the fantastic. First, there is the sense of hesitation. People have seen balloons before but never one like this one, so they don't know how to approach it. The fantastic is also characterised by a sense of the uncanny; people realize that as the balloon covers the sky, and has better colours, they also realize that they are on the verge of valuing more an inauthentic thing over a natural one. This ultimately scares them. Finally, the fantastic carries with it a sense of marvel; the sheer size of the balloon bewilders people and ultimately silences them. The following passage illustrates my point:

> There were reactions. Some people found the balloon "interesting." As a response this seemed quite inadequate to the immensity of the balloon, the suddenness of its appearance over the city, on the other hand, in the absence of hysteria, or other societally induced anxiety, it must be judged a calm, "mature" one. There was a certain initial argumentation about the "meaning" of the balloon, this subsided, because we have learned not to insist on meanings, and they are rarely even looked for now except in cases involving the simplest, safest phenomena. It was agreed that since the meaning of the balloon could never be known absolutely, extended discussion was pointless… (54)

In this classical example of postmodern discourse that destabilizes the meaning of some object by drawing attention to the way it is linguistically constituted and constructed, the balloon nevertheless emerges more obscure, fascinating, and fantastic the more the narrator tries to distance the reader from hard fact: a balloon is sometimes just a balloon, not a cigar, and not someone's mother either (homage to Freud). This passage presents us with the fantastic at the level of deconstructed meaning that parodies, on the one hand, not only calm and rational reactions to the balloon, but also the idea of absolute knowledge which the same people want to dismiss by unanimous decision, as if to say, "we cannot know the meaning of the balloon, ergo, end of story." The indirect implication is that there must be a meaning to the balloon, but since it is not within anybody's reach, it is pointless to waste time talking about it. A sense of people's pragmatism thus clashes with their offering a real solution to the problem with uncertainty, in spite of their intention to do so.

Another passage follows a different typographical layout than the rest of the text. We are presented with a list of opinions about the balloon marked by ellipses, mathematical symbols such as an "X" for the unknown, and other odd elisions, such as a line of superimposed dots. This heightens the mysterious feeling that the significance of the balloon is greater than its banal meaning; its ability to transcend rational thinking is even more emphasized. As if he were a reporter, the narrator parodies the critics:

> It was also argued that what was important was what you felt when you stood under the balloon; some people claimed that they felt sheltered, warmed as never before, while enemies of the balloon felt or reported feeling, constrained, a "heavy" feeling. Critical opinion was divided:

"monstrous pouring"
      "harp"
XXXXXXX "certain contrasts with darker portions"
      "inner joy"
"large square corners"
"conservative eclecticism that has so far governed modern balloon design"
::::::::::::::::::::::::: "abnormal vigor"
"warm, soft, lazy passages"
"Has unity been sacrificed for a sprawling quality?"
"Quelle catastrophe!"
"munching"
(57)

Although the narrator insists that logical argumentation mediates between the balloon and the meaning ascribed to it, the reason for the balloon's presence, including an interpretation of its meaning, is revealed only in the last paragraph. There, the narrator shifts the narrative voice from the first or third person, to the second person "you." Thus, Barthelme experiments with narration: quoting *verbatim* his characters' opinions and feelings while deconstructing the balloon's meaning by playfully replacing sign with referent, symbol with semiotics, first level narration with second level narration (who says what to whom and when). The narrator, through his sudden address to his beloved, brings her into the story, thus bypassing the increasingly fantastic setting and making a move toward the world of rationality, his world. Until that point, the female presence was rendered absent through signs that can be said to be suggestive of a lack. Her presence is even hardly suggested by any sign. It can, in fact, be argued that the woman's absence is mirrored in the way the balloon floats in the air without a clear goal. Moreover, if ever there is a clear statement about the literal purpose of the balloon, it is made by negation: "The purpose of the balloon was not to amuse children." (57) Symbolically, the woman's absence is felt only as she hovers, or as some would say, through a kind of ghosting, in movement that relies on the energy of a negative dialectics: "What was admired about the balloon was finally this: that it was not limited or defined." (57) As the narrator shifts his attention from the balloon to the woman, he addresses her directly and unsentimentally in the closing lines. The fact is that, while people relate in a relational way to their environment, however cozy or uncanny it may be, in terms of universal amorous feeling there is only one bottom line: either you love or you don't. Only in this acknowledgement can rational thinking be reestablished beyond any doubt where both parties are concerned. As the last paragraph illustrates:

> I met you under the balloon, on the occasion of your return from Norway, you asked me if it was mine, I said it was. The balloon, I said, is a spontaneous autobiographical disclosure, having to do with the unease I felt at your absence, and with sexual deprivation, but now that your visit to Bergen has been terminated, it is no longer necessary or appropriate. Removal of the balloon was easy, trailer trucks carried away the depleted fabric, which is now stored in West Virginia, awaiting some other time of unhappiness, some time perhaps, when we are angry with each other. (58)

While the woman remains silent in the face of the man's return to his senses as he lists all the facts about the balloon, how he put it up, how he took it down again, and then where he stored it, she yet speaks beyond the text, through the text, and above the text, as did Eve, and Scheherazade, and a host of other smart ladies. Where does this leave the fantastic, one may ask? Here, I would have to say that the fantastic is only as fantastic as we care to fantasize about or imagine it. In Barthelme's story, it is brilliantly suggested that if the woman remains silent, it is not because she is strange or because she has nothing to say, but because she can afford the luxury of saying nothing, as she stands there before the man who understands her, and who ultimately bows to her. That mutual recognition of each other is as fantastic as it gets.

References

Barthelme, Donald. *Sixty Stories.* London: Minerva, 1969.
Clark, Stuart. *Thinking with Demons: The Idea of Witchcraft in Early Modern Europe.* Oxford: Clarendon Press, 1997.
Hejinian, Lynn. *The Language of Inquiry.* Berkeley and Los Angeles: University of California Press, 2000.
***Epistemology, 5 Questions**.* Edited by Vincent Hendricks and Duncan Pritchard. Copenhagen: Automatic Press, 2008.
Todorov, Tzvetan. *The Fantastic: A Structural Approach to a Literary Genre.* Translated by Richard Howard. Ithaca: Cornell University Press, 1975.

Kim Toft Hansen

Identifying the Junction
The idea of Reason in Fantasy

I hate it when there's magic involved; it complicates the hell out of a case.
Simon R. Green, Hawk & Fisher (1990: 66)

Introduction

"All fiction is fantasy", Lucie Armitt writes, "insofar as narrative scenarios comprise an interiorised image (one having existence only in the author's head) projected outward onto a blank page." (Armitt, 2) Armitt indirectly embraces a problematic definition of fiction where it becomes an autonomous realm separate from the "real" world. If fiction is nothing but fantasy, it poses a string of questions about our epistemological framework for comprehending reality. The suggestion that what exists only in an author's head is fiction and what is at hand outside the mind constitutes reality establishes a purely material concept of reality where opinions, ideas, and basic thoughts become fictional. Such a clear distinction between fiction and unattached reality seems to be the leftovers of a new critical intrinsic study of literature where there exists no bridge to reality and opinions about social reality. Armitt, furthermore, does not seem to uphold this intrinsic study of fiction. Alternatively, she conceptualises fantasy – here, as a fictional genre – "to have a collective social and cultural significance" (ibid., 4) and so she defines fiction as containing traits of a basic cultural reality. By definition, then, fantasy fiction must have a positive affiliation with reality. This article attempts to clarify how this is likely.

Initially, to be able to establish the theoretical outline of the fantasy genre I will employ the concept of *modality of fiction*, which is a basic approach that defines fiction as having an immanent relationship to external reality. Accordingly, I will characterise the way fantasy sets up a world, and therefore genre analysis will be principally formal and without, for the most part, psychological explanations about the existence of this genre. I do not, however, reject psychological explanations, but instead set out here to explain how fantasy -- as is any other type of fiction in setting up a world anew -- is dependent on a historical, epistemological framework that is defined through a modal link to the world. This takes us through the concepts of myth and realism, across the different modal views in the Old and New Testaments, to the related study of fantasy and crime fiction and the juncture of the two in Simon R. Green's novel *Hawk & Fisher* – the first volume of a series in which logic and magic exist side by side. As a result this article has two goals. One is to derive a historical, epistemological justification for the existence of the genres of fantasy and crime fiction, separately, with emphasis on fantasy fiction. The other is to provide an analysis of the juncture of the two.

Setting up a World

"Fantasy (at least as most often constructed)," Peter Hunt writes, "concentrates on worlds other than this one: alternative worlds – desirable, if unattainable options." (Hunt, 4) Peter Hunt is, more than, for example, Lucie Armitt, rather cautious in the attempted explanations of the genre as always meaning something else, which is implied in his noticeably formal definition of fantasy. Criticism has a tendency to insist on the "more than meets the eye" solution: "Invented worlds cannot be 'merely' places of wonder and delight: they must mean something else (morally, rather than inevitably) if they are to be interesting or valuable." (ibid., 5) This resistance to psychoanalytical approaches to fantasy, the main criticism Rosemary Jackson has of Tzvetan Todorov's analysis of the fantastic (Jackson, 61), is also reflected in my suggestion of a modal explanation of fantasy. Psychology has its benefits, and the outcome is predominantly plausible, though there seems to be an excessive focus on the meaning of fantasy rather than on the formal construction of setting up a world anew. The application of the *modality of fiction* can augment the comprehension of genre fiction, such as the fantasy genre, by explaining the social conditions preconceived in the genre without resorting to commonplace interpretations. So the main goal here is to describe the construction of "alternative worlds" in fantasy fiction; yet psychological models, nevertheless, cannot and should not be discarded. As we turn to the historical framework of fantasy fiction, a general social psychology comes in handy.

By and large *modality of fiction* defines fiction as having on the one hand a vertical, diegetic axis, but on the other, a horizontal, mimetic axis. Fiction is at the same time an assertion about something diegetically self-reliant and something mimetically self-eroding. The boundaries of fiction thus become fluid and the axis of world representation can be parametrically more or less mimetic since, as Lubomír Doložel writes, the "actual world exists prior to, and independently of, textual activity" (Doložel, 24). We have *the* world before we can conceive *a* world. This has indeed strong similarities with Paul Ricoeur's theory of fiction, where the configured text "is grounded in a preunderstanding of the world of action, its meaningful structures, its symbolic resources, and its temporal character" (Ricoeur, 54). According to Ricoeur's theory it would never be possible to make sense out of fiction did we not first make sense of the world. Primarily, then, reality becomes the mimetic root cause of the existence of fiction, but secondly – if we apply Theodor W. Adorno's aesthetic concept of *relative autonomy* – the world of art and fiction dislodges itself from the real world. To define fiction as having relative autonomy highlights the fact that by separating fiction from the actual world, it simultaneously affirms the world outside the fictional world. With the fictional world as *firstness*, it verifies its *otherness* that is the historical world – and correspondingly fiction is continuously historical. This historicity is precisely what is setting the historical, epistemological framework for fictional representations, and at base, fiction – borrowing Ricoeur's concepts – prefigures and refigures reality within its own boundaries in its separation from reality. This historicity is also what helps us to explain the social preconditions in fiction and, hence, fantasy.

Alternative Worlds

Although Peter Hunt does consider some variations of defining fantasy as having roots in childhood fears, his theoretical approach is chiefly formal and historical. Furthermore, in defining fantasy, his concept of "alternative worlds" shares some close similarities with my concept of modality of fiction. He also stresses the relative nature of fantasy:

> The assumption that fantasy is childish because you may not need to know much about this world in order to read about an invented one overlooks the obvious fact that knowledge of this world is necessary to *invent* one. Fantasy is, because of its relationship to reality, very *knowing*: alternative worlds must necessarily be related to, and comment on, the real world. (7)

In its relativity, then, fantasy has a noticeable origin in the real world in distancing itself from this world. "If there is virtually no connection between the real and the fantastic, ... then we arrive at the absurd and nonsense." (ibid., 8) Essentially, language binds all literature – no matter how absurd or alternative – to reality and if it did not, literature would be incomprehensible. Moreover, Hunt delineates this relationship by means of what he calls *a realistic focalizer*: "For example, in Oz, however wild the premises of physical laws, the story centres on Dorothy and her desire to get back to her familiar home." (ibid.) This realistic focalizer is, in this case, what makes fantasy understandable for us, though it still is a characteristic trait of fantasy that the alternative world setting is clearly marked by a boundary, or what Lucie Armitt calls "beyond the horizon." (Armitt, 4) In reality the horizon is always a horizon that can never be reached, but fantasy fiction goes beyond this horizon when it sets up an alternative world. Beyond the horizon "the fantastic is the norm." (Hunt, 11) In terms of phenomenology, Husserl introduced the concept of horizon which can be helpful in our case: "A horizon comprises of a set of interpretive categories available to the person from a long biography of socialisation and acculturation" (Bruhn Jensen, 23), and fantasy does in fact go beyond these interpretive categories as it transgresses or widens the firm possibilities of the actual historical world. In addition, this alternative world beyond has its distinctiveness by being "set up" by language, often by very careful specifications: "Very often, places are very precisely described or mapped, emphasising the gap between the real and the unreal worlds." (Hunt, 11) The alternative worlds need such close inspections, almost naturalistic in style, to set up the *otherness* of time and space. Substantially, the result is frequently an actual map of the world, e.g., Tolkien's Middle Earth or Krynn in the Dragonlance series, but mainly the alternative conceptuality of the fantasy world is established through consolidating descriptions. They mark out the alternativeness of the world and in doing so "fantasy requires some concept of realism before *it* can exist." (ibid., 15) If we apply realism as a historically reliant mode, then realism – though stylistically variable – takes its basis from what we believe to be possible at a specific time and, thus, fantasy becomes historically dependent even though it relies on impossibilities. It does not make sense to identify a ghost story as fantastic if the story was written at a time when ghosts were thought to exist.

Magic and Rationality

Considering Simon R. Green's fantasy novel *Hawk & Fisher* we come across a strange case of conflicting modes of construction. On the one hand, the novel clearly differentiates itself from our world by its creation of a secondary, entirely fictional place called Haven where scientifically impossible creatures roam and magic is an option for those that possess the power. The apparent and self-evident presence and acceptance of such creatures and magical powers are of course an indispensable ingredient of fantasy and, accordingly, in Simon R. Green's novels as well. Yet the presentation of the world in *Hawk & Fisher* is initially based on Todorov's concept of *hesitancy*. At the outset the detectives Hawk and Fisher are hunting for a vampire that, allegedly, has been terrorising the city, but Hawk has his doubts:

> He'd never seen one of the undead, and didn't know anyone who had. He wasn't altogether sure he believed in such things, but then, he didn't disbelieve in them either. In his time he'd known demons and devils, werewolves and undines, and faced them all with cold steel in his hand. (Green, 8)

To begin with, there seems to be basic hesitancy that produces two initial solutions (belief versus disbelief), though the hesitancy is at once obliterated by the obvious expectancy about demons and devils. By the end of the chapter Hawk can add vampires to his list. On the other hand, Hawk and Fisher are detectives with a firm belief in the powers of rationality, which in fact produces a fundamental fictional paradox where logical rationality coexists with magical powers that defy reason.

The story is straightforward: Hawk and Fisher are invited to a party at a sorcerer's house where they are supposed to guard a politician, but under mysterious circumstances the politician is found dead, apparently murdered. Nobody has been inside the house except the invited guests, so it seems that Hawk and Fisher have a limited number of suspects, a fundamental locked room mystery. Yet Hawk and Fisher cannot – it becomes apparent – trust anyone. The sorcerer who reassures them that his safety spells would have detected intruders is also a suspect. Consequently, any conclusion becomes possible based on the existence of magic, and therefore Hawk says: "I hate it when there's magic involved; it complicates the hell out of a case." A rational man has a hard time dealing with the irrational. Nevertheless, rationality works and the murder is solved, and as we shall see here the coexistence of fantasy and crime fiction, based upon myth and realism, respectively, does not have to be as contradictory and impossible as presumed. Now we intend to establish fantasy as connected to myth and the Old Testament, and then we will approach crime fiction as linked to realism and the New Testament. Finally, we will identify the juncture of the two in what we can define as *the dialectics of realism*.

Myth, Realism, and the Bible

Lucie Armitt suggests this idea: "It is interesting that, though the Old Testament section of the Bible is full of wonderful fables and dreams, the New Testament insists on realism, almost to the exclusion of any other mode of writing." (Armitt, 14) However, she never develops this thesis. Nevertheless, it is interesting to look further into these differences between the two most important literary works in western societies.

This literary creation of a world, which we have touched upon, exists in most fantasy fiction, but the basic mode of creation takes its point of departure from religious thinking. In fact, most religions have a creational myth and the three most important religions in western society – Christianity, Judaism and Islam – have similar stories of creation. It is then interesting that the Old Testament, as does almost any book of fantasy, implies a narrative of creation, but this is not the only parallel between fantasy and the Old Testament. The narratives of the Old Testament are, as Armitt points out, fables and dreams, though most literary criticism refers to the Old Testament as mythical, or what Northrop Frye alongside myth calls "a story about a god." (Frye, 33) Basically, the Old Testament is about God as an abstract figure, though often anthropomorphical, and what we have left are the mere words of God. Accordingly, God is then a figure of the mind and therefore in some ways a *fantasy* in Armitt's sense of "having existence only in the head," and this is logically quite correct and adequate whether or not you are a believer since God is something immaterial in which to believe.

This immateriality is reduced in the New Testament at the point at which God becomes material: He is incarnate – made flesh – in the figure of Jesus. Where the Old Testament is the story of an absent god, the New Testament insists on presence. Although the Christian Bible contains the Judaic narrative of creation, the Old Testament in itself consists of the story of *world creation* and distant words of God to be interpreted through dreams, fables, and mythological representation for the most part. In contrast, the New Testament is the story of *world existence*, the life of Jesus, more than creation. The absence and presence of the figure of God defined through the differences between the Old and the New Testament, respectively, is the difference between internal conceptions and external existence. In a Platonic sense the variance in representation is a move from the idea to the material, from the metaphysical spirit to the predominantly physical body, and in this way from mythic representation to realistic presence.

The basic theological budge makes an interesting leap in a more realistic direction, though the "obvious exception to this rule, of course, is the Book of Revelation, in which fantasy is given free rein." (Armitt, 22) However, the main point here is that Christian culture has in its key scripture the coexistence of myth and realism, the metaphysical and the physical, the fantasy notion and material presence of God. This is essentially a paradox, but the paradox is solved by what is called *Christology*, the traditional interpretation of Jesus as both human and divine. In this sense, of course, we cannot consider it as realism in terms of, for instance, nineteenth-century realism, but it falls more along the line of *evangelical realism*. Thomas F. Torrance argues for an *a posteriori* knowledge of the presence of God within the revelation of Christ, which he calls evangelical realism. (Torrance, 11) As a mode of practicality, the New Testament stresses its realism through basic witnesses and, of course, the pre-eminent example is the resurrection of Jesus where, at first, Mary Magdalene actually *sees* Jesus. Witnesses are regarded as presentation of evidence and the New Testament also relies on this act of documentation. In fact, the Bible – both testaments – becomes a mixture of two historical modes, in Northrop Frye's terms, the *mythic* and the *high mimetic*. This also seems to initiate the patterns of development in western societies where a certain realism becomes necessary in both artistic, philosophical, and scientific progression. The coexistence of mythical interpretations of the world on the one hand and realistic conceptions of existence on the other hand can be thought of as the early germs of secularisation.

In the most positive sense, then, Christianity – in western societies – bridges myth and realism, if we understand realism in the philosophical sense of existing *in* the world without our subjective awareness. Nevertheless, medieval theology and positivism display the disasters of either radical myth or radical realism, respectively. On the one hand, fundamentalist Christianity – up until the Renaissance – illustrates the distortions of literal theology and twentieth-century fascism on the other – most accurately delineated in Adorno and Horkheimer's *Dialectics of Enlightenment* – demonstrated the failure of a biased focus on philosophical realism. This in no way attempts to subscribe to Christian ideology; instead it is first a localization of a formal coexistence of myth and realism, and secondly, it is an attempt to understand the epistemological framework of the two genres in question here. This has, of course, its benefits in considering *fantasy* and *crime fiction*.

Western cultures have evident preconditions for both the mode of myth and the mode of realism, although the existence of the modes is in no way exclusively western. However, the modes do have particular variations and distinct historical traits as fictional expressions. First, we take a brief look at the universality of myth and fantasy, and secondly this is considered as having specific developmental variations as a result of nineteenth-century scientific naturalism.

Dialectics of Realism

Mythologies exist in every culture. They are all specific attempts to explain the unexplained, where we come from and where we are going, and so they are primarily basic modes of living. Myths travel and there are several universal myths, but certainly most of them acquire distinct traits within a particular culture. Consequently, most of the stories in the Old Testament can be traced back to other cultures and in this way the myths are in some ways the general narratives about being human and living collectively. The most important accounts in most mythologies are essentially the explanation of why there is something rather than nothing; this, then, is a justification of the existence of the world.

There is, however, as Frye explains in his *historical criticism*, a historical development away from myth toward a realistic interpretation of the world. However, at the outset, myth and realism have parallel intentions of explaining the existence of being. Frye writes that "as the modes of fiction move from the mythical to the low mimetic and ironic, they approach a point of extreme 'realism' or representative likeness to life." (Frye: 134) The ideals of verisimilitude in this explanation rest upon how similar to *us* the fictional characters are; the more similar, the closer we get to the low mimetic mode where the hero of the story is on par with both *us* and nature. "Realism, or the art of verisimilitude," Frye continues, "evokes the responses 'How like that is what we know!'" (ibid., 136), which corresponds to my explanation of realism as connected to the possibilities of a specific time. Summing up, Frye specifies that myth "is one extreme of literary design; naturalism is the other," which also resembles my definition of fiction and world representation as parametrically more or less mimetic. Frye places the exact move away from the mythical and larger-than-life hero historically, as "the Renaissance brings the high mimetic mode into the foreground." (ibid., 34) During the Renaissance where the more important steps toward a scientific explanation of the world were taken, fiction – in Frye's words – takes a large step towards the realistic. And in following Frye's modal development of fiction, it seems quite possible that this development also follows the process of secularization with the prodigious modernization in Martin Luther's reformatory work. This indicates that both the scientific and the theological development during the Renaissance – most likely in connection to each other – triggered the vehement attention to realism in nineteenth-century literature and science.

Throughout the nineteenth century – when enlightenment and rationalism took their greatest leaps and the secular societies were born through revolutions – we locate a *double impact of naturalism*. In the second half of the nineteenth century, natural science, predominantly epitomized through Darwinism, established itself as the dominant scientific mode of explanation on the basis of eighteenth-century rationalism, which in some ways comprises the historical reasons for naturalism. Combining the two gives us Zola's notion of literature as a laboratory.

On the other hand, the early nineteenth century was an era of romanticism where mythologies certainly become a central interest. The instigation of modern fantasy, though, has its root – according to both Armitt and Hunt – in the Renaissance period, though the same can be said of realism. Nevertheless, the particular interest in rationalization and naturalism, on the one hand, and the irrational in fairy tales on the other gained their distinct features from nineteenth-century historicity. However, the basic scientific focus on the world is what in the end eradicates – or at least overrules – myths as credible explanations of existence; this move is perhaps the most important shift in the birth of a particular fantasy genre. Mythical thinking is not obliterated; instead, it tiptoes from mythology into fairy tales and fantasy which then become genres that deal with the impossibilities of scientific realism. This is the double impact of naturalism in the sense that it can be understood as the historical, epistemological framework for both the mode of realism and the mode of myth and fantasy.

This scientific development also has its impact on modern perception of the human mind. Here, the psychological point of view of fantasy makes a great deal of sense. Nineteenth-century science also facilitates the advance of clinical psychology, which gave rise to Freud's work on the unconscious. In many ways, Freud's work is formally similar to the theological concept of *Deus absconditus* (the hidden God) (Saarinen, 134). As Lucie Armitt notes:

> Where the medieval dream takes its inspiration from belief in God, psychoanalytical readings of dream structures take their inspiration from the belief in the unconscious. As faith systems, the two have much in common, despite appearances to the contrary. God is unseen, unknowable, and His/Her existence impossible to prove; all three things can equally be said of the unconscious. (33)

Fantasy, dreams, God, and the unconscious are then rendered unseen and unknowable, though the practices of psychoanalysis, theology and literary interpretation are all – in some ways – attempts to gather worldly explanations of these phenomena. First, this of course shows the close connection between literary interpretation and psychoanalysis, but secondly, this connection also verifies the basic idea that phenomena – either fiction, factual or religious – have their deep roots in human existence. In this way, the double impact of naturalism on both myth and realism explains the dialectics of realism, which in turn explain the ways in which myth is realism and vice versa.

For the staunch believer, the scriptures are not understood as a collection of myths but as a selection of real accounts; cultural myths of a society are also appreciated as reality. Both myth and realism are historically influenced in such a way that the epistemological framework determines what can be said to be real. To paraphrase Adorno and Horkheimer's dialectics of enlightenment and myth, realism reverts back into myth and thus realism and myth become dialogically and dialectically tied to each other. What we from a naturalistic point of view appreciate as myth becomes fantasy, and what is understood as possible becomes realism. As a result, the genres of fantasy and realism are dialectically bound together, which eventually influences crime fiction considerably.

Theodicy and Crime Fiction

In its most popular version, crime fiction is tied to a concept of realism. Of the many classifications of realism, two become important in crime fiction: firstly realism as fictional mode and, secondly, realism as philosophical concept. These interpretations of realism are, of course, tied together because realism as a philosophical concept is prefigured in realism as a fictional mode. This is evident when we consider the world as the otherness – the first cause – of the fictional world. In crime fiction, philosophical realism is manifest in the detective character and his/her view of the world in which there must exist some recognition of the possibility of acknowledgement. Solving a crime presupposes the opportunity to connect ideas with the material of the world. In this sense *the clue* becomes the obvious link between the idea and the material since the clue directs the mind towards recognizable truth. Crime fiction does not have to be modally realistic, though it often is; the novel *Hawk & Fisher* demonstrates that rationality and philosophical realism are no enemy to fantasy, and we will return to this point below.

This evidence-based realism in crime fiction is very similar to the witness-centered realism of the New Testament, as described above, and in this connection there exist hypotheses about crime fiction as a particularly Christian genre[1]. The assertion "without Christianity, no crime fiction" (Christensen, 2) poses a noteworthy question. The extended focus on realism in the New Testament answers the question to some extent, though ethically crime fiction builds upon several Christian values that can be found in, and perhaps are initiated by, the New Testament. The prerequisite for the massive societal mobilization – when, for instance, a murder is committed – is the basic idea of the inviolability of the individual regardless of the social status of the victim. (Christensen, 3) The human being and life itself carry universal values that seem to be initiated by the ethics and mutual solidarity in Christian thought where in death (or murder!) we are all equal in the eyes of God. If we accept this as an epistemological precondition arising from Christian thinking, this is also a prerequisite for the systematic tracing and mapping of crime and criminal intent, and therefore it becomes a requirement for the establishment of crime fiction.[2]

It might, nevertheless, be argued that the crime fiction genre was established at a time when theological metaphysics were retreating and the secular society was in embryo, though Risto Saarinen indicates that crime fiction deals with the same questions posed in the

---

[1] Not much has been written about this question, though it keeps turning up in crime fiction and to a lesser degree in crime fiction critiques. A Danish parish priest, Johannes H. Christensen (2006) has put this view forward in a sermon. The Finnish theologian Risto Saarinen has also touched upon the question in both an article about the surplus of evil in the welfare society (2003) and a conference presentation. (2007) I will note when I draw upon these although I have expanded the original analysis.

[2] Nevertheless, crime fiction does in fact exist outside Christian cultures and, existed before western crime fiction. For instance, the Chinese *Dee Goong An* (Gulik 1976) and a Jewish version – though in this case generally within a Christian culture – does pose a question about the assertion that crime fiction is a basically Christian genre. A current, popular Jewish version of crime fiction would be Jonathan Lethem's *Motherless Brooklyn* (1999). We then must deal with the question of how these ideas of law, order, and fictional representation are handled; however, this is a question for another study. Additionally, we can argue that the inviolability of human nature also has its roots in Stoic thought.

New Testament. (Saarinen 2003, 132) However, the focal point of the creator shifts from God to the social welfare system. The *problem of theodicy* – the defense of God despite the fact that evil exists – is of greatest importance in Christianity where God is depicted as merciful. Martin Luther poses the question of how we can find a merciful God when there is evil about. (Saarinen 2007, 10) Saarinen continues: "Murder mysteries are not interested in the existence of God, but rather with the fundamental issues of mercy. Although they do not find the merciful God, they emphasize asking similar questions as Luther." (ibid., 11) His term for this is *secular theodicy* where – instead of blaming God for the existence of evil – we blame the system and, in doing so, crime fiction asks this basic question:

> A traditional theodicy often modifies one of the following three propositions in order to make them compatible: 1) God is good, 2) God is omnipotent, 3) there is real evil. A secular theodicy formulates, analogically, three propositions: A) our society and people in it aim at being good, B) our society has enough resources for good life and education for everybody, C) there remains too much real evil. (Saarinen 2003, 134)

If we have a caring welfare system, why do people still commit evil deeds? If we do not have God to blame, we can blame the system.

In the same way as nineteenth-century naturalism relegated myth to fantasy, it almost seems to dispatch Christian thinking into crime fiction. The enhanced success of crime fiction exists predominantly in the twentieth century, where God is declared dead and the social welfare system is in the making. Interestingly enough, says Johannes H. Christensen, there exists no tradition for crime fiction outside Christian culture. (Christensen, 4)[3] The historical epistemological

---

3 This is, though, not entirely correct. In fact Chinese literary history reveals an interest in crime fiction as early as the eleventh century, but you could of course argue that what Christensen refers to may be a certain Western version of crime fiction. There are several observable differences between the two versions (for further analysis see Hansen 2009).

framework of both fantasy in a negative sense and crime fiction in a positive sense – in its reliance on philosophical realism – seem to stem from the same increased focus on naturalism and scientific development, which ultimately is tied to the dialectics of realism. Where myth and realism as modes are negatively joined in their focus on possibilities and impossibilities, the dialectic connection between fantasy and crime fiction comes from the fact that the alternative world of fantasy goes "beyond the horizon" and most popular worlds of crime fiction keep a philosophical and somewhat material realism within range. This is, then, no theological or metaphysical argument, but instead focuses on the fact that there are sociological reasons for the existence of particular genres. Therefore, it seems quite plausible that Wsetern crime fiction can be considered – in its basic ethical and some formal considerations – a comparatively Christian genre, whereas fantasy is at first sight mythically universal. The latter, however, needs secular thinking and naturalism to become fantasy and not myth. In myth the horizon *is* realistic; without a certain scientific realism on the one hand fantasy cannot exist on the other. However, though fantasy and crime fiction seem diametrically opposed, they coexist in Simon R. Green's novel *Hawk & Fisher*.

Defining the Junction

Hawk & Fisher is the first novel by Green about two detectives working in the fantasy world of Haven. The most interesting aspect of this novel is its combination of the fantasy and crime fiction genres. This thus becomes an indirect discussion about reason and irrational elements existing side by side, but the central question is whether one or the other has the upper hand. Does reason overrule fantasy and myth, or are they on an equal footing?

We have already analysed the novel's formal creation of an alternative world so it would be most interesting now to explore its treatment of truth within a world where nature seems to defy naturalism and logic. Since *Hawk & Fisher* is primarily a fantasy novel, it contains a weighty discussion about the condition of truth. First and foremost, Hawk and Fisher's detection process is guided profoundly by methodological motivations; the indispensable tool is "a careful, methodical search." (Green: 13) As in any crime story, the truth is well hidden: "The trouble with searching for clues was that half of the time you didn't know what you were looking for until you found it." (ibid. 59) The motive and intention of the murder are concealed which – in the words of Saarinen – has Lutheran echoes: "God is a *Deus absconditus*, a hidden God, whose goodness remains a mystery for us. In secular theodicy... [c]rime authors outline a *homo absconditus*, a humanity whose real intentions remain hidden." (Saarinen 2003, 134)

Crime stories deal with uncovering the intentions of the criminal; this is, in fact, the same process of acknowledgement that is reflected in 1 Corinthians 13:12. Paul says, "For now we see in a mirror dimly, but then face to face; now I know in part, but then I will know fully just as I also have been fully known." Another parallel is Plato's allegory of the cave where hidden intentions – the Idea behind what we see – are discovered after the escape into the light. The acknowledgement of truth is en*light*enment and evidence is hidden until the detective uncovers it, but the difficulty or challenge of this – as reflected in Green's statement earlier – is the self-evident character of truth as soon as it is uncovered. The detective is never sure where to look before he *knows* where to look, which is where rationality comes into Hawk's and Fisher's methodology: "In a case like this we need to be very sure of our facts... You can never tell what's going to turn out to be significant." (Green, 70)

Rational acknowledgement of facts is routine or as Hawk utters it "I don't believe in songs or legends" (ibid., 118); songs and legends are infused with myth, which is useless in the attempt to uncover truth.

Truthspells and Rationality

Nevertheless, magic is involved and unquestioned. Repeatedly, Hawk and Fisher are assisted by magical tools throughout their investigation. We first see this when they obtain knowledge about the impending crime to be committed by the witch Visage, but it is unclear what she thinks is happening. Magic and rationality come to the aid of the detectives throughout the novel -- for example, a "forensic magician" (ibid., 87) investigates a crime scene -- but the most significant alliance of magic and forensics is the notion of a truthspell. As a last resort, as more murders are committed with no sign of a solution, Hawk and Fisher order the sorcerer Gaunt to set up a truthspell. Nobody is pleased with the idea, given that truthspells – as Gaunt here reveals – are indeed questionable. In many ways, in fact, they are similar to truth serums and polygraphs:

> Truthspells are difficult things to put together. All the current versions produce nothing but the literal truth. They don't allow for nuances, half-truths and evasions. And then of course there's subjective and objective truth… (25)

Truthspells, then, call into question issues that have been at the heart of epistemology for centuries, mainly, the problem of connecting the subject with the object. Here, however, the question is asked from a magical point of view. As a last resort, Hawk and Fisher decide to use the truthspell despite its potential drawbacks; the result is disappointingly useless. Nothing new is gained. Subsequently, the sorcerer Gaunt suggests that maybe Hawk "didn't word the questions correctly" (ibid. 142), and it appears Gaunt is right. First of all, there were two murders committed, but Hawk and Fisher incorrectly presume that there is only a single killer. Hawk says: "I asked everyone if they killed Blackstone *and* Bowman. And of course each killer could truthfully say no; they'd only killed one man, not both." (ibid., 164) In fact, there were two different murderers at hand, but Hawk's question allowed them to justifiably deny being the *single* killer. In this way magic is bypassed by the logic of the answers and the questions; the logical realism and rationality of the investigation have the upper hand, though this time they do not help the investigators. However, logic and reason do eventually help Hawk and Fisher: Hawk can turn around the questioning by stating that, logically, there *must* be two killers. In hindsight, rationality does work; realism and rationality overrule myth and fantasy although the novel twists the argument again at the end of the story.

The character Hightower is one of the murderers; he turns out to be a werewolf and therefore is guilty of the most atrocious of the crimes. (I note here that the first victim – judging from the minimal amount of blood – was evidently not the victim of a bestial werewolf. Subsequent murders clearly indicate the raging temperament of a werewolf.) The second murderer is then proven – through complicated rationality – to be Haven's local hero Stalker, who was connected to the killings personally and politically. Hawk's final rational argument ties every strand together in an intricate denouement, leaving no plot point aside. At first, his technique leads to a violent brawl in which Stalker is killed. However, he gains the upper hand using rationality rather than elements of mythology and fantasy.

Having uncovered the truth, Hawk nevertheless refuses to make public the guilt of Stalker: "He was one of the greatest heroes ever to come out of the Low Kingdoms," says one the survivors. "He really did do most of the things the legends say he did." Hawk replies: "And that's why we're going to say Hightower was responsible for all the deaths. No one really blames a werewolf. Haven needs legends like Stalker more than it needs the truth." (ibid., 170) Ultimately, the myths about the legendary Stalker are of greater importance than the truth about the murders.

Legends of Democracy

Implicitly, then, in employing political murders in fantasy crime fiction, *Hawk & Fisher* also becomes an interesting philosophical argument about the foundations of democracy and the coexistence of realism and myth. At the very moment we enter Haven, latent democratic values are surfacing. The first murder victim, Councillor Blackstone, led the way to clean up Haven's lawlessness: "He'd done more to clean up the city of Haven in his one year as Councillor than the rest of the Council put together." (ibid., 22) The fledgling foundation of the city is an electoral system, and the criminal interests of the underworld in every way contradict the values underlying the election rally. Therefore, the city guards – as Hawk and Fisher are called – must keep crime at bay despite the corruption already in the system. Purging corruption and crime is the work of the detectives and the basis of Haven's embryonic democracy. The novel, then, provides an alter-

THE IDEA OF REASON IN FANTASY

native basis for discussing the major tenets of democracy, a discussion Hawk willingly joins:

> the idea that every man and woman should have a say in how the country should be run: that was staggering. There's no denying the system has its drawbacks, and I've seen most of them right here in Haven, but it has its attractions too. (44)

In part, this fantasy novel becomes a fictional laboratory for a debate about the basis of democratic values, a debate that benefits from occurring in a fantasy world. The alternativeness and dissociation of fantasy create a relatively autonomous realm historically separate from the real world. This, in turn, affords the opportunity to assemble a democracy afresh, virtually free of historical perspective and hindsight. This is the first element of the philosophical argument embodied in *Hawk & Fisher*.

The second element is the value of legends. In Hawk's opinion, legends are essential and significant in cultures such as Haven. The result is then that the construction of democracy – based on certainties and a sense of righteousness and justice – is, at first, based on ill-proven ideals as in Haven. Secondly then, democracy in its idealistic qualities becomes a myth in itself, which in the end – after the ideals have been proven pragmatically worthwhile – can result in a rationally outlined democratic practice. Paradoxically, democracy subsequently reverts from the rational to idealistic components that are integrated into the material system of justice, which then form the ever-changing, enduring and pragmatic nature of democracy: a system with drawbacks and attractions.

In conclusion, the elementary organizing argument of the novel is – in its formal characteristics – similar to Adorno's and Horkheimer's dialectics of enlightenment, where myth and enlightenment are the preconditions of each another. The process of enlightenment has its benefits in egalitarian values, which in many ways form the basis of democracy. However, these values change over time and new systematisations emerge, which then revert to the idealism that must be incorporated into the material system. According to this view, democracy is dependent upon both idealism and material manifestations, static and dynamic values, and, for our purposes here, myth and enlightenment. The latter is generally tied to philosophical realism and materialism, whereas myth is attached to idealism and elements of fantasy. In final analysis, there is no preferential treatment of rationality and realism or legends and mythological generalizations in either the dialectics of enlightenment or democracy in general, or in Green's novel in particular. However, realism and mythology, in brief, are prerequisites for each another.

Concluding Remarks

I have made four points in this article. First, I identified the paradox of linking two opposing genres: fantasy and crime fiction. This is a paradox to the extent that fantasy is guided by the creation of a world "beyond the horizon," as Lucie Armitt says, whereas crime fiction can create a world apart from the historical world. However, because it focuses on investigation and truth, the fantasy world can be scientifically motivated by a sense of philosophical realism. *Hawk & Fisher* combines the two genres successfully, avoiding an absurd or inconsistent ending. The boundaries between the two genres and modes of thinking are more fluid and the links are stronger than might be first apparent.

My second point is that the two modes of fiction – myth and realism – can be seen as having a single point of origin. The underlying foundation, defined in terms of a historical, epistemological framework, is located in the Christian Bible. The mythical proportions of the Old Testament coexist with the evidential and evangelical realism of the New Testament. This is not to say that fantasy and crime fiction are specifically Christian genres. However, the necessary framework is present in the Bible and offers western culture the means to foster a special relationship between myth and realism. This is defined as *the dialectics of realism*: both modes of representation are connected to historical thinking and scientific possibilities. The mythic is defined by historical impossibilities and the realistic is clarified by historical possibilities. Both modes as seen as ever-changing and historical.

THE IDEA OF REASON IN FANTASY

My third point: throughout the nineteenth century, western culture moved steadily toward a secular social structure with less clerical power and greater public influence on political constitutions. Science and the understanding of reality were relegated to the realm of positive knowledge and quantitatively intelligible facts, which – in many ways – superceded knowledge from mythic sources. This philosophical realism found its equivalent in the aesthetic realism of the nineteenth century, providing – both philosophically and aesthetically – the foundation for the genesis of the crime fiction genre. During the same timeframe, a romantic point of view surfaced, with a specific interest in fantasies, the occult, and the mysterious; in many ways, it took on the weight of the philosophically mythical. As a result of these developments, the ideas and modes of realism and myth were infused into at least two genres of realism -- crime fiction and fantasy. Just as realism and myth are dialectically interlinked, so are the genres of realism (built on historical possibilities) and fantasy (established upon historical impossibilities).

Ultimately, the juncture of the two modes of thinking and the two genres within Simon R. Green's *Hawk & Fisher* by no means creates a paradox, though the coexistence of reasonable logic and fantastic magic would imply the opposite. The interaction and junction of the two are, perhaps, predetermined in western culture by biblical Scripture, but the Bible is by no means the only source of junction. I have shown that both the Old and New Testaments are primary focal points of the western epistemological framework. Whether you are a believer or not, that is still the core of our cultural heritage, and it is the framework upon which many traditional cultural events and ways of life are based. The concept of reason in fantasy, then, does not seem as hard to believe and embrace.

References

Adorno, Theodor W. *Ästhetische Theorie*. Frankfurt am Main: Suhrkamp Verlag, 1972.
Adorno, Theodor W., and Max Horkheimer. *Dialectic der Aufkläring*, Frankfurt am Main: Fischer Taschenbuch Verlag, 1971.
Armitt, Lucie. *Fantasy Fiction: An Introduction*. New York & London: Continuum, 2005.
Christensen, Johannes H. "23. søndag efter trinitatis", *Sermon, Church of Skovshoved*, November 19, 2006.
Doložel, Lubomír. *Heterocosmica. Fiction and Possible Worlds*. London: The John Hopkins University Press, 1998.
Frye, Northrop. *Anatomy of Criticism*. Princeton: Princeton University Press, 2000.
Green, Simon R.. *Hawk & Fisher* 1990 In *Swords of Haven – The Adventures of Hawk & Fisher*. London: Penguin Books, 2006.
Gulik, Robert van. *Celebrated Cases of Judge Dee (Dee Goong An). An Authentic Eighteenth-Century Detective Novel*. New York: Dover Publications, Inc., 1976.
Hansen, Kim Toft. "Fra synd til skyld. Krimiens kulturelle rødder." In *Bogens verden*, 1 (2009): 36-42.
Hunt, Peter. "Introduction: Fantasy and Alternative Worlds." In *Alternative Worlds in Fantasy Fiction*. Edited by Peter Hunt et al. New York and London: Continuum, 2001.
Jackson, Rosemary. *Fantasy – The Literature of Subversion*. London and New York: Routledge, 1981.
Jensen, Klaus Bruhn. "The Humanities in Media and Communication Research." In *A Handbook of Media and Communication Research. Qualitative and Quantitative Methodologies*. Edited by Klaus Bruhn Jensen, Klaus Bruhn. London and New York: Routledge, 2002.
Lethem, Jonathan. *Motherless Brooklyn*. New York: Vintage Books, 1999.
Ricoeur, Paul. *Time and Narrative*. Vol. 1. Chicago: University of Chicago Press, 1990.

Saarinen, Risto. "The Surplus of Evil in Welfare Society: Contemporary Scandinavian Crime Fiction." In *Dialog: A Journal of Theology*, 42, 2 (2003): 131-135.
Saarinen, Risto. "The Surplus of Evil in Welfare Society. Suffering and Theodicy in Today's World." Conference presentation, Själens Landskap – The Landscape of the Soul, 18. Nordic Conference for Hospital Chaplains June 13-16., 2007, Borgå, Finland.
Todorov, Tzvetan. *The Fantastic. A Structural Approach to a Literary Genre*. New York: Cornell University Press, 1973.
Torrance, Thomas F. *Reality & Evangelical Theology. The Realism of Christian Revelation*, Eugene, Oregon: Wipf and Stock Publishers, 2003.

Gunhild Agger

"The Snow Queen" and the White Witch

Hans Christian Andersen's Fairy Tale and C. S. Lewis' Narnia Chronicles

"The Snow Queen", 1845, is a fairy tale by Hans Christian Andersen built on a structure strikingly similar to fantasy's double worlds; it exhibits characters later interpreted in fantasy. We meet Kay and Gerda, the protagonists, in a normal, primary world with families, apartments, a church, and a school. They play and gain knowledge of the world. However, Kay is brought to a secondary world by the Snow Queen, who represents a threat to life, harmonious growth, and to emotions such as love. Gerda's quest to find Kay leads her through various fantastic life forms. In the end, the concept of pure reason, symbolised by the Snow Queen, is challenged and overcome. The children return to their home, changed by the events they have experienced. But this doesn't mean the end of the Snow Queen. She keeps reappearing, both in other fairy tales by Hans Christian Andersen,[1] and not least in the works of other authors.

All of C.S. Lewis' *Narnia Chronicles,* 1950-56, are structured along similar principles and exhibit similar characters and themes. The protagonists are ordinary children whom we meet in the primary world. By magic means they approach the realm of Narnia, a secondary

---

[1] For example, "Iisjomfruen," 1862. In this tale the ice virgin is a principle of nature and an incarnation of a human longing for death, rather than a representative of reason without sensibility.

world created by Aslan, the huge lion, who bears crucial similarities to Christ. In this world, the children are the protagonists or act as helpers for protagonists from Narnia. The White Witch, who has strong echoes of the Snow Queen, represents a fascinating symbol of power and evil, opposing Aslan and the vision of moral order in Narnia.

My primary aim in this chapter is to highlight "The Snow Queen" as one of the first examples of fiction enfolding central elements of the fantasy genre. I will analyse its structure, characters, and themes seen from this angle, making use of *The Narnia Chronicles* as a backdrop. I shall discuss metanarratives and their functions and historical questions of genre development by examining "The Snow Queen" and its reception in an English context, considering the relationship between Hans Christian Andersen and C.S. Lewis. The analysis of "The Snow Queen" will be put into perspective by *The Narnia Chronicles*, and vice versa.

Other researchers have drawn attention to the relationship between Andersen and Lewis. It has mostly been on a referential basis, with observations that deserve to be scrutinised. As I see it, we find fundamental ingredients of the fantasy genre as early as 1845 in "The Snow Queen." Against this background it is not surprising that later authors, among them C.S. Lewis, were inspired by it. It is not my aim to trace the origin of the characters or the topos of vision. But I would like to elucidate the way in which Hans Christian Andersen elaborated on this, as it seems to have been an inspiration of lasting impact. Quoting the beginning of Hans Christian Andersen's "Snow Queen," I hope that "when we get to the end we shall know more than we do now."[2]

Immortal Characters and Metanarratives

In 1952 Carl Erik Soya, a popular Danish writer, published an essay called "De udødelige" ("The Immortals"). In the beginning, Soya is seeking an idea for an immortal short story. As always, when immortality is concerned, the devil pops up, offering his services. The au-

---

2   Andersen: hca.gilead.org.il/snow_que.html: 1. Quotations from "The Snow Queen" in this essay are from this edition.

thor accepts being transported to an Annual General Meeting of the I.O.I.C.F. (International Organization of Immortal Characters of Fiction). The setting of the meeting is the Glass Mountain, presumably in Southern Germany. The delegates are received by the porter from Macbeth. The President of the General Meeting is the frog from Aesop's fable. The chairman is Santa Claus. Among the attendees, the author notices "Don Quijote, Sancho Pancha, Hansel, Gretel, the Witch, Little Red Ridinghood, the Wolf, the Wicked Queen, Snow White, the Seven Dwarfs, the Little Mermaid, the Emperor (the one who didn't wear any clothes), Oedipus (with empty orbits), Aladdin, Hamlet, Gulliver, Alice, the four musketeers, Sherlock Holmes accompanied by Dr. Watson..." (Soya 1952, 173; my translation)[3]

One of the key issues of the General Meeting is the admission of new members. Tarzan, Donald Duck, Mickey Mouse, and Charlie Chaplin have applied, and the question is whether they have proven themselves worthy of immortality. The existing members make no haste, but first and foremost, they have difficulties agreeing about the criteria for immortality. The devil and the author leave before the decision is taken. The devil assures the author that they will be admitted: "They are Americans - they have dollars!" (Soya 1952, 179) However, this is not the only point of the essay. Others are:

- that literary immortality depends on the characters created by an author;
- that these characters are more likely to be remembered than the author himself;
- that various versions of these characters will emerge as time goes by, mixing characters and circumstances;
- that it is not always possible to trace the original versions; and
- that - perhaps - it doesn't matter, as important characters tend to live on anyway.

What has this to do with Hans Christian Andersen's "The Snow Queen" and C.S. Lewis' *Narnia Chronicles*? From the list above we recognise the Wicked Queen and the Witch. They had already merged into

---

3   Jensen 1999, 532 has drawn my attention to this essay.

the character of the Snow Queen more than one hundred years before Soya wrote his essay, and only more so in the *Narnia Chronicles*.

What Soya in a very illustrative fashion claims in this essay is confirmed on a more theoretical level by Stephens and McCallum in their discussion of retelling stories. They open it by stating, "When compared with general literature, the literature produced for children contains a much larger proportion of retold stories." (Stephens and McCallum 1998, 4) When texts are retold, they bring something from the pre-text, the original context, with them, forming "re-versions," which may be various forms of reproductions of the pre-text, configuring new accents, or versions that mock the pre-texts in various ways. Examples from Cinderella to Robin Hood from various ages and conveyed by various media testify to this. Stephens and McCallum call these repeatedly retold texts "metanarratives": "a metanarrative is a global or totalising cultural narrative schema which orders and explains knowledge and experience." (Stephens and McCallum 1998, 6) Such metanarratives provide the frame for retelling stories. The concept of "metanarrative" corresponds to the concept of "metaethic" in the Western sphere. The latter is disclosed in the notion of canons, and because of that it is rather conservative.

Accepting this understanding of connections and interrelatedness, the crucial question is whether it makes the pursuit of relationships a futile endeavour. I think not. Although it is not possible to trace the original versions, and although the combination of pre-texts, metanarratives, and metaethics establishes quite a chaos, it is always interesting to examine various versions of the same genre, the same character, and indeed the same fundamental plot. This raises the question of essential or mythical elements in stories retold during centuries, and of change caused by the impact of different circumstances. Stephens and McCallum do not give up, either. Remaining on a high level of abstraction, they propose three concepts to distinguish between various registers, preferred by various authors. They are:

1. The hieratic register "is apt to be figurative, especially metaphorical or allegorical, and implicitly grounded in transcendent significances." (Stephens and McCallum 1998, 11) It is concerned with religious or mythological narratives.

2   The epic register "is grounded in more mundane or material significances, normally set within firmly hierarchical social institutions." (ibid.)
3   The demotic register is also mundane, but "apt to be metonymic and event-focused." (ibid.) Within this frame, the authors call attention to the fact that humanist ideology has been a strong power in the retelling tradition. Using these concepts they have investigated some of the most widespread retold stories in their book. With this in mind, let us turn to the history of fantasy.

Concepts of Genre and Intercultural Flows

The concept of genre is mentioned by Stephens and McCallum as "a still looser form of pre-textual context." (Stephens and McCallum 1998, 5) However, the concept of genre is more than that since it delivers a certain structure and a certain preunderstanding, not necessarily as "loose. " Often the concept plays a major role in the way in which the narrative is created and received.

In her dissertation *Den fantastiske fortælling i dansk børnelitteratur 1967-2003* (*The Fantastic Tale in Danish Children's Literature from 1967 to 2003*), Skyggebjerg draws attention to the two different conceptual traditions in the understanding of the fantastic genre. The German tradition has coined the term "Fantasiestücke," used by E.T.A. Hoffmann to characterise his "Nussknacker und Mausekönig" and "Das fremde Kind." When introduced in a French translation in 1828, Hoffmann's term was replaced by "contes fantastiques' ("fantastic tales").

Other concepts in the German tradition, not referred to by Skyggebjerg, but necessary to consider, are "Märchen" and "Abenteuer." "Märchen," meaning "traditional folk tales" was applied by the Grimm brothers and from there expanded.[4] "Abenteuer" derives from the Latin "adventura" and is related to the French term "aventure," the

---

4   In *Duden* 2003, Märchen is defined as „im Volk überlieferte Erzählung, in der übernatürliche Kräfte u. Gestalten in das Leben der Menschen eingreifen u. meist am Ende die Guten belohnt u. die Bösen bestraft werden."

English "adventure," and the Danish "eventyr," all with the primary meaning implying an unusual, strange, and exciting event, appealing to the imagination. (cf. Duden 2003, 77; *Petit Laroussse* 1968, 88; *The Concise Oxford Dictionary* 1964, 20; *Ordbog over det Danske sprog* IV 1922, 559) Where "Märchen" according to *Duden*'s definition implies fantastic events or characters, "Abenteuer" is just on the edge of the fantastic dimension. In Danish tradition, "eventyr" as a literary term became synonymous with the German "Märchen."

The concept of "fantasy" was celebrated by English Romantics, among them Samuel Taylor Coleridge. Today it has a variety of applications: "fantasy, a special case of fiction, breaks one or more of the rules that govern 'real' life as we ordinarily define it and so invents an altered reality that must be true to rules of its own" ... Fantasy is valued for the link that it provides to stories of the past." (Culliman & Person 2005, 275)

In his essay "On Fairy Stories," Tolkien starts with a pun on these fundamental concepts: "I propose to speak about fairy stories, though I am aware that this is a rash adventure." (Tolkien 1964, 2) He finds the definitions in *The Oxford English Dictionary* unsatisfactory because of its limited understanding of the genre. The implications of mere "fairy" are disturbing: "Stories that are actually concerned primarily with "fairies," that is, creatures that might also in modern English be called "elves," are relatively rare, and as a rule not very interesting. Most good "fairy stories" are about the adventures of men in the Perilous Realm or upon its shadowy marches." (Tolkien 1964, 4) Therefore, Tolkien would rather replace "fairy" with "Faërie, the Perilous Realm itself." (ibid.)

Skyggebjerg defines the fantastic tale as a tale that "implies a meeting between reality and magic." This meeting can be structured in several ways (cf. Nikolajeva 2000) and can have various consequences for the protagonists, but "the opposition between reality and magic is always pivotal for the way in which the story is interpreted." (Skyggebjerg 2005, 310) Skyggebjerg emphasises the narrow relationship between the fairy tale -- both the artificial tale and the folk tale -- and the fantastic tale or the literature of fantasy. Both allow for the existence of the marvellous (Todorov 1970) without any hesitation. The emerging concepts mentioned above display that the first half of the nineteenth century was a crucial period for the development and understanding of this kind of literature.

It is obvious that the history of major genres is international. It is meaningless to consider the national development without accounting for the international perspective. In an article about methodological problems, Emer O'Sullivan delineates the international movements of the fantasy genre from a bird eye's view: "Taking Germany and the genre of fantasy as the focal point for a thumbnail sketch, we can say that this genre, which was subsequently to become one of the key genres of children's literature, was founded in Germany with E.T.A. Hoffmann's *Nussknacker und Mausekönig* (1816) but its further development took place in other countries. Hans Christian Andersen initially carried on the heritage of German Romanticism in the field of children's literature in Denmark in the early nineteenth century, and the tradition of fantasy reached new heights in mid-nineteenth century England with the works of George MacDonald and Lewis Carroll and, somewhat later, Edith Nesbit. (O'Sullivan 2002, 39)[5] Later, Astrid Lindgren launched fantasy in Sweden in the form of Pippi Långstrump; it was translated into German in 1949 and helped to start a renewed creation of fantasy.

"Some scholars date the rise of modern fantasy from the first half of the nineteenth century, when Hans Christian Andersen used elements of traditional stories in authoring literary tales." (Cullinan & Person 2005, 275) Here, Andersen is assigned the role of transformative link between the development in Germany and England, so his influence seems to be a well-established fact of literary history. In 1835 Andersen published his first fairy tales and stories in Danish, and from that time new collections appeared throughout his lifetime. Hans Christian Andersen's stories were quickly translated into German and English. As early as 1835-37, *Wonderful Stories for Children* appeared in Mary Howitt's translation, continuing with the second series in 1838, and the third in 1845. Other editions appeared during the 1850s. (cf. Cullinan & Person 2005, 35) Jens Andersen,

---

5   The article has been translated into Danish, cf. O'Sullivan 2002 b, 73.

one of the latest biographers of Hans Christian Andersen, gives him credit for his very modern way of promoting his books, timing the publication with foreign visits, readings, and even autobiographies. Hans Christian Andersen's visit to England in 1847 was in this way synchronised with the appearance of *The True Story of my Life - A Sketch* (Andersen II 2003, 118), and his meeting with Charles Dickens was reported as a climax of the literary visit.[6]

Jackie Wullschläger claims that there was a division of labour between the Grimm brothers and Hans Christian Andersen in the way in which they conveyed the fairy tale. The Grimm brothers spread "the power of legend" whereas Hans Christian Andersen "invented the literary fairy tale, writing his own stories, such as 'The Little Mermaid' and 'The Little Match Girl,' striking a near-archetypal resonance but overlaying them with a Christian, nineteenth-century morality and sentimentality that married well with the tastes of Victorian England." (Wullschläger 1995, 100-01) Both, however, had an effect not only on children's literature, but on Victorian literature in general. In this way, the influence of Hans Christian Andersen was assimilated into the contemporary Victorian culture to the point of assimilation, so that no one would know where it originally came from: the fairy tales of Hans Christian Andersen would merge into metanarratives.

In examining Andersen's relationship to genres, it is important to note that he constantly experimented, retelling fairy tales that he had heard as a child or discovered later in life, exploring and combining various kinds of fairy tales with the historical tale, the fable, the parable, the legend, the myth, the symbolic or allegorical tale, and poems. As we shall see, he also mixed elements from various types when he retold a story. Additionally, when compared to the traditional folk tale, an unhappy ending is more the rule than the exception in Andersen's oeuvre. By experimenting with genres and mixing elements, Andersen explored a number of ways in which the traditional "even-

---

6   Hans Christian Andersen's second visit to England took place in 1857. In terms of contacts and friendships this second visit could not compete with the first one. During his stay with the Dickens family, their relationship decayed disastrously. (cf. Andersen 2003 II, 196-205)

tyr" could be transformed. In doing so, among other things he anticipated the fantasy genre.

Discussing the relationship between children and grown-ups, it is interesting that neither Hoffmann nor Andersen, exclusively or even primarily, wrote for children. During the period 1835-1842, Andersen used the term "fairy tales, told for children." However, this term was abandoned in *New Fairy tales* from 1844. Several times he pointed out that his fairy tales also offered something for grown-ups, and in some cases the address to the grown-up reader overshadowed his interest in children. A guideline for his understanding can be found in his own reflections: "I seize an idea for older people, and then tell it to the young ones, while remembering that father and mother are listening and must have something to think about." (cf. Weinreich 2006, 213 and Cullinan and Person 2005, 34) From 1849 on, Andersen used the term "Historie" (tale) to describe all of his tales: "*Historier* - det Navn, jeg i vort Sprog anseer at være det bedst valgte for mine Eventyr i al deres Udstrækning og Natur." (Mortensen 2003, 36) ("*Stories* - the name I consider the best choice in our language for my fairy tales to their full extent and nature." My translation.)

The key term in "fairy tales, told for children" as well as in the "tales" is the idea of a narrator appealing to the ear. Andersen's excessive use of oral expressions demonstrates the strategy: "See saa! Nu begynde vi." (Andersen I 2003, 303) ("Look! Now we begin." My translation); this expression has found no equivalent in English. Andersen used the spoken language as a way of confirming his ability to see the world from the angle of the child, the thing, or the animal -- in brief, from a neglected but rewarding perspective. Andersen certainly had a dual target group in mind.

In "On Fairy Stories," J.R.R.Tolkien strikes a similar note: "In my opinion fairy stories should not be specially associated with children." (Tolkien 1964, 14) Considering their conceptual closeness, it is not surprising that C.S. Lewis agrees: "The whole association of fairy tale and fantasy with childhood is local and accidental." (Lewis 2006, 20) Naturally, both of them admit that the development of fantasy has been striking in children's literature, but both deny the close identification of fantasy with children's literature. Instead, they focus on tales of "Faërie," targeting two audiences united by their shared capacity of using the imagination.

Linking Andersen and Lewis: A Brief Survey

On the basis of current research, I have noted a few general observations of the connections between Hans Christian Andersen and C.S. Lewis. Let me establish the context of these links and add some others. C.S. Lewis himself is not very explicit regarding this source of inspiration. A.N. Wilson, one of several biographers, carefully lists the circumstances of his literary production, but Hans Christian Andersen is not on his list. However, in the above-mentioned essay on children's literature, Lewis draws attention to his reading as a child ("When I was ten, I read fairy tales in secret." [Lewis 2006, 19]) We may assume that the fairy tales of Andersen were among them. If not, the knowledge of Andersen might have been conveyed by other authors since the fairy tales of Andersen, as documented above, were assimilated into Victorian literary culture.

The origin and connotations of witches in the *Narnia Chronicles* have been an object of discussion for decades. Margery Fisher quotes one of the dwarfs in *The Silver Chair*: "Those Northern Witches always mean the same thing, but in every age they have a different plan for getting it." (Fisher 1975, 374) In this connection she suggests that "C.S. Lewis means the White Witch, the enchantress of *The Silver Chair* and the tempestuous Queen Jadis in *The Magician's Nephew* to be three aspects of one truth." (ibid.) As to inspiration, according to Fisher, Lewis may have drawn on George MacDonald's *Phantastes*, Hans Christian Andersen's "Snow Queen," and *Sir Gawain and the Green Knight* for his image of the White Witch, whereas the inspiration for the Green Witch rather seems to be Spenserian. Fisher's aim is to characterise, not to analyse in any depth. Other researchers have observed the similarity, e.g., Ying Tojier-Nilsson in her book *The Wonderland of Fantasy*. She draws a parallel between Kay in "The Snow Queen" and Edmund in *The Lion, the Witch and the Wardrobe*, but doesn't elaborate upon it. (Tojier-Nilsson 1981, 87)

In a convincing analysis, Cathy McSporran points out that there are ancient precursors of both witches. Lilith is their ancestor, and consequently both the serpent and Eve play a role as two great tempters. (McSporran 2005, 195) According to McSporran, Lewis is sceptical of female liberation, obviously preferring the traditional relationships between the sexes. Accordingly, Susan is treated rather harshly by the author because she has been "too keen on growing up," thus deliberately eliminating the childlike element in herself. (McSporran 2005, 200) This makes her brothers and her sister Lucy distance themselves from her.

Maria Nikolajeva concentrates on the topic of time, so crucial in the genre of fantasy. The usual pattern is that the story starts in everyday life, briefly depicting the protagonists' situation at home or in school. Soon the protagonists are transported to the secondary world where normal time is suspended, and where a special task awaits. This being fulfilled, the characters return to the primary world. Nikolajeva points out that this constitutes a "convenient narrative device" for the author (Nikolajeva 2000, 127), but also that the structure delivers a representation of the concepts of chronological or profane time as well as archaic or ritual time.

In *The Lion, the Witch and the Wardrobe* that constitutes Nikolajeva's primary example, the function of the White Witch is to stop time, thus stifling natural development, preventing growth -- and keeping children as children forever. When time is restored, spring breaks out and growth is possible again. However, in Narnia the concept of adolescence and of being grown-up is rather thin. The obstacles rather than the results attract interest, which is a common feature in fantasy. The return to the primary world means that the whole game can start over again, as is indeed the case in the following Narnia Chronicles, until the protagonists cannot return again because they have outgrown childhood.

Nikolajeva points out that Andersen's tale is more erotic than Lewis'. She regards Edmund as a parallel character to Kay, but emphasises the seduction act on the part of the White Queen, symbolised by the Turkish Delight enjoyed by Edmund. (Nikolajeva 2000, 130) Nikolajeva interprets rather crudely food as a parallel to sexuality: "Meals in myths and fairy tales are circumlocutions of sexual intercourse." (Nikolajeva 2000, 129) It seems to me that in *The Narnia Chronicles* food more often represents the lifeline to dailiness[7]: during all their adventures, the protagonists need something to eat and drink. This provides a link to the ordinary world. In the midst of adventures and perils it may be comforting to think of a cup of tea, sardines and toast, both for the protagonists and for their audience.

However, in certain cases the connection to sex *is* evident. With Edmund, the sexual allusions are as obvious as in "The Snow Queen" where, as Nikolajeva observes, Kay is seduced by a kiss. She also points to the different endings of the two stories. Kay's rejection of childhood is equal to death, and Gerda's tears make childhood come back to him. When they reach home, however, they are changed. They have grown up (with the possibility of becoming lovers), yet remain children at heart. According to Nikolajeva, this combination is not adopted by C.S. Lewis. Nikolajeva is right as far as Susan is concerned. (cf. Cathy McSporran) This does not mean that it is not possible to learn from experiences in the secondary world; Eustace is an example. In *The Voyage of the "Dawn Treader,"* he is at first a nuisance, but in due course he matures. In *The Silver Chair* he is changed; and in the short time between the two stories, his behaviour to Jill has ameliorated.

Skyggebjerg clearly understands "The Snow Queen" as a forerunner of fantasy, claiming that it "indeholder ansatser til en struktur som er typisk i fantastiske fortællinger for børn." (Skyggebjerg 2005, 89) ("contains dispositions of a structure typical of fantastic tales for children." My translation) Skyggebjerg realises the double world structure of the tale and stresses that Gerda's travel from the primary to the secondary world has a great significance. Her objection to an interpretation of "The Snow Queen" as a fantastic tale is that the meeting between the real world and the magic world is not the pivotal point. I agree that the story is complex, but to me it seems that this meeting is crucial.

---

[7] A term from Paddy Scannell in *Radio, Television and Modern Life,* Oxford: Blackwell, 1996.

FAIRY TALE AND NARNIA CHRONICLES

Finally, it should be mentioned that "The Snow Queen" is not the only Andersen-related narrative retold by Lewis. Among all the fairy tales and adventures rearranged in *The Narnia Chronicles* there is the legend of Holger Danske (Ogier the Dane) in *The Silver Chair*. Legend says that Holger rests as a statue of stone in the basement of Kronborg Castle. When danger arises and he is needed, he will be resurrected and will overcome the enemies of the nation. This legend was re-told in a tale by Hans Christian Andersen in 1845, and the whole structure of *The Silver Chair* might be said to mirror this legend. The protagonist has been turned into a kind of stone in the Underland and reawakens at the time of danger, when Narnia is threatened by the Green Witch.

"The Snow Queen"

"The Snow Queen" was published in 1845 in the second volume of *New Fairy tales*, 1844-45. The first volume was comprised of tales such as "The Nightingale" and "The Ugly Duckling." In the final volume were "The Red Shoes" and "The Shepherdess and the Chimney Sweep." "The Snow Queen" was published in the second volume with "The Fir Tree." All of them are some of the best-known tales by Andersen. It is easy to find similarities in themes, style, and perspective among these tales, as numerous researchers have found, from Rubow in 1964 to Mortensen in 2003. In this context, I shall concentrate on "The Snow Queen."

As far as genre is concerned, "The Snow Queen" is called "Et Eventyr i syv Historier" ("a fairy tale in seven stories"). (Andersen 2003, 303) It is clearly an example of Andersen's mixing elements from various subgenres and of his taste for exploring subgenres. Seven is a magic number, implicitly referring to the myth of creation and, thus, to the seven days of the week. Seven is a mirror of mythical time as well as everyday time, and both are crucial in this context. The device of using seven stories parts or segments is one of the reasons why it is difficult to characterise "The Snow Queen." Let us follow the critical tradition in Danish research and examine the segments in chronological order.[8]

The first part has an apparently innocent subtitle: "der handler om Speilet og Stumperne" ("which describes a Looking-glass and the Broken Fragments"). This is also the case with the other subtitles: they are suggestive, but not revealing. The genre of the first part is a sort of prologue delivering "the commencement of this story." The looking-glass is fabricated by the demon to distort perception: "everything good or beautiful" shrinks to nothing and vice versa: "everything that was worthless and bad increased in size." This invention is the cause of much devilish laughter governed by the principle: distortion is ridiculous.

As noticed by Ib Johansen, the shattering of the looking-glass is akin to the myth of falling, in a cosmic setting, but in a peculiar incarnation. (Johansen 2000, 100) Evil avoided is the distortion of the angels. But it causes a greater evil since the smallest fragment of the mirror contains the same power as the original mirror. Being fragmented, it becomes part of the human condition in risking to host such a piece. The victims are attacked in two ways: their vision is distorted, and their hearts can become "cold like a lump of ice." In this way, distortion of vision and lack of feeling are combined. And once exposed to them, remedy is rare.

The subjects of the next stories deal with possible remedies. They deal with the things that happen when you – in Karlsen's words -- become alienated from yourself and others. (Karlsen 2000, 21) The implication of the mythical approach in this opening story has been absorbed by language. In Danish, we still speak of the "fragment of the magic mirror in the eye" as an expression of being able to see only the negative side of things, and the image has also been a fertile factor in modern literature (e.g., in the case of Villy Sørensen).[9]

The second segment repeats the device in an apparently innocent subtitle. In this case, it is "A Little Boy and a Little Girl," conveying the

---

8   This procedure is followed in all the very different articles about "The Snow Queen," assembled in Barlby, 2000.

9   In his analysis of modern retelling stories in this article, Gemzøe distinguishes between different kinds of intertextuality: common and specific versions, genre, style, and epoch.

essence of the two sexes, Adam and Eva, as though they were children in the Garden of Eden. Kay and Gerda are introduced. They live in "a large town, full of houses and people." They attend school, play, and are occupied with everyday life. Though they are not rich, they have access to a tiny garden, really only a box placed across the water-pipe. This box contains kitchen herbs and sweet peas as well as the central symbol of love, a rose bush. The first part of this story anticipates the end of love, introducing nature's dichotomy of summer and winter, between roses, flowers and frost, snow and ice. Already at this point a rift between the children is introduced. Both children have seen the bees, but Kay is fascinated by the "white bees swarming." He asks his grandmother about the queen bee and boasts that he can cope with her: "Only let her come!" After that, the materialisation of the Snow Queen "fair and beautiful" (3) takes place before his eyes, and consequently Kay is vulnerable to being hit in the eye and heart by a fragment of the looking-glass. He is also vulnerable to subsequent abduction by the Snow Queen. Gerda is not attracted. A line of magic poetry from her favourite hymn seems to protect her: "Roses bloom and cease to be,/ but we shall the Christ-child see." (ibid.) As we shall see, not all flowers are like roses.

The looking-glass changes Kay from a participant into an observer. His imaginative power is frozen. Instead of inventing new ways of seeing himself, he imitates and mimics others. In this way he becomes a willing victim of the Snow Queen, having no allies except reason: he "tried to say a prayer, but he could remember nothing but the multiplication table." (4) Andersen's vocabulary is concrete. In the prologue, we heard that lovely countrysides appeared like "boiled spinach" seen through the looking glass. Consequently, Gerda looks "ugly" to Kay when she cries, and he has no eye for the beauty of the roses any more: one rose is worm-eaten, and another is crooked.

Curiosity and fascination led to Kay's change of character. The observing attitude paved the way for his abduction, which is carried out as a seduction: the first kiss makes him ignore the cold around him, and the second kiss makes him forget Gerda, his grandmother, and his home. Parents play no role here, as the importance of individual development is stressed. The children, their counterparts, and helpers are at the heart of the story. The danger of annihilation is signalled by the Snow Queen: "Now you must have no more kisses, or I should kiss you to death." Kay's perception has changed completely: the Snow Queen is to him lovely, intelligent and "perfect," and he sleeps at her feet.

In the third part, Gerda's quest to find Kay begins.[10] Spring and sun have prevailed, and the natural conditions for finding him are positive. Gerda is receptive to the language of the animals; swallows and sparrows guide her. Her quest confronts her with various characters and settings, making it possible to investigate different attitudes to the moral question that arose with the disappearance of Kay: how should you live your life? This question is answered in a number of different ways during the next three stories, mirroring possible perspectives for Kay and Gerda as if nothing had happened.

Gerda's first stop is the Flower Garden. Every time she gets the chance to meet anyone, Gerda tells her story to that point. Sometimes she gets a response in the form of hints or helpers, sometimes not. In any case, she continues telling her story. Contrary to the former dichotomy, in the flower garden selfishness prevails. Gerda is almost conjured into forgetting her quest. In spite of the spell, however, Gerda is eventually appalled by the lack of roses. No garden without roses! She calls them forth, and they assure her that Kay is not dead. This is the only positive help she gets.

In this story, the further exploration of genres continues. Every flower is allowed to tell its own little metaphorical story, reflecting its own nature, reminding the reader of the idyllic, but isolated, universe in the garden of the woman who could conjure. The narcissus gets the last word, mirroring the general idea in the garden: "I can see myself, I can see myself." This narcissistic universe is clearly rejected by Gerda: "Oh, how I have wasted my time." Gerda must realise that "it is autumn" (6) and that the conditions for finding Kay consequently will be harder.

The fourth story does not advance Gerda by much. Again she tells her story, first to the crow, later to the prince and princess of the castle.

---

10 Johansen 2000 enhances this point of view in the title of his article.

It is a tale of trial and error: She believes the prince to be Kay, but is disappointed. The prince is occupied elsewhere. Within this story are two others, exhibiting Andersen's ongoing experiments with genres in this context. The first embedded story is a fairy tale about the prince and princess, which ten years later was retold as "Clodpoll." This tale is in the tradition of a folk tale. The clever princess opposes convention. Her only wish is not to get bored in her marriage and life at court. Therefore, she chooses an entertaining husband and makes a kind of moral choice: to have fun! She exhibits a hedonistic way of life. The second story-within-a-story is the satirical fable about the crows, their marriage, and choice of way of life. As "one crow always chooses another crow," they have preferred "the position of court crows, with all that is left in the kitchen for yourselves" (11) to freedom. This choice implies a voluntary limitation on life.

Having been detained in the Flower Garden and at the Castle, Gerda has experienced different types of life, but as yet has met no helpers or allies on her quest. Though kind, the inhabitants of the castle are more occupied with their own family sphere. Gerda gets a golden coach to lead her on and is given boots and a muff, servants and cakes. These turn out to be of little help, but they do move the story to a new phase.

The fifth part has a Gothic and ironic twist since Gerda is caught in the woods by robbers, who were attracted by her golden coach. Objecting to society, the merry robbers and outlaws in the woods seek their own society. All of Gerda's newly acquired servants are killed! She herself barely survives, and only with the help of a "self-willed and obstinate" robber-girl. Again Gerda tells her story. In a way, the robber-girl mirrors the Snow Queen: she is strong, independent, self-willed; she gives orders and she is the ruler in her robber-mother's realm. Even her mother obeys her. The difference is that the robber-girl is also led by her emotions. And she appears as the most resolute helper to this point. She provides Gerda with her reindeer, fur boots, and her mother's mittens; the robber-girl decides to take Gerda's lovely muff for herself.

Gerda has now experienced oblivious idyll, hedonism, and outlaw's rejection of society. The sixth segment brings her nearer to the end of her quest, going through an imaginary Lapland and Finland. Following in the hoof prints of the reindeer, both the Lapland Woman and Finland Woman appear to be helpers. The Finland Woman even knows what has happened to Kay. She has insight in the mechanisms of the looking-glass and into the limitations of her own art: "I can give her no greater power than she has already; don't you see how strong that is? How men and animals are obliged to serve her, and how well she has got through the world, barefooted as she is. She cannot receive any power from me greater than that she now has, which consists in her own purity and innocence of heart." (15) In contrast to Kay, Gerda remembers the Lord's Prayer. She is a believer, and even the hostility of the Snow Queen's domain does not affect her: little angels spring forward to keep her from being annihilated by the threatening snowflakes.

In the seventh story Gerda's quest ends. She finds Kay, the object of her hope and love. The Snow Queen, her main adversary, has departed for the South.[11] There is no direct confrontation between the two females, which makes redemption easier -- and more uncertain, as the Snow Queen might return at any moment. Kay is occupied by trying to solve a riddle in "the icy game of reason." (16) The key word is "Eternity"; it is a solution not quite obvious to Kay, who is more concerned with facts, measures, and tables.

Even if Kay does not acknowledge Gerda at first, she redeems him by crying. Her tears melt the lump of ice in his heart. When she repeats the lines about the roses and the Christ-child quoted in the first story, Kay weeps, and with his tears the splinter of glass disappears. When icy, he could not find the key word. Now, it forms itself. "Eternity" thus connects itself to life, in opposition to the condition of living death.

The return hastily and satirically repeats the previous stages in short glimpses. The crow is dead, and the robber-girl has set out to see the world. Returning home, Kay and Gerda realise that they are grown-ups, "yet children at heart." This confirms the assumption that the story of the quest is a formation process in which Kay is liberated

---

11   She is attracted to the southern countries even if her home is in the North. (cf. Johansen 2000)

and maturity is brought about, but not at the expense of the element of childhood. Preserving the inner child in the process of change seems to be the core of the tale.

The elements in "The Snow Queen" pointing to later fantasy tales are partly placed in the structure, partly in the characters, partly in establishing thematic dichotomies, pointing to the overruling themes. The fact that the structure is reminiscent of fantasy's double worlds is made clear in the second story, which emphasises everyday life. Kay and Gerda start out living in a town in a normal, primary world where they play and live in small apartments, go to church, and attend school. The primary world provides a frame for the plot since the story ends with their return. Gerda's quest leads her through various fantastic life forms, which become the basis of her experience.

Though the Snow Queen is the title character, she is not the main protagonist. Neither is Kay, who is brought to the secondary world by the Snow Queen. The main protagonist is Gerda, who sets out to find Kay. Both Kay and Gerda are children in the process of adjusting to being grown-ups, and the relationship between them is a central focus. A multitude of fantastic beings, humans, animals, and creatures in between -- even snowflakes -- act as helpers and adversaries. Among them, the Snow Queen is a mighty symbol of power without a heart, a symbol of the power of destruction.

Through all dangers Gerda is led by her heart, her trust in the positive forces of nature and her belief. The concept of pure rationality is challenged. A parallel between the secluded worlds she visits and aspects of life in the primary world is drawn and in some cases parodied (e.g., the life of the tame crows and the robbers). A series of dichotomies, essential to fantasy, are established:

reason	- emotion
abstract knowledge	- belief
desire for power and things	- love
artificiality	- nature
evil	- good

In concentrated form, these dichotomies exhibit the overruling themes: the possibility of falling (betrayal) and the moral challenge (how to develop and still be true to yourself).

"THE SNOW QUEEN" AND THE WHITE WITCH

The Narnia Chronicles

C.S. Lewis' *Narnia Chronicles* are structured along similar lines and exhibit similar characters and themes in a more stable form; the fantasy genre has developed its conventions since 1845. The protagonists are ordinary children, siblings, a boy and a girl as in "The Snow Queen." We first meet them in the primary world where they behave as ordinary children. By magic means, and due to a certain disposition of the imagination, they approach the realm of Narnia, a secondary world created by Aslan, a lion and Christ-like figure. In this secondary world, the children are protagonists, e.g., Digory and Polly in the 1955 *The Magician's Nephew* and the Pevensie siblings in *The Lion, the Witch and the Wardrobe*, of 1950.

Sometimes, the children act as helpers for protagonists from Narnia as do Eustace and Jill in *The Voyage of the "Dawn Treader"*, 1952, and in *The Silver Chair*, 1953. Having passed the tests and finished the quest in Narnia, they return to their point of departure, sometimes wiser, sometimes oblivious to past experiences in the secondary world. The children are similar to Gerda and Kay. Often the boys are a little more audacious and curious than the girls (as is Kay); this disposition leads them into temptation or even treason, a position from which they fight to liberate themselves. Lucy mirrors Gerda in her belief in the power of imagination, originally ridiculed and rejected by the older children.

The secondary world has its own myth of creation and its own development in time. In Narnia, the children meet institutions, creatures and beings, who mirror the primary world in many ways. Society is a medieval kingdom. The most obvious lookalike of the Snow Queen is the White Witch, who represents the same fascinating qualities, being a symbol of evil and abuse of power, able to turn her adversaries into stone. If we adopt the author's chronology and not the actual date of him writing the books, this new incarnation of the Snow Queen first appears as Queen Jadis in *The Magician's Nephew*. Her name has the following connotations: 1) jade, a beautiful stone that might be associated with power, ruthlessness, coldness; 2) French - jadis, "au temps jadis" (a long time ago), accentuating the mythical quality of the queen.

FAIRY TALE AND NARNIA CHRONICLES

Led by curiosity, Digory, the boy, makes the fatal mistake of releasing her, not knowing the consequences: the appearance of evil in the newly created world of harmony. Ignoring Digory's friend Polly, she addresses Digory arrogantly, trying to lead to his downfall in the Garden of Eden. The myths of falling and redemption provide the structure of the plot, where Digory is tempted and tried and at last overcomes his initial fall. In the redemption process, tears appear as a sign of sincerity: "But when he had said 'Yes,' he thought of his Mother, and he thought of the great hopes he had had, and how they were all dying away, and a lump came in his throat and tears in his eyes." (Lewis 1995, 131)

In *The Lion, the Witch and the Wardrobe*, the image of the White Witch unfolds as part of the structure; her realm of coldness, cruelty, and despotism is opposed to all that Narnia was meant to be. The character of the White Witch is explicitly identified with winter. As her realm means "Always winter and never Christmas" (Lewis 1988, 23), the relationship to the Snow Queen is obvious from the beginning, and confirmed by later traits and events. The White Witch lives in an ice castle, surrounded by stone animals and various beings such as wolves and dwarfs. When she first appears to Edmund, she is white, beautiful, and attractive, but cold. The combination of sexual appeal and living death is emphasised by the first description of the White Witch: "Her face was white - not merely pale, but white like snow or paper or icing-sugar, except for her very red mouth." (Lewis 1988: 33) She offers her fur mantle to Edmund and seduces him with a magic potion and Turkish delight, appealing to his ambition and selfishness in a rather sexy manner. In his fascination and disposition Edmund surely resembles Kay. Consequently, the White Witch supplies him with the wrong vision, the lack of the ability to discern good from evil, and he falls.

In their search for redemption, Nature provides helpers for the children (birds, beavers, the season of spring, etc.), but nature also shows her dark side in the form of dwarfs, wolves, and winter, helping the White Witch. However, the children have an omnipotent helper in the shape of Aslan/Christ. Sacrificing himself, he is resurrected stronger than ever. Edmund is redeemed, Narnia is rescued and the children can return to their ordinary world.

The White Witch is defeated when *The Lion, the Witch and the Wardrobe* ends. However, she reappears both in legends later referred to (in *Prince Caspian* 1951, where the dwarf Nikabrik is punished for his belief in her superiority) and in other incarnations (in *The Silver Chair* as the Queen of Underland, the Green Witch). In this context, as in *The Lion, the Witch and the Wardrobe*, she plays a vital role as the main opponent to the rule of Aslan.

In the overruling themes, which are the possibility of falling-betraying and the moral challenge, we distinguish the same dichotomies in *The Narnia Chronicles* as in "The Snow Queen." And in the same way, they are elucidated in a way palatable to children and one that does not frighten away grown-ups from listening.

Similarities and Differences

The comparison reveals striking similarities concerning structure, characters, and themes, and these similarities have been highlighted during the previous pages. Summing up, the hieratic register forms the backdrop in both cases, and with it the metaphorical and allegorical allusions. In "The Snow Queen" as well as in *The Narnia Chronicles*, the Christian ideals of love, self-sacrifice, and resurrection serve as the bases for opposing evil and restoring harmony. However, Andersen emphasises that change nevertheless has been brought about during the quest. In both cases, the epic and the demotic register play a larger role than the hieratic register, exhibiting institutions out of order, grotesque traits, paralleling circumstances in the primary and the secondary world.

This does not mean that all is the same. The eagerness of exploring genres related to the fairy tale so eminent in "The Snow Queen" is replaced in *The Narnia Chronicles* by a firm and steady structure that repeats itself during the series, with the exception of *The Horse and his Boy.* There, the primary world is only alluded to. The styles are different. The oral language so typical of Hans Christian Andersen is also present in the chronicles of Lewis, but the dominant way of narrating is much more even and smooth, both in the narrator's language and in the remarks and replies of the protagonists. The striking concreteness of Andersen is absent.

But this is a subject for further study.

References

Andersen, Jens. *Andersen: En biografi.* 2 vols. København: Gyldendal, 2003.
Andersen, H.C. *Eventyr og Historier.* 3 vols. Vol. 1: H.C. Andersens *Samlede værker.* Edited by Klaus P. Mortensen. København: Det Danske Sprog- og Litteraturselskab og Gyldendal, 2003.
Cullina, Bernice E., and Diane G. Person. *The Continuum Encyclopedia of Children's Literature.* New York: Continuum, 2005.
Barlby, Finn. *Det (h)vide spejl* Analyser af H.C. Andersens "Sneedronningen. København: Dråben, 2000.
Fisher, Margery. *Who's Who in Children's Books.* London: Weidenfeld & Nicolson, 1975.
Gemzøe, Anker: "Tavshed og ord. Om Villy Sørensens "Ægget." In *Kritik* 147: 33-43.
Jensen, Bo Green. *Det første landskab. Myter, helte og kunsteventyr.* København: Rosinante, 1999.
Johansen, Ib. "*Quest*-struktur og sort og hvid magi i H.C. Andersens "Sneedronningen." In *Det (h)vide spejl* Analyser af H.C. Andersens "Sneedronningen.", edited by Finn Barlby. København: Dråben, 2000.
Karlsen, Hugo Hørlych. "Spejlene og de indre veje". In *Det (h)vide spejl* Analyser af H.C. Andersens "Sneedronningen.", edited by Finn Barlby. København: Dråben, 2000.
Lewis, C.S. *The Magician's Nephew.* London: HarperCollins, 1995.
———. *The Lion, the Witch and the Wardrobe.* London: HarperCollins 1988.
———. *The Horse and his Boy.* London: HarperCollins, 1995.
———. *Prince Caspian.* London: HarperCollins, 1995.
———. *The Voyage of the "Dawn Treader,"* London: HarperCollins, 1995.
———. *The Silver Chair.* London: HarperCollins, 1995.
———. *The Last Battle.* London: HarperCollins, 1995.
———. "On three ways of writing for children." In *Children's Literature* I. Edited by Peter Hunt. Abingdon: Routledge, 2006.

McSporran, Cathy. "Daughters of Lilith: Witches and Wicked Women in *The Chronicles of Narnia*". In *Revisiting Narnia*. Edited by Shanna Caughey. Dallas: Benbella Books, 2005.

Mortensen, Klaus P. "Indledning." In H.C. Andersens *Samlede værker* I. Edited by Klaus P. Mortensen. København: Det Danske Sprog- og Litteraturselskab og Gyldendal, 2003.

Møller, Hans Henrik. "Hvordan staver man til evighed?" *Det (h)vide spejl*. Edited by Finn Barlby. København: Dråben, 2000.

Nikolajeva, Maria. *From Mythic to Linear Time in Children's Literature*. London: The Children's Literature Association and The Scarecrow Press, 2000.

O'Sullivan, Emer. "Comparing Children's Literature". In *German as a Foreign Language*, no. 1 (Summer 2002): 33-56.

O'Sullivan, Emer. "Komparative studier i børnelitteratur". In *Nedslag i børnelitteraturforskningen* 3. Roskilde: Roskilde Universitetsforlag 2002.

Rubow, Paul V. *H.C. Andersens Eventyr*. København: Gyldendal, 1967.

Skyggebjerg, Anna Karlskov. *Den fantastiske fortælling i dansk børnelitteratur 1967-2003*. Roskilde: Roskilde Universitetsforlag, 2005.

Soya, Carl Erik. "De udødelige". In *Hvis tilværelsen keder Dem*. København: Borgen, 1952.

Stephens, John, and Robyn McCallum. *Retelling Stories, Framing Culture. Traditional Story and Metanarratives in Children's Literature*. New York: Garland Publishing, 1998.

_____. "Pre-texts, Metanarratives, and the Western meta-ethic". In *Children's Literature* IV. Edited by Peter Hunt. Abingdon: Routledge, 2006. (Chapter 1 reprinted from the above mentioned book.)

Todorov, Tzvetan. *Introduction à la littérature fantastique*. Paris: Seuil, 1970.

Tojier-Nilsson, Ying. *Fantasins underland*. Klippan: Efs-förlaget, 1981.

Tolkien, J.R.R. "On Fairy Stories." In *Tree and Leaf*. London: HarperCollins, 1964.

Weinreich, Torben. *Historien om børnelitteratur.* København: Branner og Korch, 2006.
Wullschläger, Jackie. *Inventing Wonderland.* London: Methuen, 1995.

Jørgen Riber Christensen

Peter Pan from Barrie to Disney

> *I don't want ever to be a man," he said with passion. "I want always to be a little boy and to have fun. So I ran away to Kensington Gardens and lived a long long time among the fairies."*
> – J.M. Barrie, *Peter Pan*

J.M. Barrie's (1860-1937) 1904 play *Peter Pan* and its many adaptations (including film) have become part of the Western world's cultural heritage. All of these versions use the concept from fantasy of the double universe (Neverland) to interpret and describe the changes in our mental landscape. In this article, the *Peter Pan* tradition (in a number of interpretations) will be examined in light of psychoanalytical theories. My goal: to demonstrate how Barrie's original text and its later transformations have worked on the therapeutic and ontological levels for generations of readers and audiences to cope with their growing up and development. Throughout its history, *Peter Pan* has been adapted to explain a child's development and role in the family. Discussions range from the classical Oedipus conflict through narcissism, tweening, changing gender roles, and the dissolution of the nuclear family.

The versions of *Peter Pan* considered in this article are:
- Barrie's play *Peter Pan or The Boy Who Wouldn't Grow Up* (1904-1928) and its novelisation, *Peter Pan and Wendy* (1911);
- Disney's animated film *Peter Pan* from 1953;

- Steven Spielberg's film *Hook* from 1991;
- Disney's animated sequel *Peter Pan Return to Neverland* from 2002;
- P.J. Hogan's film *Peter Pan* from 2003;
- Geraldine McCaughrean's novel *Peter Pan in Scarlet - The Official Sequel* from 2006;
- J.M. Barrie's biography of his mother, *Margaret Ogilvy – by Her Son,* from 1896;
- Bradley Raymond's *Tinker Bell*, the Disney film from 2008 about the early development of Tinker Bell.

Bruno Bettelheim and the Therapeutic Function of Fairy Tales

In 1976 Bruno Bettelheim published an apologia for the genre of folk tales: *The Uses of Enchantment: The Meaning and Importance of Fairy Tales*. Bettelheim mentions the importance of parents and other people who take care of children, and a supplement to this is passing on one's cultural heritage in the form of good literature such as fairy tales. Bettelheim contrasts this with knowledge passed on through school books, as they support and further the development of even a young child. Bettelheim also writes in "The Struggle for Meaning," the introduction to the book, that he gained insight from his therapeutic work with severely disturbed children. His aim was to restore a sense of meaning to their lives. He advocates telling fairy tales to children, and while doing so he connects fairy tales to psychoanalysis:

> Through the centuries (if not millennia) during which, in their retelling, fairy tales became ever more refined, they came to convey at the same time overt and covert meanings – came to speak simultaneously to all levels of the human personality, communicating in a manner which reaches the uneducated mind of the child as well as that of the sophisticated adult. Applying the psychoanalytic model of the human personality, fairy tales carry important messages to the conscious, the preconscious, and the unconscious mind, on whatever level each is

> functioning at the time. By dealing with universal human problems, particularly those which preoccupy the child's mind, these stories speak to his budding ego and encourage its development, while at the same time relieving preconscious and unconscious pressures. As the stories unfold, they give conscious credence and body to id pressures and show ways to satisfy these that are in line with ego and superego requirements. (5-6)

One of Bettelheim's points is that fairy tales make it possible for the child to connect the anxieties and desires of its unconscious mind to the conscious mind; fairy tales provide ways to do this via images and topoi. This acknowledgement of anxieties and repressions, or giving symbolic form to existential problems, is necessary for the child to mature. Here, Bettelheim gives his opinion of the function of psychoanalysis and compares it to the way fairy tales can positively affect a child's development in the face of problems and sorrows:

> Psychoanalysis was created to enable man to accept the problematic nature of life without being defeated by it, or giving in to escapism. Freud's prescription is that only by struggling courageously against what seems like overwhelming odds can man succeed in wringing meaning out of his existence. (8)

The bulk of *The Uses of Enchantment* consists of analyses of a wide range of fairy tales. *Peter Pan* is not mentioned, though. Each of the fairy tales analysed is connected to a psychological problem or to a step in a child's development. For instance, the tale of "The Three Little Pigs" is tied to the Freudian concepts of the pleasure principle and the reality principle. In the brief but detailed analysis (Bettelheim, 41-45) of this folk tale, Bettelheim compares it favourably to the fable of "The Ants and the Grasshopper." There is a threefold progression in "The Three Little Pigs." The first two lazy pigs' behaviour is governed by the pleasure principle as they seek instant gratification and avoid facing reality. They quickly build shelters that are not wolf-proof and they consequently get eaten. They represent the early id-dominated personality that must be surpassed in the child's development. Therefore, Bettelheim writes that the pigs' violent end is acceptable and understandable by the child. The third pig, which laboriously builds a house of bricks, represents the ego-controlled personality with a superego. This pig is consequently able to recognise the reality principle and can negotiate with the demands of its own needs and those of external reality. The third pig outsmarts the wolf, and just as the two first pigs are left behind in the development of the mind, so the ravenous id-dominated wolf, which belongs in the oral stage of the development of the child, is boiled and eaten by the pig. Bettelheim sees true maturity in this outcome as an element of pleasure is integrated into the mind. In contrast, the fable of the unhappy grasshopper and the cynical and puritanical ants does not recognise the pleasure principle at all. The lesson of this fable, which is pedagogically spelled out, is that it is wrong to enjoy life when it is good, as in the summertime.

One of Bettelheim's points in his analysis of "The Three Little Pigs" is that this fairy tale demonstrates the value and advantages of growing up. The surviving pig is the eldest and most mature; the fact that the three pigs are "little" makes it possible for the child to identify with them and also to realise the advantages of growth and development towards maturity.

Perhaps the most salient feature of Peter Pan is that he is the boy who did not grow up. One may then ask the question: Does Barrie's tale demonstrate the value of arrested development and in this way contradict "The Three Little Pigs"?

Margaret Ogilvy – by Her Son

In *Margaret Ogilvy,* Barrie's 1896 biography of his mother, he describes in the first chapter "How my mother got her soft face." He also discusses how his thirteen-year-old brother, David, died. Barrie himself was half this age when it happened in 1867. His mother went into mourning and was "always delicate from that hour." (7)

When his sister tells him to go into his mother's bedroom to try to cheer her up by telling her that she still has a boy, Barrie writes about the incident:

> The room was dark, and when I heard the door shut and no sound come from the bed I was afraid, and I stood still. I suppose I was breathing hard, or perhaps I was crying, for after a time I heard a listless voice that had never been listless before say, "Is that you?" I think the tone hurt me, for I made no answer, and then the voice said more anxiously "Is that you?" again. I thought it was the dead boy she was speaking to, and I said in a little lonely voice, "No, it's no' him, it's just me." Then I heard a cry, and my mother turned in bed, and though it was dark I knew that she was holding out her arms.
>
> After that I sat a great deal in her bed trying to make her forget him, which was my crafty way of playing physician. (12-13)

Barrie seeks to make his mother laugh, and he keeps an account of how many laughs he has produced with a stroke for each. He is also jealous of his dead brother:

> It was doubtless the same sister who told me not to sulk when my mother lay thinking of him, but to try instead to get her to talk about him... At first, they say, I was often jealous, stopping her fond memories with the cry, "Do you mind nothing about me?"(15)

In a grotesque and morbid way Barry practised to be and look like his dead brother. He secretly put on his brother's clothes, went into his mother's bedroom, and whistled like his brother. This identification with the dead brother stayed with Barrie, and he wrote: "When I became a man he was still a boy of thirteen." (19)

A reading of Barrie's biography of his mother can distil certain aspects of its author's experiences that are relevant for an understanding of *Peter Pan*. The locus of character formation is the family, and the very existence of this biography and obviously also its content stress Barrie's close relationship with his mother, though this must be rephrased as Barrie's *efforts* to establish such a relationship. He was not very successful as his dead brother David was an obstacle. Barrie's love for his dead brother was ambivalent; it was tainted by a jealousy that paradoxically manifested itself as Barrie's identification with David in his attempt to win the mother's love. Finally, David was the boy who refused to grow up. He was the original Peter Pan, who "was still a boy of thirteen." In classical Freudian terms, here we are dealing with the Oedipal conflict, and also with a fixation that demonstrates the refusal to grow up. This takes the form of David remaining a boy of thirteen for ever, so this may also indicate that Peter Pan's refusal to grow up is a denial of Thanatos, or the Freudian death wish.

Peter Pan – from Prehistory until Dispersal

It is difficult if not impossible to identify the "official" version of *Peter Pan*. The genesis of the text and its main character is clouded. In his 1928 dedication to the play *Peter Pan, Or The Boy Who Would Not Grow Up*, Barrie enigmatically describes the background of the Peter Pan story. "To the Five – A Dedication" is made to the five Llewelyn Davies boys, George, John, Peter, Michael, and Nicholas, although they are addressed only by the numbers 1 to 5. The dedication begins, "Some disquieting confession must be made in printing at last the play of Peter Pan; among them this, that I have no recollection of having written it." (3) Barrie also writes that he has lost the original manuscript: "I know not whether I lost that original MS. or destroyed it, or happily gave it away. I talk of dedicating the play to you, but how can I prove it is mine?" (5) Barrie is, however, clear about the source of Peter Pan: "I always knew that I made Peter by rubbing the five of you violently together, as savages with two sticks to produce a flame." (3) In some detail he recounts the way in which the early stages of the character and tale evolved: out of his games with the five boys.

Barrie textualised these adventure games in *The Boy Castaways of Black Lake Island*, of which only two copies were printed in 1901, illustrated with Barrie's own photos. Of these two copies, one survives. Barrie writes of how the other disappeared, "(there was always some devilry in any matter connected with Peter) instantly lost itself in a railway carriage." (Barrie, 1928:8) The Captain Hook figure is present in *The Boy Castaways of Black Lake Island*, but his name is

Captain Swarthy and in the photos he is a black man. He did not meet his end with the crocodile. The large dog (Nana) is there, and she also seems to be protecting the children, though the dog also appears with a tiger's mask. Wendy is not in *The Boy Castaways*, nor is Peter Pan himself.

The fairy Tinker Bell is a creation of *The Boy Castaways of Black Lake Island*: "Even Tinker Bell has reached our island before we left it. It was one evening when we climbed the wood carrying No. 4 to show him what the trail was like by twilight. As our lanterns twinkled among the leaves No. 4 saw a twinkle stand still for a moment and he waved his foot gaily to it, thus creating Tink." (13)

Barrie's loss of memory and of the manuscript of the original *Peter Pan* may seem not unlike repressions and Freudian errors. When writing about the loss of the manuscript in the dedication, Barrie has included this passage, "A safe but sometimes chilly way of recalling the past is to force open a crammed drawer. If you are searching for anything in particular you don't find it, but something falls out at the back that is often more interesting." (13-14) The passage is echoed within the play:

> She [Mrs. Darling] does not often go out to dinner, preferring when the children are in bed to sit beside them tidying up their minds, just as if they were drawers. If WENDY and the boys could keep awake they might see her repacking into their proper places the many articles of the mind that have strayed during the day, lingering humorously over some of their contents, wondering where on earth they picked this thing up, making discoveries sweet and not so sweet, pressing this to her cheek and hurriedly stowing that out of sight. When they wake in the morning the naughtinesses with which they went to bed are not, alas, blown away, but they are placed at the bottom of the drawer; and on the top, beautifully aired, are their prettier thoughts, ready for the new day. (19)

The metaphor of tidying a drawer is repeated when Mrs. Darling performs the function of repression ("tidying up") in her children's minds.

In another version of the same passage, Barrie is more explicit about this function of repression, "When you wake in the morning, the naughtiness and evil passions with which you went to bed have been folded up small and placed at the bottom of your mind." (Barrie 1911, 8)

Barrie's vagueness about the genesis of *Peter Pan* may be due to repression. This article uses the optics of classical Freudian psychoanalysis to look under the textual surface. Barrie's lack of precision and closure about the genesis of *Peter Pan* may be positively rephrased because *Peter Pan* exhibits the vagueness of the unconscious. It becomes an open text that is dynamic through time and cultural history. There is not and never was a finite or "official" *Peter Pan*. It negotiates with the climate of each period in which it is read, performed, and reproduced.

Even before others created versions of *Peter Pan,* the history of the Barrie's text is confusing, though six distinct versions can be identified. The early history begins with *The Boy Castaways of Black Lake Island*, and the character Peter Pan himself appeared in print in 1902 in a novel written for adults called *The Little White Bird or Adventures in Kensington Gardens*. Here, a story is told about a baby called Peter Pan, who has adventures in Kensington Gardens with the fairies and birds. In 1904 a play, *Peter Pan*, was produced in London. Barrie constantly rewrote the play, and though this play was produced every Christmas, Barrie did not hesitate to change the manuscript. In 1906 Barrie republished the Peter Pan chapters from *The Little White Bird* as a separate children's book, *Peter Pan in Kensington Gardens,* illustrated by Arthur Rackham. A novelisation of the play followed in 1911. It carried the title *Peter and Wendy*, and contained notable changes and addition of scenes, characterisation, and comments from the author. In 1924, the title was changed to *Peter Pan and Wendy*, and again later to simply *Peter Pan*. Barrie published the play with the dedication to the Llewelyn Davies boys in 1928, under the title *Peter Pan or The Boy Who Wouldn't Grow Up*. However, it should be noted that this is only one version of the play.

The Classical Oedipal Conflict in Peter Pan

Barrie's own versions of *Peter Pan* are fantasy discourses about family life. They function in the therapeutic and ontological way that Bruno Bettelheim described, as they deal with the young (male) child's place in the nuclear family structure. This discourse focuses on the Oedipal conflict, and it has significant parallels to Freud's writings produced simultaneously with Barrie's production of *Peter Pan*. Insofar as the secondary fantasy world, Neverland, is related to the Freudian unconscious, it is the training ground for the child's early development. The theme of the text is (not) growing up, and it is connected to infantile development and family structure. Some passages in *Peter Pan* echo Sigmund Freud's psychoanalytical writings. For instance, Freud's tripartite structure of the functions of the mind: id, ego, and superego is reflected in the following passage, in which Neverland is an adventurous rendering of the unconscious; the superego that pops up near the end of the passage is less attractive (e.g., "verbs that take the dative"). Typically the ego is dynamic and volatile, as Barrie describes the child's mind:

> I don't know whether you have ever seen a map of a person's mind. Doctors sometimes draw maps of other parts of you, and your own map can become intensely interesting, but catch them trying to draw a map of a child's mind, which is not only confused, but keeps going round all the time. There are zigzag lines on it, just like your temperature on a card, and these are probably roads in the island, for the Neverland is always more or less an island, with astonishing splashes of colour here and there, and coral reefs and rakish-looking craft in the offing, and savages and lonely lairs, and gnomes who are mostly tailors, and caves through which a river runs, and princes with six elder brothers, and a hut fast going to decay, and one very small old lady with a hooked nose. It would be an easy map if that were all, but there is also first day at school, religion, fathers, the round pond, needle-work, murders, hangings, verbs that take the dative, chocolate pudding day, getting into braces, say ninety-nine, three-pence for pulling out your tooth your-

> self, and so on, and either these are part of the island or they are another map showing through, and it is all rather confusing, especially as nothing will stand still. (Barrie 1911, 9)

The function of repression through parental authority has already been mentioned, and an explicit Oedipal wish fulfilment runs through the text -- the son wins the mother and becomes the father -- and the result of the Oedipus conflict is turned upside down. Barrie's *Peter Pan* is an Oedipal discourse in which the son is victorious. He can win the mother without having to grow up. Peter Pan, as a representation of the son, wins a mother figure, but he does not achieve a strong superego through identification with an all-powerful father figure. Therefore, he does not grow up. The childhood stage represented by Peter Pan is not to be eradicated by the Oedipal father. If it were, the child would grow into the latency period and later into adulthood.

The child's antagonist in the Oedipal conflict is represented by two figures in the Peter Pan text, traditionally and fittingly played by the same actor in stage versions. Mr. Darling is the pre-Oedipal father, and Captain Hook is the Oedipal and castrating father. Mr. Darling is consistently depicted as weak, and he is humiliated to the extent that he lives in the kennel. The captain with his hook on the other hand is a somewhat charming representation of the Freudian unconscious fear of castration. However, in this wish fulfilment world the tables are turned, and it is Peter Pan who symbolically castrates the Oedipal father figure:

> "I cut off a bit of him."
> "You!"
> "Yes, me," said Peter sharply.
> "I wasn't meaning to be disrespectful."
> "Oh, all right."
> "But, I say, what bit?"
> "His right hand."
> "Then he can't fight now?"
> "Oh, can't he just!"
> "Left-hander?"

> "He has an iron hook instead of a right hand, and he claws with it." (43)

Hook is not yet disarmed, though humiliated and traumatised:

> "Peter flung my arm," he said, wincing, "to a crocodile that happened to be passing by."
> "I have often," said Smee, "noticed your strange dread of crocodiles."
> "Not of crocodiles," Hook corrected him, "but of that one crocodile."
> He lowered his voice. "It liked my arm so much, Smee, that it has followed me ever since, from sea to sea and from land to land, licking its lips for the rest of me."
> "In a way," said Smee, "it's sort of a compliment." (53)

Mrs. Darling is to some extent transformed into Wendy in Neverland as the object of Oedipal desire:

> "Lovely, darling house," Wendy said, and they were the very words they had hoped she would say.
> "And we are your children," cried the twins. Then all went on their knees, and holding out their arms cried, "O Wendy lady, be our mother."
> "Ought I?" Wendy said, all shining. "Of course it's frightfully fascinating, but you see I am only a little girl. I have no real experience."
> "That doesn't matter," said Peter, as if he were the only person present who knew all about it, though he was really the one who knew least. "What we need is just a nice motherly person."
> "Oh dear!" Wendy said, "you see, I feel that is exactly what I am."
> "It is, it is," they all cried; "we saw it at once." ... (65)

In the chapter "The Happy Home," Peter and Wendy can now pretend to be a married couple and yet retain a mother-son-relationship so that the Oedipal wish fulfilment is circumscribed by family life:

> "Ah, old lady," Peter said aside to Wendy, warming himself by the fire and looking down at her as she sat turning a heel, "there is nothing more pleasant of an evening for you and me when the day's toil is over than to rest by the fire with the little ones near by."
> "It is sweet, Peter, isn't it?" Wendy said, frightfully gratified.
> "Peter, I think Curly has your nose."
> "Michael takes after you."…
> "Peter, what is it?"
> "I was just thinking," he said, a little scared. "It is only make-believe, isn't it, that I am their father?"
> "Oh yes," Wendy said primly.
> "You see," he continued apologetically, "it would make me seem so old to be their real father."
> "But they are ours, Peter, yours and mine."
> "But not really, Wendy?" he asked anxiously.
> "Not if you don't wish it," she replied; and she distinctly heard his sigh of relief. "Peter," she asked, trying to speak firmly, "what are your exact feelings to me?"
> "Those of a devoted son, Wendy."
> "I thought so," she said, and went and sat by herself at the extreme end of the room.
> "You are so queer," he said, frankly puzzled, "and Tiger Lily is just the same. There is something she wants to be to me, but she says it is not my mother." (92)

Peter finally defeats Captain Hook, whom the crocodile eats. The narrator has stopped the crocodile's ticking clock. He writes it is not to disgrace Captain Cook in his hour of death. The clock as a symbol of time and growing up has been stopped now, for after Peter's defeat of the Oedipal father, his development has stopped and his infantile existence has been preserved. Peter Pan can now identify with this Oedipal father figure, and the Oedipal dream has come true in Neverland:

> The general feeling was that Peter was honest just now to lull Wendy's suspicions, but that there might be a change when

the new suit was ready, which, against her will, she was making for him out of some of Hook's wickedest garments. It was afterwards whispered among them that on the first night he wore this suit he sat long in the cabin with Hook's cigar-holder in his mouth and one hand clenched, all but for the forefinger, which he bent and held threateningly aloft like a hook. (134-35)

Through Peter Pan, the Edwardian child could negotiate with the Oedipal phase and the repressions it caused, and the child could probably better come to terms with its place in the family structure and its own development, which included an Oedipal defeat. The question asked earlier in this article -- does *Peter Pan* contradict the lesson from "The Three Little Pigs?" -- can be answered "no." *Peter Pan* confronts the repressions gained from the Oedipal conflict, but this is done in the fantasy, secondary world of Neverland. This confrontation is, despite the violent symbolism, therapeutic in the same way as Freudian dreamwork is: it operates through a fantastic narrative using dream symbolism. The emphasis on father and mother figures is a reflection of a patriarchal family structure. As this family structure changed during the century, new versions of *Peter Pan* with other foci of attention appeared.

Disney's Peter Pan: Fairies and the Preservation of Childhood

Barrie's own versions of Peter Pan are not only the foundation of all later versions, but also the best known. His novels are widely read. The play has never lost its popularity, and it has become part of Christmas traditions alongside Dickens' *A Christmas Carol* outside Britain. There is a fairly large number of film adaptations. The first is from 1924, directed by Herbert Brenon, but so far the classical adaptation is Disney's animated *Peter Pan* from 1953, directed by Clyde Jeronimi.

Tinker Bell is one of the charms of this Disney film. She was animated by Marc Davis to be a winged pixie. In the original stage version, Tinker Bell was only a moving point of light, and when she and

Peter first visit Wendy in the nursery in Bloomsbury, Wendy complaints that she cannot see her. However, Tink stands still for a second, and Wendy exclaims, "I see her, the lovely! where is she now?" (Barrie 1928, 32) Tinker Bell is, however, described in greater detail in the novel: "a girl called Tinker Bell exquisitely gowned in a skeleton leaf, cut low and square, through which her figure could be seen to the best advantage. She was slightly inclined to *embonpoint.*" (Barrie 1911, 37) Tinker Bell's appearance has become decidedly more sexual, and Marc Davis' version was criticised for stressing this aspect too much, especially when it was rumoured that Marilyn Monroe posed for the fairy. Actually, it was Margaret Kenny who (in a bathing suit) posed for Tinker Bell. As a resident of Neverland, Tinker Bell is without morals. Since she is Peter Pan's personal fairy, her jealousy towards Wendy is passionate and deadly, as when she makes the lost boys shoot down the flying Wendy with an arrow, with Tootles firing the near-fatal shot. Tinker Bell's sexuality, cruelty, and aggression seem to belong not only to Neverland, but also more generally to the unconscious.

The tempting and dangerous nature of fairies is seen in folklore, art, and in literature. One of the precursors of Barrie's episode in which Peter goes to live with the fairies in Kensington Gardens might have been Thomas Tickell's (1685-1740) 1722 heroic poem "Kensington Garden." It documents the creation and passing of a fairie kingdom in Kensington. A parallel to the Lost Boys can be seen in these lines:

> By magic fenc'd, by spells encompass'd round,
> No mortal touch'd this interdicted ground;
> No mortal enter'd, those alone who came
> Stol'n from the couch of some terrestrial dame:
> For oft of babes they robb'd the matron's bed,
> And left some sickly changeling in their stead.
> It chanc'd a youth of Albion's royal blood
> Was foster'd here, the wonder of the wood. (Tickell)

The cultural history of fairies is tied to the concept of loss and passing. Fairies always belong to earlier generations, and people always do not believe in fairies anymore. Over time, fairies have diminished in size, and their realm has diminished in nature, from literature and art to the realm of childhood, represented mainly by children's literature. In cultural history fairies tend to appear when history changes from one paradigm to another, so that fairies may be said to be connected to anxiety created by modernity – whatever it is deemed. Already in the seventeenth century, antiquary John Aubrey (1626-1697) expressed this idea:

> Before Printing, Old-wives Tales were ingeniose, and since Printing came in fashion, till a little before the Civill-Warres, the ordinary sort of People were not taught to reade. Now-a-dayes Bookes are common, and most of the poor people understand letters; and the many good Bookes and variety of Turnes of Affaires, have put all the old Fables out of doors: and the divine art of printing and Gunpowder have frightened away Robin-goodfellow and the Fayries. (Christensen 1988, 12)

Fairies accompany transition. More precisely, in a transitional phase consisting of three stages -- departure, passage and arrival -- they are part of the first step, and as such they are metaphors of departure. Fairies are, in other words, part of a transitional stage, but they are reactive, because they look backward. This understanding of fairies is relevant when explaining the presence of Tinker Bell in *Peter Pan*. A dominant theme here is the fear of leaving childhood, and Tinker Bell is there to preserve Peter Pan's infantile existence. She jealously guards Peter against Wendy, who in the Disney film is presented as a girl, not a woman or a teenager. Disney's *Peter Pan* goes along with Barrie's premise about the value of childhood. The very form of this adaptation – an animated film – caters to a children's audience, and the prominence of Tinker Bell in the adaptation may indicate that *Peter Pan* is a children's film. Although Peter Pan himself in most versions of the text is relatively stable, the characters of Tinker Bell and Wendy, and the dialogue between these characters, change from version to version, especially in recent adaptations of *Peter Pan*.

Steven Spielberg's Hook: Narcissism

The focus in Steven Spielberg's 1991 version of *Peter Pan*, *Hook* is neither on Wendy nor Tinker Bell. This is a family film. It explores the parental role of the father, and as such it also describes the situation of children in families during the last part of the twentieth century. In earlier versions of *Peter Pan,* father figures were quite important, as the father was doubled into the pre-Oedipal Mr. Darling and the Oedipal Captain Hook. In Spielberg's version an additional father figure has come on stage. Now, surprisingly, Peter Pan has grown up, and he himself has become a father.

Hook is a sequel to Barrie's *Peter Pan* with strong pastiche elements. Peter Pan, now called Peter Banning (played by Robin Williams), has grown up in London to become a yuppie-style merger and acquisitions lawyer. He has a son and a daughter, and he is married to Wendy's granddaughter, but has totally forgotten his childhood. It appears that Wendy has adopted all the Lost Boys from Neverland. Captain Hook (Dustin Hoffman) kidnaps Banning's son and daughter in order to lure Peter Pan to Neverland for a final showdown. Banning is dragged there by Tinker Bell (Julia Roberts). The pirates humiliate him in front of his children; he is unable to fly, and it is only later with the help of the Lost Boys and Tink that he realises his identity as Peter Pan. When he thinks the happy thought that he is a father, he is able to fly, and he finally defeats Hook again. Until this happens, Peter Banning/Peter Pan remains estranged from his children, especially from his son Jack. This boy takes to Hook, and actually adopts him as a kind of father. Hook creates Jack in his own image, dressing him in a Captain Hook costume. Near the end of the film, Peter Pan flies back to London with his children.

Hook is the narcissistic version of *Peter Pan*. Peter Banning is the present-day absent and remote father, and Captain Hook is the surrogate father figure or stepfather. The Lost Boys have become politically correct in their ethnic diversity, energetic on skateboards. They are the narcissist's peer group. The original Peter Pan-Oedipus conflict has been reformulated. The father figure is so weak that the son does not go through a classical conflict. There is no castrating patriarchal antagonist, so the son does not reappear on the other side of the conflict with a powerful superego, as was the case with the classical Oedipus conflict.

Peter Banning is unable to fulfil his duties as the father in a nuclear family. As such his immaturity and egoism make him a Peter Pan, and it seems to be the message of this film that it is necessary to grow up to function socially and psychologically. The reluctance to mature has in popular psychology been termed the Peter Pan syndrome. In 1983, Dr. Dan Kiley published *The Peter Pan Syndrome: Men Who Have Never Grown Up*. *Hook* is a narcissist discourse. Peter Banning is not the patriarchal superego figure, but rather a convergence of child and adult. When Peter Banning becomes Peter Pan, this is a regression to an earlier stage in his mental development.

The narrative structure of *Hook* is similar not as much to other adventure or fantasy films, but rather to disaster movies, e.g., Spielberg's *War of the Worlds* (2005) or Michael Bay's *Armageddon* (1998). In these films, the premise is that you cannot save the world until you have realized that the true meaning of life lies with your own family. The chief focus of *Hook* is on family values. The film is a reflection of the crisis of the nuclear family while at the same time a defence of it. *Hook* has lost the subversive and anarchic discourse of the original *Peter Pan*, but it directs the attention of its audience to the problems of children who cannot find role models or father figures within their families. Jack identifies with Hook as a father figure, but Hook is as much id (a pirate) as superego (captain). Consequently, Jack will be left with a mind that does not distinguish so consistently between superego and id, as is the case with the narcissist.

Return to Neverland: Gender Reversal and the Last Stand of Childhood

The Disney production *Peter Pan Return to Neverland* (2002), directed by Robin Budd, is a sequel to Disney's 1953 *Peter Pan*. The significance of the time setting is complicated. The action of the film takes place in 1940 during the Blitz of London. Wendy Darling is an adult; she is married with two children, twelve-year-old Jane and four-year-old Danny. Her husband leaves for war.

The film is historical in several ways. It relates to the original Edwardian *Peter Pan*; it relates back to Disney's 1953 version; it is a Second World War film; at the same time, the themes are relevant to its release date. The nuclear family is threatened because the father is absent, and the concept of childhood itself is similarly threatened; Jane Darling does not recognise its values.

Jane is the main character of this film. She was already introduced to readers and Peter Pan near the end of Barrie's novel (though she does not appear in the play):

> Years rolled on again, and Wendy had a daughter. This ought not to be written in ink but in a golden splash.
>
> She was called Jane, and always had an odd inquiring look, as if from the moment she arrived on the mainland she wanted to ask questions. When she was old enough to ask them they were mostly about Peter Pan. She loved to hear of Peter, and Wendy told her all she could remember in the very nursery from which the famous flight had taken place. (Barrie 1911, 147)

In *Return to Neverland* Wendy uses the stories about Peter Pan therapeutically during the bombing raids to comfort her children, but Jane reacts against this and against the fact that she and her brother are to be evacuated. She persists in saying that she does not believe in Peter Pan. However, one night Hook kidnaps Jane, thinking she is Wendy. As in Spielberg's *Hook,* he intends to use the girl as bait to defeat Peter Pan. Later, in Neverland Peter rescues Jane, but she fails to fill Wendy's type of traditional role, and she is unable to fly or to believe in fairies. She even comes close to betraying Peter to Hook. When he and the Lost Boys are captured by the pirates, however, Jane strikes an alliance with Tinker Bell and saves the day. She now becomes the first Lost Girl. She can return to London to be reunited with her family, and, happily, her father has come home from the war.

Jane's development is the subject of *Return to Neverland*. She has become a female hero, and as such gender roles have been reversed. *Return to Neverland* is an updated version of *Peter Pan*. Another contemporary aspect of the film is the dissolution of the nuclear family. However, this threat to the family has been narratively weakened as it has been historically distanced. It is not divorce, but the Second World War -- with the father fighting away from home and the children removed to the country -- that undermines the nuclear family. Jane is too serious about her familial responsibilities; she has become a combination of the nurse, Nana, who in the film is Nana-Two, and a mother in relation to her younger brother.

Jane refuses to be a child, and the premise of the film is that if you do not recognise your childhood and childish imagination, you cannot grow up. It is not until she has used the secondary fantasy world of Neverland (in Bettelheim's sense) that she is able to appreciate and contain her childhood and move on. In this sense *Return to Neverland* mediates between Barrie's infantile fixation and the next film version of *Peter Pan* to be considered in this article. *Return to Neverland* may actually be seen as an argument against the age concept of tweens in its appreciation of childhood as a necessary step in development. When Jane says, "I'll always believe in you, Peter Pan," she can grow up.

Peter Pan 2003: Tweens

In the Disney animated *Peter Pan,* the Darling children (Wendy, Michael, and John) seemed to form one collective main character; in *Hook,* the protagonist was clearly Peter Banning/Peter Pan. In P. J. Hogan's Peter *Pan* (2003), Wendy has moved into the limelight. The two father figures in this film are played by the same actor, Jason Isaacs.

Whereas Wendy in Barrie's play had to fulfil the role of the surrogate mother in an Oedipus conflict, she has to deal with her own puberty in Hogan's *Peter Pan*. As such she is a representative of the tween generation, which refers to children between middle childhood and adolescence, generally in the age range of eight to twelve years old. The tween concept is as much at home in marketing as in developmental psychology, but tweening may be appropriate in *Peter Pan*. However, tweening is as much about saying hello to adulthood as saying goodbye to childhood. Hogan's film focuses on this transitional stage. In particular, Wendy is depicted as a tween, but the Peter Pan character himself (Jeremy Sumpter) is defined by his age. At the time of filming, Jeremy Sumpter was fourteen years old, and his voice may at times be heard breaking on camera. In other words, the timeless childhood quality of Wendy and Peter has been abandoned here. Barrie's *Peter Pan* was about not losing childhood; but as childhood has already been lost in Hogan's version, we may ask what the premise of this film is? The answer may be that the 2003 version of *Peter Pan* has moved on with the times. The film may indicate that the boundaries between ages have become weakened. Old-age pensioners behave as if they are young; adults enter into the experience economy as if they were children; and childhood itself is under attack with marketing geared specifically to tweens. (de Mesa)

Hogan's *Peter Pan* may be regarded as a continuation of Spielberg's *Hook* because Peter Banning is a grown-up for whom it is beneficial to regain infantile behaviour. He, too, is placed (be)tween adult and child, but it is in Hogan's *Peter Pan* that the tween concept is stressed, and it is foregrounded in the thematics of the film. The Oedipal conflict in the 2003 version of *Peter Pan* has lost ground, as Wendy is not so much desired by Peter as a mother figure. Rather, Wendy is presented as a subject rather than an object of desire. For instance, the film has a scene that is neither present in Barrie's play nor novelisation: Peter Pan hovers over Wendy's bed in the nursery. She discovers this, but takes it to be a dream. When at school she draws a picture of the incident, her teacher is shocked; she understands the dream to be romantic or Freudian.

Tinker Bell is desexualised in this film as the sexuality has been moved to Wendy, yet the role of fairies has been upgraded. Probably this was influenced by fairies in films such as Charles Sturridge's *Fairy Tale – A True Story* (1997) and Nick Willing's *Photographing Fairies* (1997). After Tinker Bell has swallowed the poison Hook intended for Peter, there is a magnificent, sentimental, and pompous sequence in which Peter asks children all over the world to shout "I do believe in fairies" to revive Tinker Bell.

Peter Pan in Scarlet: The Official Sequel

The title of Geraldine McCaughrean's 2006 sequel to *Peter Pan* includes the words "*The Official Sequel.*" *Peter Pan in Scarlet* is just one of many sequels and adaptations. In 1929 James Barrie bequeathed the copyright of *Peter Pan* to the Great Ormond Street Hospital for children, and the royalties have been a substantial source of income for the hospital since then. The copyright expired in 2007, and in order to continue receiving income from *Peter Pan,* the hospital held a competition to find an author for a sequel. Geraldine McCaughrean won the competition with a sample chapter and plot outline.

The novel is set in 1926, and the Lost Boys have become the Old Boys living comfortable and established lives in London, except for Michael Darling, who was killed in the First World War. These men and Wendy Darling start to suffer from nightmares connected to Neverland, nightmares that are so real that they produce physical objects such as cutlasses and even a crocodile. With the help of a fairy from Kensington Gardens, the Old Boys and Wendy fly to Neverland after they have shrunk to child size by putting on their own children's clothes. Slightly, who has daughters, turns into a girl during the process. Neverland has changed into a kind of Narnian winter. In Neverland, they meet with Peter, who has become bitter, and a mysterious circus master, Ravello, who late in the novel is revealed to be Hook. He has survived as a shadow of a man inside the crocodile's belly. The children, Peter Pan, and Ravello undertake a long quest to find treasure, and Ravello nearly succeeds in changing Peter Pan into a new Captain Hook before the Lost Boys are reunited with their mothers. These women have also travelled to Neverland, which has finally regained its health; it is summer again. Everyone except Peter Pan and Captain Hook can now return to London.

As in Barrie's original texts, there are Freudian elements in *Peter Pan in Scarlet*, but not to the same degree. Dreams are included to demonstrate how the repressed (Neverland) returns in them, and the Oedipus conflict is there, but as was the case with other recent versions, it is muted, as are the father figures. The Oedipal father figure Hook has been almost reduced to an unravelling woollen cardigan; instead *Peter Pan in Scarlet* focuses on mother figures. The dissolution of the nuclear family noted in other later sequels is present here, too. The mothers are presented tragically as they have all lost their children and mourn for them in what Ravello/Hook calls the Maze of Witches, but the true name of it is the Maze of Regrets. A feeling of loss permeates the whole novel. Mothers have lost their children, children their mothers, and childhood is left behind. This sense of loss pervades the book, and the shadow of the First World War looms over everything. Both Michael Darling and most of Hook's pirates were killed in the war. Michael's death is a biographical note, as one of the Llewelyn Davies boys, George, was killed, and another, Michael, drowned himself. The Lost Boys do grow up, and they die. The denial of Thanatos found to some extent in the original *Peter Pan* has lost ground in this darker version, where neither childhood nor family life endure.

Tinker Bell – Only Fairies

In Bradley Raymond's *Tinker Bell* from 2008 (produced by The Walt Disney Studios), the upgrading of fairies seen in P. J. Hogan's *Peter Pan* from 2003 is so strong that there is no Peter Pan at all in this film, only fairies, and Wendy only appears a few seconds with no spoken lines near the end of the film. There are no lost boys, rather the boys are lost as an audience, as this is purely a girls' film.

Tinker Bell is a prequel to Barrie's *Peter Pan*, or rather a prequel to just one of the characters in *Peter Pan*. In the original theatre production of *Peter Pan,* Tinker Bell's character was merely represented by a spot of light reflected by a small mirror off stage; here she goes centre stage with her own feature-length film. The plot of *Tinker Bell* is about the little fairy's acceptance of her place in the world; or rather her own lack of acceptance of her place. Tinker Bell does not fit into the realm of the fairies. She is far too self-centred to subject herself to its feudal hierarchy where every fairy has its allotted and predestined place dependent on its one talent. In the film the fairies have the function of changing the seasons on earth, and to be able to do so there is a strict division of labour where each class of fairies is in charge of an aspect of nature and its cycle. In a scene reminiscent of the sorting hat in *Harry Potter and the Philosopher's Stone*, Tinker Bell is chosen to become a tinker, as this is her talent. When she discovers that, unlike many of the other fairies, the tinkers are not allowed to go to the mainland, she becomes dissatisfied with her lot, and her ambition to rise in the hierarchy of the fairies from now on takes over. After several failed attempts, one of which is globally catastrophic, she actually manages to rise in the world of the fairies. Tinker Bell has destroyed all the preparations for spring by an accident caused by her ambition and by the interference of a rival fairy, and spring has to be postponed one year, as there is no time to prepare for spring all over again. However, to make good her mistake Tinker Bell tinkers with various objects lost from the human world on the mainland, and her successful solution is to introduce Fordist assembly lines in the fairy world. Now an industrially prepared spring can be taken to the mainland, and Tinker Bell and the other tinkers are allowed to go there with the other fairies. Thus, Tinker Bell's ambition has been fulfilled, and she has actually risen in the rigid class system of the fairies.

It may seem contrary to the conception of fairies as natural agents belonging to a pre-industrial world that Tinker Bell can introduce Fordist methods in their kingdom (see John Aubrey's description of fairies' antagonism to modernity on p. 207), but Bradley Raymond's *Tinker Bell* attempts to reconcile this contradiction by making Tinker Bell's methods depend on reusable and renewable raw materials, as it is stressed how she reuses discarded objects. In this way Tinker Bell may seem to unite the mythical fairies, nature and an acceptable industrial development. Though this solution may seem facile, it is nevertheless an attempt not simply to deny modernity.

Where the earlier Disney production *Peter Pan Return to Neverland* (2002), directed by Robin Budd, may be read as a defence of the concept and necessity of childhood in the face of the age concepts of tweens, *Tinker Bell* can be understood as an attack against childhood and an acceptance of the concept of tweens. Tinker Bell herself as the main character is conceived in London at the first laugh of a baby, as she should be according to the fairy lore of Barrie's *Peter Pan*. When the baby laughs, a seed from a dandelion is blown to fairyland. Here it becomes the young and immature Tinker Bell, who after her appointment as a tinker goes to her new house, puts on clumsy garments made of leaves only to change it off-screen into a short, close-fitting dress, and reappear a moment after as a sexually mature young woman. Her behaviour and language reflect the one found in many television series about and with American teenagers, but her professional ambitions may belong to the executive floor.

Childhood is not only denied in the film: it is attacked fiercely in a scene, where Tinker Bell – to prove her talent as a fairy of nature – seeks to teach a fledgling to fly. Not by making the little bird think happy thoughts, but by shouting at it and shaking it. The bird repeatedly refuses to grow up, leave the nest and fly, and it even regresses back to its very early childhood by rebuilding its egg around itself from the broken shell. This scene is stylistically out of tune with the rest of the film, as Tinker Bell seems surprisingly aggressive, until one realises that her anger is directed at the little bird's attempt to remain a child and its Peter Pan-like refusal to grow up. It is childhood Tinker Bell shouts at, not the bird.

Tinker Bell is eventually allowed a happy ending in her own film; but her struggle to reach it is traumatic with its humiliations, failure upon failure and social exclusion. Tinker Bell's ambitions are those of a young egocentric teenager, and her morals seem infantile. The combination of these weaknesses in Tinker Bell's character overshadows her final success, and the exposition that Bradley Raymond's *Tinker Bell* gives of a representative of the tween generation, whose behaviour almost stops the natural circle of the seasons, may not be without educational value to the development of its audience. Also in this version of *Peter Pan* there are therapeutic and ontological values to be found.

Peter Pan is an open and dynamic text that is and has been rewritten many times. The double universe is its central narrative device and also its fantasy characteristic. The dialogue between the Darlings in Bloomsbury and Neverland is also a dialogue between growing up in a family and the mental mechanisms connected to personal development. Barrie's concept had from the outset such an open nature that it invited rewriting. This history of all the versions of *Peter Pan* from *The Boy Castaways of Black Lake Island* to *Peter Pan in Scarlet* and *Tinker Bell* is also the social and psychological history of childhood and family life. It is also more than that: each generation of readers (children and adults) have been able to use a version of *Peter Pan* to better understand the complexities of childhood in both therapeutic and ontological ways.

References

Books and Plays

Barber, Benjamin R. *Consumed – How Markets Corrupt Children, Infantilize Adults, and Swallow Citizens Whole.* New York: W.W. Norton and Company, 2007.

Barrie, J.M. *Margaret Ogilvy – by Her Son.* London: Hodder and Stoughton, 1896.

_____. *The Plays of J.M. Barrie.* London: Hodder and Stoughton, 1928.

_____. *Peter Pan: Peter and Wendy* and *Peter Pan in Kensington Gardens.* Harmondsworth: Penguin Classics, 2004. (Original editions: *Peter and Wendy,* 1911, and *Peter Pan in Kensington Gardens,* 1902.)

Bettelheim, Bruno. *The Uses of Enchantment – The Meaning and Importance of Fairy Tales.* Harmondsworth: Penguin, 1987. (First published 1976).

Christensen, Jørgen Riber. *Psycho – Analysis and Texts.* Copenhagen: Gyldendal, 1987.

_____. *Fairy Tales.* Copenhagen: Gyldendal, 1988.

de Mesa, Alicia, "Marketing and Tween." Online at: http://www.businessweek.com/innovate/content/oct2005/id20051012_606473.htm Accessed August 17, 2007.

Kiley, Dan. *The Peter Pan Syndrome: Men Who Have Never Grown Up.* New York: Dodd Mead, 1983.

McCaughrean, Geraldine. *Peter Pan in Scarlet - The Official Sequel.* Oxford: Oxford University Press, 2006.

Tickell, Thomas. "Kensington Garden." Online at http://www.poemhunter.com/poem/kensington-garden. Accessed August 15, 2007.

Peter Pan In and Out of Time. Edited by Donna R. White and C. Anita Tarr. Toronto: The Scarecrow Press, 2006.

Films

Budd, Robin Budd. *Peter Pan Return to Neverland*. DisneyToon Studios, 2002.
Bradley, Raymond. *Tinker Bell*. The Walt Disney Studios, 2008.
Hogan, P.J. *Peter Pan*. Universal Pictures, 2003.
Jeronimi, Clyde. *Peter Pan*. Walt Disney Pictures, 1953.
Spielberg, Steven. *Hook*. Amblin Entertainment, 1991.

Ole Ertløv Hansen

Fantasy
A Cognitive Approach

Fantasy can be described as a narrative about the normal situated in the unreal. Humans meet fairies, elves, and orcs; they fight the mightiest dragons and the most horrible monsters in order to save the "world." The fantastic is retold and relived generation after generation.

Fantasy as a concept and a genre has a strong connection to the specific human ability to fantasize, to imagine the impossible as possible, to give narrative forms to the threats of the 'Unheimliche' (uncanny), and to be fascinated by marvellous wonders, and fantasy is based on these human capabilities. Bolter & Grusin state: "In computer graphics as in print, fantasy illustration expresses a strong desire for immediacy, the desire that one's waking or dreaming imagination should come true." (Bolter & Grusin 2001, 135-36). Thus, fantasy can be seen as the remediation of dreams and nightmares.

Many of these dreams and nightmares share a relationship with a-thousand-year-old myth and tradition and have become a kind of collective recounting and remembering of the unreal, which challenges reason. Fantasy as a genre is not tied to one or a few media; it has found its way to all known media through the ages from mythological murals to videogames. If fantasy is to be seen as the remediation of dreams and nightmares, which in their nonmediated forms are purely mental, an obvious place to start examining fantasy is in the media that come close to mimicking the way we think and imagine things, or in other words media that mimic mental forms. In the twentieth and twenty-first centuries, especially, there are two kinds of media that can blend the real and the imagined: filmmaking and computer games.

In 1916 Hugo Münsterberg pronounced that filmmaking came close to mimicking the human experience of the world and the inner reality of the human mind. And as computer graphics and interface devices became ever more advanced in the late twentieth century, Virtual Reality (VR) and the concept of immersion assured us that not only could we visualise and relive our dreams and the products of our imagination, we could step right into them. We could interact with them in real time. So it is no surprise that in film and interactive media we find a huge number of fantasy or fantasy-related works.

In this chapter I will discuss the characteristics of the remediation of dreams and nightmares within films and computer games. Using a cognitive theoretical framework, I will give a general overview of their narrative forms and describe the devices and designs that make them fantastic.

The Fantasy Narrative

The first step towards a characterisation of fantasy is to take a closer look at the fantasy film and fantasy computer game on a general metalevel: their narratology.

Fantasy itself can be categorised by genre: myth, saga, legend, fable, and the adventure. (Høgh 2003) Almost all existing fantasy stories are narrated in the way of the canonical narrative (Branigan 1992):

Introduction of setting and characters
Explanation of a state of affairs
Initiating event
Emotional response or statement of a goal by the protagonist
Complicating actions
Outcome
Reactions to the outcome

Although there might be minor variations within the overall structure, the causality and internal coherence of the structure can neverthe-

A COGNITIVE APPROACH

less be recognized as the fundamental structure of the fantasy film genre. If we examine the different parts of the narrative structure more closely, we see that the characters, especially the protagonist, have a fundamental role in developing the narrative. Especially in relation to the fantasy adventure, the protagonist and his relation to other characters are essential and fundamental.

In the early twentieth century, Vladimir Propp made a thorough analysis and set up a morphology of the Russian folktale. He pinpointed thirty-one narrative functions and eight dramatic characters that constituted the folk tale as a genre[1]. His work inspired many other narratologists and has become the standard for the development and use of analytical and dramaturgical tools when writing stories, particularly tales of adventure.

Propp's eight dramatic characters can be recognized in most fantasy fiction:

The hero
The helper
The villain
The false hero
The donor
The dispatcher
The princess
The princess' father

Propp's thirty-one narrative functions are basics of almost all fantasy narratives:

0. Initial situation
1. Absentation: Someone goes missing.
2. Interdiction: Hero is warned.
3. Violation of interdiction

---

[1] Propp 1927 (http://changingminds.org/disciplines/storytelling/plots/propp/propp.htm).

FANTASY

4. Reconnaissance: Villain seeks something.
5. Delivery: The villain gains information.
6. Trickery: Villain attempts to deceive victim.
7. Complicity: Unwitting helping of the enemy.
8. Villainy and loss: The need is identified.
9. Mediation: Hero discovers the loss.
10. Counteraction: Hero chooses positive action.
11. Departure: Hero leaves on a mission.
12. Testing: Hero is challenged to prove heroic qualities.
13. Reaction: Hero responds to test.
14. Acquisition: Hero gains magical item.
15. Guidance: Hero reaches destination.
16. Struggle: Hero and villain do battle.
17. Branding: Hero is branded.
18. Victory: Villain is defeated.
19. Resolution: Initial misfortune or lack is resolved.
20. Return: Hero sets out for home.
21. Pursuit: Hero is chased.
22. Rescue: pursuit ends.
23. Arrival: Hero arrives unrecognized.
24. Claim: False hero makes unfounded claims.
25. Task: Difficult task proposed to the hero.
26. Solution: Task is completed.
27. Recognition: Hero is recognised.
28. Exposure: False hero is exposed.
29. Transfiguration: Hero is given a new appearance.
30. Punishment: Villain is punished.
31. Wedding: Hero marries and ascends the throne.

Propp analysed the role of the hero, the villain, and the other characters. The focus on the hero has been even more explicit in the Jungian-inspired writings of Joseph Campbell[2] and his book *The Hero*

---

2   Campbell, Joseph. *The Hero With a Thousand Faces*, New York: Bollingen, 1949.

A COGNITIVE APPROACH

with a Thousand Faces, which Christopher Vogler[3] rewrote as *The Writer's Journey: Mythic Structure for Storytellers and Screenwriters.* Campbell's works have been consulted often by Hollywood filmmakers. His books have also had a great influence on the design of narratives in computer games (e.g., Rollings & Adams 2003; Fullerton et al. 2004; Miller 2004), those connected to fantasy fiction.

> The hero's development may follow these steps (Rollings & Adams 2003, 135):
> Limited awareness
> Increased awareness
> Reluctance to change
> Overcoming
> Committing (typically at the plot's first turning point)
> Experimenting
> Preparing
> Big Change (typically at the plot's point of no return)
> Consequences
> Rededication (typically at the plot's third turning point)
> Final Attempt
> Mastery

According to contemporary film theory (e.g., Branigan 1992; Bordwell 1990; Grodal 1997, 2007), the canonical narrative is an innate mental scheme that belongs to all humans. It is a logical and natural structure in which we organize and represent information about the world and the events happening in it. The widespread use in fantasy fiction of the rigid structures described by Propp and Campbell indicate that fantasy fiction does not want to challenge us as we hear, see, and experience the story. The plot and characters are schematic. Although one finds many talking animals, trees, and chimeras, they always obey the structure and fit neatly into a category. So if fantasy

---

3   Vogler, Christopher. *The Writer's Journey: Mythic Structure for Storytellers and Screenwriters.* Studio City, CA.: Michael Wiese Productions, 1992.

fiction is so schematic, and if the only function of all the fantasy figures is to act anthropomorphically, why does fantasy fiction make us want to see, read, and play more and more often?

Let us take a closer look at contemporary film theory. It is also known as cognitive film theory, which acknowledges that watching a film is an active cognitive process. Although cognitive film theory is not espoused by a homogeneous group of scholars, the existing approaches share presuppositions about the process of viewing films. In general, most critics presuppose that watching a film is dependent on some innate and some culturally acquired mental schemata. The story (also called the fabula) is constructed by the viewer on the basis of the plot (also called the syuzhet) and its use of stylistic elements. Plot and style are the material parts of the film; the story is only a mental construct of the viewer. In order to carry out the construction process, the viewer uses his or her set of schemata, which can be divided into prototypes, templates, and procedures.

Prototypes are, for example, birds and humans; templates may be the canonical narrative; and procedures handle the motivated shifting and adding of prototypes and templates to the ongoing construction of the fabula. A procedural schema, though, can be seen as a series of hypothesis and inferences. Motivation, which is another central concept within cognitive theory, also has subdivisions. Bordwell originally made distinctions among realistic, compositional, transtextual, and artistic motivation. These categories have been applied to early formalist narratology (Schepelern 1972), but they are given new meaning and function within cognitive theory; they are changed into mental processes and cognitive categories. They are not seen as something one can read into the text, but as something one applies to the text in order to understand it. Consequently we may anticipate that we do have an understanding of the 'real' (e.g. prototypes), a set of assumptions about causal relations (e.g. templates) but also a culturally acquired 'textual capital' and an ability to handle and reflect upon the unknown.

Returning to the question about our thirst for fantasy fiction, I must introduce another point made by psychologist Mihaly Csikszentmihalyi (Csikszentmihalyi 1990). He argues that the degree to which we get involved in an activity depends on our competences in relation to the challenges the activity poses. If we do not get challenged, we get bored. If the challenges are too overwhelming, we get frustrated. It is not our hypotheses that are challenged by fantasy fiction, although it might introduce shadow characters that add nuance to the portrayals of the hero (the "good guy") and the villain ("the bad guy"). Gollum in *The Lord of the Rings: The Return of the King* (Jackson 2003) represents both of these types in one character. What do get challenged by fantasy fiction are our imaginative powers and our transtextual schemata, and this is done by the *mise-en-scene* and other stylistic elements. Fantasy fiction expands the real by compositional enrichment and the supernatural that becomes the prototype of the fantasy reality.

But how does this happen? Is it possible to find a cognitive explanation of the aesthetic powers of the supernatural and the grotesque? Earlier, I proposed that fantasy could be seen as the remediation of dreams, nightmares, and the imagination. In contrast to other ways of remediating dreams and imagination, e.g., surrealism, fantasy does not try to represent the chaotic order of events, which also might describe our experience of being in a dream state. Instead, fantasy takes on the elements of unreality that resemble the real, and enhances their appearance. In other words, fantasy stimulates our imaginative powers by the use of caricature, and that is why we are so attracted to it. Here we meet the essence of our dreams, nightmares and imagination.

Fantasy Aesthetics

The idea of art as caricature was advanced by Ramachandran and Hirstein in their groundbreaking article "The Science of Art. A Neurological Theory of Aesthetic Art." They identify a series of principles that artists use to stimulate our visual faculties. Here are some of their most interesting points.

First, Ramachandran and Hirstein argue that all art is caricature. This sounds odd, but it refers to the idea that art grabs the essence of the object under depiction and enhances it. This is connected to the so-called "peak shift" effect. This is best defined by an example: animals that learn to respond to a shape such as a rectangle do not react to a specific rectangle but to the "essence" of rectangularity. Ramachandran and Hirstein speculate that the "peak shift" has enabled art itself to change over time; a new form finds and amplifies the essence of a previous one. This may be applied to the depiction of fantasy figures: films and television programs now may amplify and enhance the essence of their character without being able to portray a specific vice or virtue. What we see on the screen is not, then, a specific hero but a representation of the essence of heroism. The ugly witch is always a sample of amplified imperfections.

Art also utilises the reinforcement that accompanies the construction of unity in the act of perception. Visually, for example, we organise input through grouping, and as soon as a group is founded the limbic system retains it. This search for unity gives us pleasure and we are, therefore, attracted to visuals that are hard to recognise.

The same holds true with, for example, the way we perceive contrast. We could assert that the more elements a work of art exhibits, the more pleasurable the experience. But the brain has a restricted number of attention resources, so if we combine that fact with the idea of art as the extraction of essence, we understand why a sketch can be more aesthetic and pleasing than a colour photograph. As Ramachandran and Hirstein say: in art "more is less". A certain amount of uncertainty in relation to what the work of art shows us makes it even more interesting. Similarly, it is not necessary for fantasy fiction to invent a new set of causalities; it will be more pleasing if it adds some uncertainty to a well-known world or reality. That is why almost all heroes are "humanoids," and if the story endows other creatures with free will and intentionality, they usually behave according to a well-known cultural mythology or set of rules. However, it is also a rule that the characters will have an extraordinary quality, an essence that will make them superior and make apparent the specific challenge they represent. As is the case with dreams, in which we process the day's impressions, fantasy fictions (and folk tales) process representations of good (heroism and sacrifice) and bad (that which challenges the social order) in order to shape desirable social and ethical behaviour.

Conclusion

In this essay I have shown that it is possible to describe fantasy fiction in terms of cognitive media theory. I have also discussed how fantasy fiction's narrative and aesthetic dimensions cue cognitive operations in the same way imagination and dreams do. Fantasy fiction is a way of trying to remediating and presenting of the purely mental states of imagining and dreaming. To accomplish this, fantasy fiction uses schematic narratives and orchestrations of characters, on the one hand, and, on the other, a widespread use of transtextual cues and an essential use of enhancing small amounts of the unreal as real within the reality of the story. This enhancing can be regarded as based on the same aesthetic functions that are made use of in caricature when the essence of good and the essence of evil are made 'visible'. Fantasy employs the mechanisms of caricature to intensify the narrative of good and evil.

References

Bolter, Jay David, and Richard Grusin. *Remediation*. Cambridge, MA: The MIT Press, 1999.
Bordwell, David. *Narration in the Fiction Film*. 1985. Reprint, London: Routledge, 1990.
Branigan, Edward. *Narrative Comprehension and Film*. London & New York: Routledge, 1992.
Csikszentmihalyi, Mihaly. *Flow – The Psychology of Optimal Experience*. New York: Harper Perennial, 1990.
Fullerton, Tracy, and Christopher Swain, et al. *Game Design Workshop*. San Francisco: CMP Books, 2004.
Grodal, Torben. *Moving Pictures. A New Theory of Film Genres, Feelings, and Cognition*. Oxford: Clarendon Press, 1997.
Grodal, Torben. *Filmoplevelse*. 2nd ed. Frederiksberg: Forlaget Samfundslitteratur, 2007.
Høgh, Carsten. "Film og Eventyr." *Kosmorama* 231 (2003): 91-107.
Miller, Carolin H. *Digital Storytelling*, Burlington: Focal Press, 2004.
Ramachandran, V. S., and W. Hirstein. "The Science of Art. A Neurological Theory of Aesthetic Experience." *Journal of Consciousness Studies* 6, nos. 6-7 (1999): 15-51
Rollings, Andrew, and Ernest Adams. *On Game Design*. Indianapolis: New Riders, 2003.
Schepelern, Peter. *Den fortællende film*. Copenhagen: Munksgaard, 1972.

Martin Knakkergaard

Browsing the Suggestive Catalogue: Music in Modern Fantasy Films

On the notion of otherness in the movies as a function of the musical dressing

One could claim that music is always the sonorous unfolding of a fantasy world regardless of the kind or style of music and how it is used. Although we hear it, music is neither concrete nor tangible. It is transient and unfolds quickly in time, slipping away as fast as it emerges. Music leaves both listener and performer in a state of constant change. It is considered its own language, but more than that, it creates parallel world that is experienced primarily as an auditory event or series of incidents. Mercilessly temporal, the world of music often serves as a retreat into the imagination. Music is always fantasy.

This article surveys the role and operation of music in modern fantasy films by investigating and analysing parts of the soundtrack of two prominent, fairly new examples of the genre, *The Lord of the Rings. The Fellowship of the Ring* (2001) and *Harry Potter and the Philosopher's Stone* (2002).

The term Fantasy or Fantasia has existed in the history of western European music since at least the Renaissance. First used to describe instrumental versions of vocal motets, the term Fantasy/Fantasia has been used increasingly to categorise music of an improvisatory or investigative nature that does not meet specific standards or norms; a Fantasy or Fantasia is more freely formed, challenging the musical standards and norms of a given epoch. In the Baroque era, the term Fantasy could be applied to a freely formed but carefully notated piece built upon extended chromatic progressions and phrases, peppered with embellishments. In the Classical era, the Fantasy grew to include and, indeed, depend upon the performer's facility, flexibility, and skill. In the Romantic era, Fantasy encompassed a wide variety of forms, ranging from the instrumental equivalent of a song cycle to improvised virtuoso variations on a given theme.

Apart from a few pieces, the genre – and term – Fantasy fell out of use in the twentieth century, possibly because the concept of formal genres and styles had become insignificant. As a result, the relatively close link between bourgeois music culture, with its enhanced cultivation of the emotive and sensuous, and Fantasy, a musical genre that reached its peak in the nineteenth century, persists.

The fact that the style and composition of film scores seem to be heavily influenced by music of the Romantic Period and imitations of it is, however, not necessarily related to the development of fantasy as musical genre. It might also be that composers who scored film music in early sound movies were educated in the traditional styles of Western European music, dominated by Romantic examples, techniques, and practices.

Music in Film

The idea that music and sound add value to film scenes and sequences, suggesting or clarifying the visual narrative, is very convincing in many ways. This axiomatic concept of film music is generally attributed to the French composer and theorist Michel Chion although this approach goes back to the early days of sound movies. (Cook, 1998)

At first glance, this point of view might imply that the score is applied to the film and not a genuine part of it, merely sharpening or completing a point made by other elements of the film. However, this is not Chion's understanding. On the contrary, he continues to maintain quite the opposite: film music - and sound - cannot be detached from the film. He makes his position clear with the apothegm: "There Is No Soundtrack." (Chion 1994). I share his view; I even claim that we cannot speak of music in film, only of references to music or musical allusion. (Knakkergaard 2009)

When watching a film, one experiences its score as an integral component of the artifact. One cannot talk of the film on one hand and its score on the other. Whenever the music is discussed separately, it is done in the same way as the dialogue, the acting, the narrative, the scenes, the settings, and so on. This type of critique views music or any other component as detached from the totality of the film, placing it into another arena. In the case of the music, this foreign context is typically that of film music as a genre, or music in general, or even, that of music theory, semiotics, and so on.

In recent years, a growing interest in silent movies has led to the establishment of societies and festivals, "culture feature programs" and dedicated websites[1]. Neil Brand, one of the leading accompanists in this field, states that the accompanist's role in the drama "… is the character you don't see."[2] In a recent interview on Danish Radio[3], Brand's point of view is supported by Ben Model, another accompanist, who was trained as both an actor and musician. His background itself supports Chion's and Brand's points of view, and does not oppose their approach. The music that accompanies silent movies becomes an element or role that is added to the film, integrating with and completing the narrative and the film as a whole.

The important issue is that music is an integrated – and integral — element in the film; it is not subject to independent reflection. This is exactly the reason why film scores can be so manipulative and suggestive within a film. To the degree that music is not heard or analysed as a detached element, the viewer's experience of the film is so much the stronger, especially if the music carries culturally indexed content. Whether a film score is original or previously composed, its main function is that of the referential, the associative, which, at a

---

1 See, e.g., http://www.stummfilm.info/, http://www.dfr.dk/
2 http://www.neilbrand.com/nbframe.html
3 http://www.dr.dk/P2/Kulturnyt/Udsendelser/2008/09/16162909.htm

subconscious level, evokes acknowledged structural archetypes within the practices of a cultural discourse. Some of these are even developed in close interaction with film as genre.

The choice — and application — of a film score energises the narrative and scenes in a way that is not merely supplemental. Music might confirm what seems already to be included, but music contributes by deepening the general feel of the scenes and events.

Music is not only capable of supplying a film with the sense of general mood and character, whether sinister and threatening, careless and joyful. It is also able to support the film's sense of tempo and anxiety and to connect different scenes and takes in terms of time, location, and geography.

In the following pages, music is viewed in the light of theory, momentarily detaching it from the film at hand, but I continue to relate it to other elements of the film.

Frame of Understanding

In this essay I will approach the question of how film music works by combining psychological, semiotic, pragmatic and cultural insights, attempting to join them into a single frame of understanding.

The *psychological* understanding of (film) music stresses the emotive and affective, gestural qualities of music, and often focuses on how musical proportions resemble the prosodic communicative practices that we have known from early childhood. In an attempt to pinpoint the psychological factors underlying the sense and perception of music, Ulrik Volgsten draws on Daniel Stern's model of the development of the self. (Stern 1985) Volgsten claims that the way we experience and value musical phrasing is tied to the sonorous aspects of preverbal vocal communication between baby and mother, enabling "the intuition of an affective core underlying the other's behaviour, an intuition of the other's affective states." (Volgsten, 2006:80) The competences that allow us to perceive simple musical phrasing are established at the earliest stages of self-development. The resulting abilities are the basis of our use and understanding of complex musical phrases and structures that are themselves built upon simpler structures. (See also Lerdahl & Jackendoff.) Volgsten refers to this as "affect attunement" and suggests that its use enables us "to denote the musical phrase in terms of 'masculine' and 'feminine,' of being 'happy' or 'sad,' or being expressive of any other kind of emotion." (ibid., 81)

Volgsten's line of inquiry lays the groundwork for the concept of film music as a trigger of regression. (Gorbman 1987) As long as the score is not heard consciously – a high ambition among many film composers – music and musical means in the broadest sense discreetly adjust the audience's mode of sensing to a prelinguistic, narcissistic state.

To a certain degree this viewpoint does not differ radically from that of Susanne K. Langer, although she does not explicitly rely upon the element of learning as precondition: Musical expression does not only resemble but evokes "the pattern of sentience—the pattern of life itself, as it is felt and directly known" (Langer 1953, 31), the dynamic form and not the specific content of feeling.

Music can also be viewed from a cognitive position, investigating the relationship between the experience of sound and sound events as carriers of - indexed - information, signs, and the organisation of a musical piece, its structure. In a broader sense this semi-*semiotic* perspective includes categories such as dynamics, intensity, frequency, speed, texture, contour, all leading to an understanding of music that resembles the way "real" sounds are interpreted. Here loudness signifies proximity or size; gradual changes in volume might also signify movement from one position to another. This is similar to the way in which frequency peaks give witness to size and especially the weight of objects, exposed or hidden.

Film music acts in much the same way as sound in general. It can endow a scene with a sense of proportion, direction, and dimension while it challenges the screen's reference to a Euclidean room by virtue of its transcendent, other-worldly status (insofar as it is non-diegetic). Being "positioned" outside the visual frames and the narrative, non-diegetic music generally appears as immersive, generating a certain atmosphere, "a kind of 'wrap-around sound'" (Donnelly 2005, 13), but at the same time it completely surrounds the film's audience and inevitably serves as a guiding interpreter of the nature and character of a scene. Even if "music makes space and time pliable, subject to contrast *or* distension" (Chion 1994, 82), the pliability is restrained by the type and means of musical expression that delimit the imminent interpretations and anchor the viewer's understanding of a scene. This is similar to the way a text is able to guide the reading of an image. (Barthes 1977, 38ff) Regardless of its "musical" character, music dominated by lower-pitched sound always seems to evoke a sense of gravity and seriousness, whereas high-pitched sound often but certainly not always evokes a light and carefree atmosphere. The high-pitched human scream, however, can also signify angst and fear.

There are fundamental elements of film music that refer to circumstances characteristic of our auditory experiences, independent of the genre and style of the music in question. Thus, part of the effect of film music is tied to sonorous implications independent of musical setting and means of excitation. However, the immersive qualities of film music also draw heavily on references to well-established categories of non-film music. In this respect the efficiency of the musical means of expression is dependent upon the audience's knowledge or sense of cultural, historical, and stylistic implications. This points towards *pragmatic* and rhetorical implications that are closely connected to musical as well as filmic discourses and dependent upon specific cultural learning.

In many films, there are obvious links of a synesthetic nature between the atmosphere and gestural aesthetics of nineteenth-century music and the grandeur and drama of the settings – and, often, the pathos of dialogue and performance. The extended use of the lower-pitched symphonic brass and contrabasses, and also synthesised "deep" sounds, gives rise to a feeling of gravity and seriousness, often supporting or engendering the sense of anxiety and worry. As part of the film's expressive means, music acts highly suggestively, indicating a powerful and mighty universe dominated by strong spiritual and paranormal elements.

Music in Modern Fantasy Films

In the case of major fantasy films, the element of musical standardisation seems surprisingly evident: Not only does the music demonstrate close affinity with western European classical tradition, it is very often written by or in the style of prominent contemporary composers such as John Williams and Howard Shore, who have distinguished themselves as composers of excellent heroic and epical scores. John Williams' highly influential scoring for major series such as *Star Wars* (all except *Star Wars: The Clone Wars* [2008]), *Indiana Jones,* (all films in the series), bear witness to this.

Thus, music in fantasy films belongs to a fantastic universe as it derives from or refers to primarily the musical discourse of the nineteenth century. As the music of, especially, the Romantic era is aimed strongly at spirituality (part of the century's preoccupation with mythological and philosophical issues), the music is well suited to provide a sense of the metaphysical and other-worldly. It can hardly be considered a coincidence that it corresponds with the dramatic universe of the nineteenth-century romantic music and poetry exemplified by Schubert's Lieder, Wagner's operas, and other works.

The Lord of the Rings · The Fellowship of the Ring

The use of archaic musical language supports the notion that fantasy is somehow a phenomenon of the past. However, the reference to the past does not bring the past to the present. Instead, the opposite occurs; the present is taken back to the past, exposing the film in an archaic atmosphere regardless of the chronological time of the film. Even films – and not only those that belong to the fantasy genre – whose dramatic situation is set in the present are very often garnished with a score that is historically anachronistic. This seems to be common to film music in general.

Howard Shore's score for Peter Jackson's *The Lord of the Rings, The Fellowship of the Ring* (2001), is a compelling example of the use of historic and archaic styles of music in fantasy films. The table below shows that, within the first ten minutes of the film, the musical setting presents many different musical idioms and allusions to music styles of the past. Some of the observations as well as other examples from the score are dealt with in greater detail in Table 1.

Table 1 The first ten minutes of Lord of the Rings, The Fellowship of the Ring:

Time	Scene-Action	Music
0:00:00	Intro–Prologue – voice-over	Gregorian chant-like but female-singing on extended drones
0:00:48	Dark screen (cont. voice-over) Title presentation → Casting of rings	Brass and noise leading to exposition of Main Theme – (signifying the Ring) nineteenth-century in shape, harmonisation and orchestration. Concrete sound (fire) is added. Main theme is continuously exposed. No noticeable rhythmic impetus.
0:01:38	Another ring was made	Sudden use of marcato and decisive rhythmic patterns. A kind of march with a strong upbeat to second beat
0:02:17	Battle scenes (voiceover cont.)	Sudden use of clear melodic lines bearing similarity to the opening of the thirteenth-century Latin hymn *Dies Irae,* exposed with a strong accentuated, almost driving rhythmic feel and heroic atmosphere supporting martial implications and leading back to the march. The march now enveloped in loud choral singing similar to the use of choir in carl Orff's *Carmina Burana* but in this context supporting the notion of war and evil. Strong double beats in Grand Cassa Return of *Dies Irae* allusions

MUSIC IN MODERN FANTASY FILMS

Time	Scene-Action	Music
0:03:57	Chopped-off hand hits the ground wearing the ring	Short motive from J.S. Bach's *Toccata and Fugue in d-minor* at first orchestrated for strings later for brass stands out shortly as part of the continuation of the section described above. Subsonic synthesised sound as the evil force is defeated and spreads an inverted mushroom wave.
0:04:20	Isildur lying on the ground; grabs the finger with the ring	Return of the main – ring – theme followed by a sequence without musical elements
0:04:46	The ring is lost in the water	Return of the main – ring – theme
0:05:20	Gollum discovers the ring "My precious" Mountains Gollum in the caves Gollum loses the ring.	Dark brass voicing Ascending melodic lines Main theme is continuously paraphrased Harmonic progressions without a significant thematic profile or contour
0:06:26	Bilbo picks up the ring.	Main — ring – theme returns
0:06:56	Scenes from The Shire	Short exposition of the leading Hobbit / Shire theme followed by harmonic progressions orchestrated for woodwinds, clarinet (for the first time), and strings
0:07:20	Gandalf is driving through the forest.	No music is heard except for Gandalf singing. Only peaceful sounds of the forest

Time	Scene-Action	Music
0:08:04	Gandalf and Frodo start laughing.	Joyful antiphonal- or vamped bass as a short prelude to the presentation of the full version of the leading Hobbit / Shire theme here performed by Irish whistle or recorder accompanied by strings
0:08:30	Gandalf starts telling Frodo news from the world.	Light variations on the Hobbit / Shire theme set out in harmonic sequences leading more and more towards a genuine folk music feel and setting. The violin / fiddle is the leading instrument supporting the sense of folk music.
0:09:58	Children gathering around the approaching Gandalf	Musical breakthrough in which the Hobbit / Shire theme is suddenly executed in a British national romantic setting and form making strong references to the works of Elgar, Holst and Vaughan Williams
0:10:15	Gandalf sets off the fireworks.	Return of the fiddle violin sequenced variations
0:10:34	Frodo and Gandalf both declare that they are glad that Gandalf is back in the Shire.	Return of the – original — Hobbit / Shire theme performed by Irish whistle, recorder or exotic flute

Besides these allusions to various music styles, forms of expression, and particular historical pieces – a feature that is not specific to music in fantasy film but quite common in mainstream film music as a whole – the music shows characteristics that can be judged on a more neutral, less idiosyncratic level, regardless of style. For example, the orchestration is generally of a low-pitched or dark character, which on the psychological level suggests a somewhat sinister atmosphere and a world of huge proportions. The tempo is slow, giving rise to the notion of the slightly reserved and dignified, but also of the threatening and tense. All in all, the style and density of the music evoke a strong feeling of suppressed power and heavy forces.

The melodic, counterpunctual, and voiced lines are generally formed stepwise, showing only few significant intervals and a prevalence of falling endings, which evoke a sense of the confined and suppressed. This is supported by the orchestration described above. Whereas the general feel and character are dark dominated by the lower registers, the themes stand out in higher registers, implying that they are clearly profiled.

The scoring is well executed and highly economical, preventing it from getting in the way of the narrative or stealing the picture. On the contrary, it mixes with the film as a whole and supports the narrative in a precise and efficient manner.

Framing the Ring

In the case of the Ring motif, the orchestral exposition of the theme leads to an impression of isolation and loneliness. The theme does not only reflect an ill-fated character by means of its narrow falling contour, it paradoxically has a kind of vulnerability. (Fig. 1) Obviously, this has nothing to do with the ring itself, but signifies that it triggers its evil magic and affects whomever is close to it, one way or another. Examples are numerous, and the musical theme occurs twice during the opening voiceover: the first, as the narrator says the ring "…betrayed Isildor to his death" [0:04:46] and the second when it is pointed out that "It was picked up by the most unlikely creature imaginable. A Hobbit. Bilbo Baggins." [0:06:26]

Fig. 1. LotR: Ring theme

However, the theme does not occur every time the ring is shown or mentioned. The adaptation of the opening motif of the Dies Irae (introduced when prehistoric battle scenes are shown), functions as a kind of *leitmotif,* suggesting the possible consequences if Sauron regains possession of the ring. (Fig. 2)

Fig. 2. *LotR:* The opening bar of Shore's adaptation with the first bar of the Dies Irae hymn below

The Dies Irae adaptation serves as an alternate sign of the ring. It seems to indicate the power of the ring and serves as a foreshadowing of death and destruction if the ring falls into the hands of Sauron. However, this motif first stands out clearly when Bilbo Baggins pulls the ring out of his pocket on Gandalf's command; he is told to leave it behind when he travels from the Shire [0:22:30]. Soon after this, we hear the motif again as the writing on the ring becomes visible to Frodo [0:29:40]. This is remarkable; the ring theme was heard when Frodo saw the ring for the first time as he entered Bilbo's house.

The relationship between the two themes seems obvious: The Ring theme is referential illustrating its magic and alluring power, whereas the Dies Irae adaptation is a connotative indication of the ring's dangerous and destructive powers. It seems that the reference to Dies Irae is deliberately included, reflecting its use in numerous other films where it almost exclusively acts as an indication of death and fall[4]. In accord with this, the theme is often heard when the Black Riders, the Nazgûl, appear.

---

[4] Among the many examples of the use of the Dies Irae theme in film music are Gottfried Huppertz' scoring for Fritz Lang's *Metropolis* (1927), Dimitri Tiomkin's music for Alfred Hitchcock's *I Confess* (1953), Miklós Rozsa's score for George Sidney's *Young Bess* (1953), Bernhard Hermann's music for Brian de Palma's *Obsession* (1976), Jerry Goldsmith's score for Tobe Hooper's *Poltergeist* (1982), Elmer Bernstein's music for Angelika Weber's *Marie Ward* (1984), Elliot Goldenthal's music for Marco Brambilla's *Demolition Man* (1993), and Hans Zimmer's music for Allis and Minkoff's *The Lion King* (1994).

Projections of the Present

Enya's *The Council of Elrond* [01:21:30] accompanies the solemn scene in Rivendale in which Arven and Aragorn declare their love for each other and Arven confirms that she will forsake immortal life in order to marry Aragorn. In a way, Enya's piece externalises the film, as the music connects with a particular field of significance: a discourse, established independently of the film and of film in general, with the everyday music heard through mass media. Music brings forward not only the notion of fantasy but also – and more importantly – ideas of purity, order, and idealised love. Enya's music draws heavily on idioms that are related closely to folklore, authenticity, and romance. The sum of these characteristics forms a sense of nostalgia, suggesting a connection between fantasy and history. Here, fantasy is an emblem of a paradise lost, and history is understood as a continuous process of decline from idealised primitivism to civilised alienation. At the same time, however, the scene reaches into current time; the conception of the one and only eternal love continues to hold the position of an idealised social institution in modern culture. The music lacks any mark of modernism and belongs unmistakably to the discourse of popular music. Its atmosphere and character are those of the romantic as embodied in the New Age music of the past two decades. Furthermore, Enya's music signifies the modern concept of ecological thinking, a sense of purity and healing, the idea of getting back to the core of nature.

The use of New Age music also takes into account the audience building a dialectic split, which joins the past and mysterious with the familiar and mundane.

Paradoxical Time

Neither the music of Shore nor of Enya refers to the apparent setting of the narrative. (Both, however, interact with the film in terms of mood and character.) None of the music in the film refers to the time or place of the narrative unless we say the Shire or Hobbit themes are historical paraphrases of folk music.

With the exception of references to the opening bar of the Dies Irae and modal tonality, the score does not correspond to the time of the narrative in any way. Even though the setting of *The Lord of the Rings* is fictional and not synchronised to historical time, the references in the film suggest the late medieval era. Similarly, there are references to the modern calendar in the case of Bilbo Baggins' birthday party. The narrative carries a sense of old but historic times, which are not paralleled in the music.

Although the Dies Irae adaptation could suggest a medieval reference, the theme has become a cinematic audial icon, signifying death and decline in numerous films regardless of the setting and time (note 4). The theme simply indicates death on the pragmatic level.

There are other correlations between narrative threads and musical agents in the film, but I will discuss only one more example here.

Twentieth-century Musical Language as Signifier of War and Aggression

Moving beyond nineteenth century musical influences, I turn now to Bartòk, Stravinsky, and Orff, and the ways in which their music has been used in contemporary films. The dramatic, rhythmic drive and modern orchestration occur mainly in battle scenes and especially in scenes involving the Uruk Hai, Isengard, or Mordor. In several cases the noise of the battle scenes and the Uruk Hais' noisy activities are underscored by modernistic or neo-classical music language. The music is also integrated with realistic sounds of battle, especially hammering and fighting. This is the case in the scene where the Uruk Hais are fashioning swords and other weapons in the open-air smithy.

The use of this technique leads to a psychologically strong effect, as the music is closely integrated into the scenes and becomes part of the sonorous surroundings. The guiding principle is a form of musicalization; the concept can be toggled so that the sounds and noises in the scene may be organised according to the music. (Knakkergaard 2009)

The extended allusions to Orff's 1937 *Carmina Burana* (used in many fantasy films) indicates a predilection for simple musical forms and clear-cut phrases, signalling a medieval universe with remnants of a heathen world, identified by a mixture of the martial and the mystic.

Summing up The Fellowship of the Ring

Generally the score of this film builds an auditory universe that is characterised by a strong element of sentiment, force, and contrast on the one hand and of ease, peace and simplicity on the other. The use of the symphonic scoring is reserved for scenes that deal with the foreign and dangerous, and with threat and horror. Although the ring theme belongs to a musical typology of intimacy and comfort, the theme acquires an uneasy quality when arranged on a rich, dark background that questions its simplicity. Contrary to this, scenes that visualise or refer to the Shire or to Hobbits are underscored by a musical language that is simple and easy to comprehend; it is arranged for a small ensemble in plain settings.

These characteristics are supported semiotically. The dynamics and density of the orchestral passages correspond to the scenes they escort, endowing them with a sense of force, intensity, and grandeur. Music performed by smaller ensembles is softer and more transparent, generally manageable and uncomplicated. Likewise, orchestral passages tend to be marked by driving rhythms enhanced by strong percussion; passages for solo instruments and smaller ensembles are typically articulated more loosely.

The scoring relies on techniques and aesthetics that are particular to Western European music culture although many of the instruments are not indigenous to Western Europe. The score supports a strong sense of tonal centre; the melodic lines and harmonic implications fall within the discourse of traditional western music in terms of shaping and tonality. The music is rich in references and allusions to famous pieces of music, enabling familiarity and a level of comfort.

Harry Potter and the Philosopher's Stone

John Williams' music for Chris Columbus' 2001 film of J. K. Rowling's bestseller *Harry Potter and the Philosopher's Stone* resembles Howard Shore's score for *The Lord of the Ring – The Fellowship of the Ring*. Williams, however, has chosen a different path in terms of the general character and feel of the music. Brighter orchestration and a less burdened movement prevail. Most of the music evokes a

BROWSING THE SUGGESTIVE CATALOGUE

light and carefree atmosphere, suggesting an overall sense of comedy and joy. The music helps the film to fit into the category of family entertainment.

The observations on the scoring of the first ten minutes of the film listed in Table 2 reveals how Williams has managed to achieve a scoring of high integrity without desisting from detailed variation that allows for deepening and characterisation of the shifting scenes. The table is followed by a more detailed discussion of these matters.

Table 2 The first ten minutes of Harry Potter and the Philosopher'

Time	Scene-Action	Music
0:00:00	WB logo	Main Theme I in Horn accompanied by stepwise melodic ladders in strings
0:00:18	Intro - Owl on Privet Drive Road sign	Melodic line (Magic Theme) in Glockenspiel
0:00:36	Professor Dumbledore comes walking out of the dark.	Traditional chromatic ladders in strings supporting anxiety and mystery. Atmosphere is not heavy or light
0:00:49	Dumbledore stops up to start switching out lights in Privet Drive.	Return of the beginning of Magic Theme in woodwind (possibly high bassoon). Symphonic orchestra harmonics supporting lights switching off.
0:01:14	Dumbledore stops switching out lights and the cry of a cat is heard.	Return of the Main Theme I in horn almost unaccompanied

MUSIC IN MODERN FANTASY FILMS

Time	Scene-Action	Music
0:01:22	Cat transforms into Professor McGonagall and joins Dumbledore.	Musical accompaniment with clear affinity to twentieth-century symphonic music (e.g., Stravinsky's *Firebird*)
0:01:59	Hagrid arrives with baby Harry Potter.	Heroic horn version of Main Theme I accompanied by chromatic runs in strings
0:02:21	Conversation between Hagrid, Dumbledore and McGonagall	Return to musical accompaniment with clear affinity to twentieth-century symphonic music
0:02:37	Dumbledore carries Harry Potter to the doorstep.	Continuation of the scoring right above but with Main Theme I added in woodwind (oboe or English Horn)
0:03:12	Dumbledore places Harry Potter on the doorstep. Harry Potter is lying on doorstep. Hagrid sniffles.	Stepwise falling melodic line gradually orchestrated broader and deeper as the tempo is falling simultaneously. Cadence-like ending. Morendo and deep strings
0:03:36	Dumbledore places letter on top of Harry Potter.	Return of Privet Drive / Magic Theme in Glockenspiel
0:03:50	Title screen	Full blown orchestral version of Main Theme II with melodic line in doubled horn
0:04:00	Harry Potter is woken up by his Aunt Petunia.	Music ends in cadence as Harry Potter opens his eyes.

BROWSING THE SUGGESTIVE CATALOGUE

Time	Scene-Action	Music
0:06:08	Snake rises a little as Harry Potter talks to it. Snake rises high up communicating. Harry Potter asks if the snake misses its family. Dudley falls into the snake's cage.	Music starts with long note in woodwind gradually broadened with more and more instruments coming in. Atmospheric and non-thematic. Accentuated ascending notes in horn Broad soft chords in strings envelope the scene sentiment. Music gets darker with a stronger impetus.
0:07:04	Snake escapes from the cage and causes panic.	Light high-pitched comedy music performed with a dry, jumping feeling.
0:07:31	Dudley discovers he cannot get out of the cage.	The light comedy music theme turns into a jumpy variation on Main Theme I.
0:07:44	Uncle Vernon discovers that Harry Potter has caused the snake's escape as well as Dudley's confinement. Harry Potter is locked up in the cupboard under the stairs.	Sudden darkening of the music with strong deep resting notes in brass and double-basses as part of a dissonant chord The music's dissonant quality stops.
0:08:13	Owl arrives with letter.	Main Theme I in horn returns accompanied by stepwise and chromatic runs in strings
0:08:50	Harry Potter hands Uncle Dudley letters but keeps his own for himself.	Music ends

Time	Scene-Action	Music
0:08:55	Uncle Dudley looks at Harry Potter's letter.	Light comedy music from above returns.
0:09:06	Owl comes flying with letter again.	Stepwise and chromatic runs in strings anticipate the return of Main Theme I.
0:09:22	Uncle Vernon tears letters into pieces.	The flow of the music is halted and is continued into pizzicato in deep strings not forming a clear continuous rhythmic pattern thus gaining a sneaky character.
0:09:38	More owls deliver letters to Harry Potter.	Return of the above stepwise and chromatic runs in strings, this time with the heroic Main Theme II on top

William's scoring of the first ten minutes is highly homogeneous although it combines musical elements of different characteristics and expressions, and is also implemented in different orchestration. This is accomplished by a strong sense of economy and a stringent use of similar or identical musical approaches towards scenes of corresponding observation. A large amount, if not most, of the film's musical themes are introduced during the opening scenes.

Generally, the music tends to refer to a consistent idiom that resembles the neoclassical tradition of the first half of the twentieth century. But it does so in a diluted form and does not restrict itself to that idiom. Some of the elements — chromatics, orchestration, and defined motives — clearly point back to the nineteenth century and to practices of, for instance, the tone poem. Another feature of the musical setting is that it resembles much of Williams' other film scores. We cannot ignore this feature, because of its possible consequences for the construction and acknowledgement of the drama.

Leading Themes

As the table above shows, there are three prominent themes in Williams' score: Main Theme I (fig. 3), Main Theme II (fig. 4), and the Magic Theme (fig. 5), are presented in the first ten minutes of the film. The two Main Themes are also used extensively in other Harry Potter films, thus functioning as signature themes.

Main Theme I (0:00:03) in some way resembles the themes of other Williams pieces, for example, *Star Wars* and *Indiana Jones*. Although written in three-quarter time, which does not apply to the other two themes, *Harry Potter* has a similar masculine, bold, heroic character. This is achieved through the choice of horns, its vivid tempo, and also through its characteristic opening interval of the fourth.

Fig. 3. Harry Potter: Main Theme I

Main Theme I is related to Main Theme II, which we hear the first time the title, "Harry Potter and the Philosopher's Stone," appears [0:03:50]. Main Theme II relates even more closely to other Williams' music and it appears to be more notably shaped to signify action and adventure. Again this is achieved by the choice of horn and by its intervallic implications. Here the rising interval is more prominent, being repeated and, the third time, expanded from the interval of a third to a fourth. The rhythmic realisation from weak to accentuated beats stresses the interval, and the theme is endowed with a sense of vitality and energy.

Fig. 4. Harry Potter: Main Theme II

The Magic Theme, which is heard in the Glockenspiel the first time we see the Privet Road sign, is connected to the others in a subtle way as it recycles some of the intervals and the meter. However, the three-quarter meter, which initially supports the connection to the other themes, is not maintained. Three-quarter time alternates with five-quarter, and with the use of the fragile Glockenspiel, establishes the theme's magic character.

MUSIC IN MODERN FANTASY FILMS

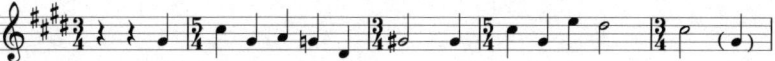

Fig. 5. Harry Potter: Magic Theme

In general, the thematic material presented at the beginning and used throughout the film, secures unity and coherence. Much of the accomplished differentiation in the musical scoring is due to the application of different orchestration techniques and settings.

Comfort, Peace, and Love

Seen from the perspective of the western European musical tradition, most of music in *Harry Potter and the Philosopher's Stone* is kept within a mildly dissonant atmosphere. There are, however, passages, that deviate from this and expose a harsher and more dissonant sound universe. Likewise, some scenes are accompanied by music of a highly consonant and soft character, generally supporting an emotive sensation in relation to scenes of sentimental content.

An example of the last type is the scene in which Harry Potter spends his first night in Gryffindor sitting on the windowsill, apparently daydreaming while the others are sleeping [0:47:38]. The beginning of the scene – before we see Harry – is accompanied by a theme that in style and character resembles the solemn and peaceful orchestral music for which prominent, twentieth-century English composers such as Elgar, Holst, and Vaughan Williams are known. To the average western European audience, the particular musical idiom probably has a sort of national and even pastoral quality signifying core values of traditional, bygone English culture. It is highly suitable to accompany scenes of the interior Hogwarts castle (with a look back at noble life in the countryside of Old England).

Fig. 6. Harry Potter. Opening bars of the sentimental theme shown above the "corresponding" passage from Stravinsky's Firebird.

As Harry Potter comes into the picture [0:47:55], the music progresses into a generally stepwise and over-arching cantabile passage, which in its opening motive is closely related to the well-known passage from *The Round of the Princesses* in Stravinsky's *Firebird* (Fig. 6). The musical disposition endows the scene with a sense of Harry's emotions, as he first looks out the window then turns towards his owl, Hedwig, to caress it. He turns again and lifts his head to look out the window dreamily (and directly into the camera). Thus the music is highly supportive and even manipulative, as it points up the emotive quality of the scene.

20th-century Musical Language as Signifier of War and Aggression - Again

To accompany the battle scene on the oversized chessboard, Williams draws upon idioms of the classical tradition of the first half of the twentieth century [01:57:11]. Unpitched percussion instruments suddenly dominate the scoring and support a feeling of danger, and aggression, and the scoring alone provokes anxiety and fear. At first, the percussion instruments form a stable, march-like core, on which the pitched instruments build lines and blocks of sound that penetrate the score irregularly. This procedure simultaneously causes more emotional effects: the heady sense of soldiers on the move, approaching quickly and requiring swift and precise responses from the chess players, Harry, Hermione, and Ron. The insertions of pitched sound cause the illusion of danger coming from more unpredictable quarters, and, at the same time, interacting with the sound effects that support the action.

As the game develops, the stringent quality of the march is abandoned and the amount of unpitched percussion is expanded. The result of these changes is a strengthening of the unpredictable character of the drama, suggesting a sense of the accidental and chaotic.

Quite remarkably, the chess scene is heralded by a short motif (fig. 7) that is heard in *The Fellowship of the Ring*: another adaptation of the Dies Irae opening motif:

MUSIC IN MODERN FANTASY FILMS

Fig. 7. Harry Potter. Grave motif resembling the opening of Dies Irae.

The motif is performed in a very slow tempo and scored in low registers outlined by horns, thus endowing the scene with a grave, heavy feeling and a sense of suspense.

Summing up Harry Potter and the Philosopher's Stone

Although the music of *Harry Potter and the Philosopher's Stone* is characterised by uniformity and integration, the use of shifting orchestration, dynamic contrast, and of nearly specific references to established music styles and works implies that the musical framing of the film compellingly directs the emotions of the audience. The shift from orchestral voicing, profiled by the familiar and reassuring sound of horn, to the frail and transparent sound of the Glockenspiel in the opening scenes, epitomises this procedure. The music is, in this respect, psychologically integrated seamlessly into the film as it supports the move from everyday life in Privet Lane to the magical universe of fantasy.

Whenever the music leaves the domain of the well-known and familiar to early modern sonorities of the twentieth century, that shift signifies anxiety and stress, and the music supports a related sense of the foreign and unknown. The arrangement of the music and the use of musical styles rest upon the assumption of different psychological responses to different types of music and different categories of sound.

Semiotically the music is shaped closely in accordance with the filmed scenes. The dream-like atmosphere, evoked by the somewhat unfamiliar sound of the Glockenspiel (played in a hesitating manner) is considerably softer and more blurred compared to a symphonic passage. The softer quality of the Glockenspiel — in contrast to the full symphonic sound — gains semiotic value that exceeds its psychological effect. In other words, the characteristic sound and expression are framed and partly isolated. Furthermore, as the sound of the Glockenspiel resembles other types of chimes, there is a connection to religious activities: chimes and bells are widely used in such cultural contexts as signifiers of gatherings, processions, sacrifices, supporting the magical moment's sense of the ceremonial and esoteric.

All in all, the scoring of *Harry Potter* does not only rely on the established film scoring practices and musical codes of western European musical discourse, but also draws heavily on codes made familiar in Williams' own body of work. The similarity to other examples of Williams' music for blockbuster films – modern classics – suggests that his music builds a genre of its own, allowing for cross-references as it plays with established musical metaphors. The music draws from a source that, in one form or another, is known to most of the audience; it leads to a form of intertextuality that allows for unconscious cross-referential links to other musical settings of fantasy films, supporting exactly the sense of the otherworldly and imaginative leading to an ever- reassuring subject positioning.

There are, however, instances where the scoring draws directly on musical archetypes that are well established within the western European discourse. Among them is the short passage where the new students walk to their rooms after their first meal at Hogwarts [0:46:04]. The scene is accompanied by martial orchestral music in the style of the American Civil War classic, "Battle Hymn of the Republic", best known for its refrain "Glory, Glory Hallelujah." As the students process, the music adds a carefree, adventurous, and slightly comical atmosphere to the scene, as if the students were setting out on a field trip. Likewise, the magic Glockenspiel music suddenly expands into rousing orchestral arpeggios — often heard in nineteenth-century tone poems — as Ollivander finds out a proper wand for Harry Potter [0:26:04]. This technique is well known from numerous Walt Disney animated cartoons.

Conclusion

The music for the two fantasy films discussed here is carefully prepared and composed to interact with the films in a way that appears highly homologous with their narratives. Whether it is the cruel and ominous fantasy world of *The Fellowship of the Ring* or the more juvenile, comedy-drama of *Harry Potter and the Philosopher's Stone*, the music supports the face value of the narrative. It adds depth to scenes by anchoring their dramatic content and never seems to question them. Thus, the music is neatly integrated and interwoven into the film artifact.

The amount of musicalization (see p. 244) is modest and only occurs eminently in *The Fellowship of the Ring*. The scoring of both films is generally kept within traditional musical expression; the soundtrack as such holds a strong musical orientation. This gives the impression that the music is autonomous and somehow detached from the rest of the cinematic elements. But, in truth, the music is carefully prepared to support and interact with the other elements: the music never stands out on its own.

Full pieces of music are the exception, suggesting that the free form and character of the musical Fantasy are the organising principle for fantasy film scoring (as well as for other films). The recurring themes and leitmotifs assume different disguises and settings but point in this direction. Any inner formal binding of the music would prevent it from integrating with the rest of the film's components. Thus, the free and formally unpredictable nature of a musical fantasy is the most viable form.

The film scores make extensive use of semiotic and pragmatic means to support the notions of proportion and dimension, as well as time, tempo, place, and locale. The music supports the emotions from the soft and sentimental through the joyful and aroused to the frightened and aggressive. In *Harry Potter and the Philosopher's Stone* the music generally suggests a strong sense of unity and coherence brought about through structural and sonorous similarity and variation. By employing highly contrasting elements and refined, differentiated orchestration, the music for *The Fellowship of the Ring* stresses the dramatic diversity of the narrative: from the careless, loving, and peaceful to the fearful, threatening and violent. In this way, the score supports the experience of a complex and troubled universe, an effect achieved by a subtle combination of psychological, semiotic, and pragmatic means.

The music is in both cases Eurocentric, supporting the notion of dramatised fantasy worlds as elements of modern western mythology. At the same time, it is quite remarkable that, apart from the use of Enya's music in *The Fellowship of the Ring*, none of the films discussed uses musical styles that can be considered up-to-date or contemporary. There are no direct references to either classical or popular music forms of the twenty-first century, no R&B, no Minimalism, no Electro. Except for the occasional use of synthesised sounds, the orchestrations make use entirely of acoustic instruments mostly belonging to the western European symphony orchestra, fostering the security of the well-known, familiar, and generally manageable[5]. This type of scoring builds a world of certainty and confidence, endowing the music – and the film – with a touch of the harmless, the absence of contemporary musical styles and expressive means secures temporal displacement, allowing us to escape from everyday life into a well-defined world of good and bad.

---

5   The use of the rock musical idiom as part of the prominent ball scene in *Harry Potter and The Goblet of Fire* (2005) [1:16:05], scored by Patrick Doyle and not by Williams, does surprisingly break with this principle. The effect can be heard as somewhat disturbing in the otherworldly atmosphere of the magic universe.

References

Barthes, Roland. *Image-Music-Text.* London: Fontana Press, 1977.
Chion, Michel. *Audio-Vision: Sound on Screen.* New York: Columbia University Press, 1994.
Cook, Nicholas. *Analysing Musical Multimedia.* Oxford: Oxford University Press, 1998.
Donnelly, Kevin J. *The Spectre of Sound: Music in Film and Television.* London: BFI (British Film Institute), 2005.
Gorbman, Claudia. *Unheard Melodies: Narrative Film Music.* Bloomington: Indiana University Press, 1987.
Knakkergaard, Martin. *The Musical Ready-Made. On the Ontology of Music and Musical Structures in Film.* In Jantzen, Christian, and Nicolai Graakjær, *Music in Advertising.* Aalborg: Aalborg Universietsforlag, 2009. (in production)
Langer, Susanne. *Feeling and Form.* London: Routledge, 1953.
Lerdahl, Fred and Ray S. Jackendoff. *A Generative Theory of Tonal Music.* Cambridge: MIT Press, 1983.
Stern, Daniel N. *The Interpersonal World of the Infant: A View from Psychoanalysis and Development Psychology.* New York: Basic Books, 1985.
Volgsten, Ulrik. *Between Ideology and Identity. Media, Discourse, and Affect in the Musical Experience.* In *Music and Manipulation. On the Social Uses and Social Control of Music.* Edited by Steven Brown and Ulrik Volgsten. New York and Oxford: Berghahn Books, 2006.

Anders Bonde

Distant Lands of Danger and Pleasure

Musical Exotica as Devices for Feminization in Xena: Warrior Princess

Since the 1990s, there has been a considerable amount of academic writing about gender issues in multiseason television shows, where strong women succeeding in professions and at tasks that are traditionally associated with men. Examples are *Sabrina, the Teenage Witch* (1996-2003); *Buffy the Vampire Slayer* (1997-2003); *Ally McBeal* (1997-2002); *The X-Files* (1993-2002); and *Xena: Warrior Princess* (1995-2001),[1] all featuring tough female characters who – more or less, and in their own distinct ways – personify a reversed gender role. (cf. Halfyard 2001, 2003) However, the identity politics of women in the media, with the general ambivalence or even reluctance

---

1   See for instance the anthologies by Inness (1998, 2004); Helford (2000); Early & Kennedy (2003); Schubart & Gjelsvik (2004); and Ross & Byerly (2004). They deal with these and other shows as well as movies and computer games. Additionally, several fanzines have been established: e.g. *Whoosh!* (http://www.whoosh.org), *Xenaville* (http://www.xenaville.com), and *Slayage* (http://slayageonline.com) devoted to the studies (and celebrations) of *Xena: Warrior Princess* and *Buffy the Vampire Slayer*.

to "challenge gender conventions too dramatically" (Inness 1998, 5), may suggest that gender reversal is not entirely fulfilled in these shows. Taking *Xena: Warrior Princess* (*XWP*) as an example, the spectator is presented with a soft-porn image of an Amazon warrior wearing a skin-tight black leather costume. Her legs are bare and her breasts emphasised as she fights one blood-dripping battle after another without getting killed. On the other hand, by placing a sexy female protagonist in a formerly masculine professional context, the show might be said to embody a liberatory feminist discourse (with a possible lesbian subtext shown in Xena's warm relation to the secondary female protagonist Gabrielle), while still appealing to adolescent and adult heterosexual males fascinated by her outfits.[2] In fact, this kind of mixed discourse has frequently been perceived as the recipe behind the success of the show, and is a major improvement compared to more traditional series featuring male characters in leading roles. (cf. Young 2005) Instead of a one-dimensional male superhero (like Superman or Batman), the spectators get a multifaceted superheroine who seems impervious to gender stereotypes. The picture of Xena as a desirable woman, using her attractive physical qualities to fool her male rivals (and arouse sexual desire in the male audience), is balanced against her heroic actions and capability to protect innocent people (i.e., unarmed farmers, powerless women, and children) from murderous warlords and thieves all by herself. Thus, Xena personifies a "one-of-a-kind" action-heroine type whose spectacular performance and strength, combined with her reticence and ability to solve problems alone, fit with conventional ideals of male heroism. Xena outclasses men at their own game of world domination. According to Janet Halfyard (2001), *Buffy the Vampire Slayer* (*BtVS*) represents a similar example of how the heroine "rewrites the rules of the heroic in relation to the female." (ibid.) Like Xena, Buffy handles all the dangers by herself, while her "scoobies" (the group of members helping her to fight supernatural and evil forces) are reduced

---

2 Various fanzine articles on the Internet confirm this notion (cf. Meister 1997, Dunn 2000 and Young 2005).

to sideline assistants, providing technical equipment, knowledge, and those things necessary for Buffy to act. This makes the role of the heroine in shows like *BtVS* and *XWP* significantly different from contemporary "girl-power" series such as *Charmed* (1998-2006), which supports "the idea of women as sociable, working best in cooperative groups." (ibid)

Gender and Other in Music

Now, the kind of "kick-ass" heroine, as exemplified in *BtVS* and *XWP*, is not limited to the narrative (i.e., moving pictures and dialogue); it is also achieved through music. Compared to television in general, the use of music in *BtVS* and *XWP* is quite substantial, not only during the opening titles and closing credits, but also incidentally, where it forms the "background" or "atmosphere" of the scenic action.[3] Hence, it seems reasonable to interrogate whether – and if so, how – music (as a semiotic resource for the making of discursive meaning) may reflect or contribute affectively to a gendered reading of the narratives in these shows. Judging from feminist studies by Susan McClary – a handful of them collected in her much influential book *Feminine Endings. Music, Gender, and Sexuality* (McClary 1991) – as well as the empirical research carried out by the British musicologist Philip Tagg in collaboration with Bob Clarida and Anahid Kassabian (cf. Tagg 1989, 2003, 2006), it makes perfect sense to distinguish between male and female tunes.[4]

During the early 1980s, Tagg did a number of tests featuring ten theme tunes from films and television programs in the United States and Great Britain, each lasting between thirty and sixty seconds.[5]

---

3   For instance, there is about 36 minutes of music in each 45-minute episode of *XWP* (Rudnick 1998).

4   It appears that McClary (1991), when proposing a modern 'musical semiotics of gender' (ibid., 8) and a 'semiotics of "masculinity" and "femininity"' (ibid., 14), was unaware of the work of Tagg (1989), which has not been mentioned at all (cf. Schwartz 1995). Yet, the latter represents, even today, one of the most elaborate empirical studies of this topic.

5   The title themes were *The Dream of Olwen* (Charles Williams 1942),

The purpose of these tests was to examine the impact of purely musical stimuli on everyday consumers of audio-visual media. Most subjects were under the age of 30 and were "non muso" students in Sweden. They had no formal musical knowledge, being academic or practical (Tagg 2003, 808), and – more importantly – had little familiarity with the tunes and their contexts. When hearing the tunes, the students were asked to write down their visual-verbal associations immediately. Their responses were subsequently grouped in a number of categories, such as "love and kindness," encompassing the subcategories "in love," "very romantic," "seductive," and "gentle." (ibid., 1989, 23). I shall go no further into detail but sum up one of the main conclusions of the tests, which came to light when the responses were classified according to the male- and female-oriented associations. Eight of the ten tunes were classified as either as "predominantly manly" or "predominantly womanly" with four tunes in each grouping; the remaining two tunes were "neither nor." The essential musical-parametric differences between the male and female tunes were then summarised (Table 1) and compressed into a general list of "gender polarities" (Table 2).[6]

Table 1

Musical characteristic	Male tunes	Female tunes
Average tempo	109 bpm	83 bpm
Surface rate	C. 400	C. 180
Phrase length	Short	Long
Phrasing	Staccato	Legato
Repeated notes	Common	None
Volume change	None	Some
Bass line	Active and angular	Quite static

The Virginian (Percy Faith 1962), *Monte Python's Flying Circus* (J. P. Sousa c. 1900), *Romeo & Juliet* (Nino Rota 1966), *Sportsnight* (Tony Hatch 1973), *Emmerdale Farm* (Tony Hatch 1972), *Sayonara* (Franz Waxman 1957), *A Streetcar Named 'Desire'* (North 1951), *Owed to 'g'* (Tommy Bolin 1975), and *Miami Vice* (Jan Hammer 1984).

6   Both tables are derived from Tagg. (2006, 175)

MUSICAL EXOTICA AS DEVICES FOR FEMINIZATION

Table 1

Musical characteristic	Male tunes	Female tunes
Offbeats and Syncopation	Common	Rare
Melodic instrumentation	Electric guitar, guitar synth, trumpet, xylophone	Strings, flute, mandolin, oboe, piano
Accompanimental instrumentation	Guitar riffs + strum, brass stabs, sequenced synth, percussion	Strings, piano, woodwind, no brass, no percussion
Tonal idiom	Rock, (diluted) jazz common	Classical, romantic common

Table 2

Male	Female
Fast	Slow
Dynamic	Static
Hard	Soft
Urban	Rural
Sudden	Gradual
Upwards	Downwards
Jagged	Smooth
Modern	Old times
Active	Passive
Outwards	Inwards
Sharp	Rounded
Strong	Weak

Concerning *BtVS* and *XWP*, discussions of music and gender are limited to a few cursory studies of the title themes, leaving incidental music unnoticed. Using Tagg's gendered stereotypes in music (Table 1) as theoretical background, Halfyard (2001) emphasises a linkage between, on the one hand, the divergent musical styles of the title themes in *BtVS* and the show's spin-off series *Angel* (1999-2004), respectively (fig. 1),[7] and, on the other, the gender coding of the main characters in these two series.

Fig. 1: Title theme in BtVS (a) and Angel (b).

---

7 All figures are transcriptions made by the author.

The similarities of key and motif between BtVS and Angel are a thinly disguised means of reasserting the eternal bond between the two characters. Although they are separated (into two series, apart from anything else), they will always be connected: the shared motif stands as a symbol of their love and also of their separation. The differences between these themes, however, are just as interesting and speak more clearly to the idea of music as identity. One of the most striking differences between the two theme tunes is their mood. Buffy's theme is for amplified rock band, and the melodic line is carried by an increasingly frenetic electric guitar. Angel's theme is more obviously lyrical, slower paced and written largely for acoustic instruments: piano and cello dominate the melodic line. One could easily argue the appropriateness of this on the grounds that Buffy is a modern girl, and therefore more likely to listen to the kind of music heard in her theme, identifying with it and being identified by it on grounds of her youth and chosen cultural environment, particularly the Bronze [nightclub]. Angel, meanwhile, is an eighteenth-century Irish vampire: rock music is certainly not "his" music in terms of his somewhat unusual age group or culture, and so a more classical and slightly Irish-folk sounding theme is one that he might identify with more readily. However, what cannot be ignored about the two themes is that it can be argued that Buffy's music is coded male, and Angel's is coded female. (ibid.)

A fairly similar, although briefer, study on "oppositional categories" in the *XWP* title theme (fig. 2) has been presented by Carolyn Bremer (1998), who argues for a musical mirroring of the duality between the masculinity of the "dark warrior" woman (Xena) and the more feminine traits of her companion (Gabrielle).[8] Thus, the vigorous opening and closing E-minor sections, symbolising the power of Xena, are identified as "masculine," whereas the lyrical middle section, emphasising

---

8   Although not referring to Tagg (1989), Bremer's characterization of a musical duality corresponds considerably to Tagg's distinction between "male" and "female" tunes (cf. Table 1).

a complementary subdominant area, is recognised as "feminine" in accordance with the softness and tenderness of Gabrielle (fig. 2).

Fig. 2: Opening/closing section (a) and middle section (b) in the XWP title theme.

> As with the characters – the entirety of each dependent on disparate, separate parts, and the entirety of the show dependent on the very different Xena and Gabrielle – LoDuca's theme music has two discrete sections which meld one into one another, which individually remain incomplete without the other. The amount of dissimilarity between the two themes is significant and unusual. One relies on a rhythmic ostinato, the other does not; one is asymmetrical (in seven/eight time), the other is in four/four (or common time);[9] one stays within a very narrow range of a minor third later transposed up ... a fourth, the other encompasses an octave plus a fifth; one is coloured by brass, percussion, and voices, the other is focused on strings and has no text or voices; one uses but two chords, the other integrates a more typical harmonic progression; one uses only three closely-related rhythmic values of eighth, quarter, and dotted quarter, the other ranges from quick embellishments to whole notes. (ibid.)

As mentioned above, *incidental* music and its potential for signifying gender roles has been omitted in both studies. Therefore, I have found it interesting to dip into a more thorough reading, concentrating

---

9   The 4/4 meter of the middle section, as noted by Bremer (1998), is not correct; rather, the meter changes to 3/4 in the melody line (cf. fig. 2b) while polyrhythms (in concordance with the 7/8 meter of the outer sections) occur elsewhere in the orchestra.

solely on the music in *XWP*, which has been composed and arranged by Joseph LoDuca (b. 1958). Unlike the musical score of *BtVS*, LoDuca includes several stylistic elements suggesting an exotic "Otherness," which accentuates further the issues of gender and femininity in *XWP*. Indeed, as asserted by Linda Phyllis Austern (1998, 26), "[t]he Western imagination has for long considered music a phantasmic language through which the unspeakably alien may be evoked, and through which the exotic and the feminised erotic have the capacity to unite in forbidden and dangerous desire."

Western art music's reflection of the conception of woman as "foreign land" is not least perceptible in the nineteenth century's intertwining of Orientalism and symphonicism (Stokes 2000, 214) and particularly in French operas such as Bizet's *Carmen* (1875) and Delibes' *Lakmé* (1883). Both of these works, according to James Parakilas (1993, 34), thematise "The Soldier and the Exotic" – that is, the European conqueror's fascination for the colonised world through escapist fantasising about the good, uncomplicated life among native people (and, not the least, beautiful women), relieving him from all his regular duties at home. By means of exotic musical stereotypes such as non-western scales, Oriental-sounding motifs, melismas, static harmonies, and the choice of orchestration, the composer reminds the viewer of distant lands, far from contemporary western culture.[10] In LoDuca's score there are comparable stylistic traits, connoting the exotic, tribal and female-powered – at least to a Euro-American audience. Corresponding to the primary settings of the show (i.e., ancient Greece, or more correctly ancient Thrace),[11] LoDuca has found inspiration in unusual (non-classical) instruments and vocal styles as well as melody and harmony with an eastern Mediterranean, notably Bulgarian flavour (Rudnick 1998); all of these elements characterise a certain kind

---

10 See McClary (1991, 56-67) for a further discussion of Bizet's *Carmen* and the musical characterization of Carmen as "the dissonant Other."

11 Thrace was a region spread over the territories of today's Bulgaria, Greece, and European Turkey. In fact, it is the same geographical area where Xena was born, according to the narrative; more precisely Amphipolis, lying in East Macedonia and Thrace, Greece. However, the show was filmed in New Zealand.

MUSICAL EXOTICA AS DEVICES FOR FEMINIZATION

of "ancient culture," "native exoticism," "Orientalism," and "distantness" – an "Other" – within an overall symphonic framework.[12] Comparing the score with the portrayal of Xena, the show seems to embody elements of a long tradition in western culture, including opera.

> Some of the most basic and powerful myths of Western culture present unfathomable female singers who would destroy the manly heroes who pass through their distant domains. Moving across the centuries, as Catherine Clément [1988] and Susan McClary [1991] point out, many of the greatest operatic heroines remain foreign object of sexual magnetism whose very Otherness and capacity to inspire obsessive love leads to tragedy and death. And as any modern moviegoer knows, the tonal languages of exoticism and magnetic femininity are strikingly similar, relying on chromatic harmony, pulsating and often syncopated rhythms, irregular metrical accents, a de-emphasis of the violin family (the backbone of Classical and Romantic art music), and sometimes scales or melodic patterns blatantly borrowed from specific foreign cultures – in short, on an aesthetically intriguing violation of Western High Art auditory norms. (Austern 1998, 26-27)

However, given the fact that the gender roles in *XWP* are – although perhaps not wholeheartedly reversed, then significantly adjusted – the relation between music and visual narrative might be substantially different. Thus, taking LoDuca's score in *XWP* as the object of analysis, the aims of this chapter are to identify the range of gendered

---

12 However, the musical Other is not limited to Eastern Mediterranean styles; there are also traits of Indian and Chinese music in season 4 as well as Irish (or Celtic) traditional dance music in season 2. Like the show's eclectic narrative, mixing Greek, Roman and medieval myths, LoDuca's score unites present and past (e.g., the "ancient Bacchae rap song" in the season 2 episode "Girls Just Wanna Have Fun"). LoDuca also calls upon Celtic and Islamic musical traditions (cf. Arenson 1998), the latter being most notable in "Stowaway" (i.e., no. 11 on *Xena: Warrior Princess – Original Television Soundtrack Volume Two*. Varese Sarabande, 1997: VSD-5883) by means of the ubiquitous bagpipe.

exoticism and to examine how particular stylistic elements different from western music may relate to the feminine angle of the show.

Feminine Mystique in the XWP Soundtrack – The Bulgarian Connection

In all six seasons of *XWP*, LoDuca has composed (or arranged) incidental music as a series of plot cues, many of them used in different episodes, whether functioning as leitmotifs or not.[13] Due to the limited scope of this chapter, a narrowing of the analytical material is necessary. Therefore, I will consider selected cues only from the first season, all featured on the first soundtrack volume.[14] The choice seems reasonable since most prominent musical characteristics defining the show are introduced here, and – what will be clear in the following analysis – particularly in the initial episode "Sins of the Past," where all the vital associations between the show's setting, title character, and sonic environment are presented.[15]

As already stated, the musical exoticism in *XWP* is, for the most part, derived from Bulgarian indigenous music [*bulgarska narodna muzika*]. To be more precise, it was derived from musical practice in Bulgaria as cultivated through professional folklore ensembles and folk music

---

13 An equal number of soundtracks have been released on the label Varese Sarabande. However, the third and fifth volumes, entitled *The Bitter Suite: A Musical Odyssey* and *Lyre, Lyre, Hearts On Fire*, make up two distinct musical episodes in seasons 3 and 5, respectively, leaving all the other musical cues in those seasons for volumes 4 and 6.

14 *Xena: Warrior Princess – Original Television Soundtrack* (Vol. 1). Varese Sarabande, 1996: VSD-5750 (hereafter abbreviated as "Soundtrack 1"). Four cues originate in the show's parent series *Hercules: The Legendary Journeys* (1995-1999), but are reused in the first season of *XWP*. That is "The Warrior Princess," "Darfus," "The Gauntlet," and "Roll in the Leaves" (appearing in the season 1 episodes in *Hercules*: "The Warrior Princess," "The Gauntlet," and "Unchained Heart"). The cues are strongly associated with Bulgarian indigenous music, which, according to the composer (cf. Damarell 1997; Rudnick 1998), appealed to Robert Tapert (the executive producer of both series) and gave birth to the score of *XWP*.

15 Surely, such a technical device is not uncommon; a similar trend can be observed in *Angel* (cf. Mills 2000, 33).

schools, supported by socialist governments since the end of the Second World War. (Silverman 1983, 58)[16] In fact, an ensemble like this represents the principal influence for the distinctive sonic environment of *XWP*. I refer to the Bulgarian State Radio and Television Female Vocal Choir (entitled, in French, *Les Mystère Des Voix Bulgares*) – a composite choir comprised solely of female singers recruited from folk music festivals around the country. Their voices sound distinctly non-western, they present Bulgarian lyrics and music with an extraordinary vocalisation technique, and therefore represent an unusual musical background for a television show aimed primarily at an American audience. Originally, the adjective *mystère* ("mysterious") referred to a distinctive way of polyphonic singing, characterised by an open-throated resonance without classical vibrato, and embellished with ornamentation such as trills and mordents (different kinds of "voice shaking"), as well as "glottal stops," – the latter sounding like a short transitory yodel and used as a device for separating the tones.[17]

---

16 What has become known in Bulgaria as *narodna muzika* (people's or indigenous music) is actually traditional music from the ethnographic regions of Thrace and Rhodopes in southern Bulgaria and northeastern Greece. According to Carol Silverman (1983), "Thracian music has come to be the 'national music' of Bulgaria because of an ongoing Thracian influence in the government-sponsored institutions (ensembles and music schools), which has contributed 'to a marked standardization and homogenization of folk music throughout the country." (ibid., 59) Due to the political changes in Eastern Europe in 1989-90 and the opening to the West, Bulgarian indigenous (notably vocal) music suddenly became an object of popularization and commodification outside Bulgaria, too, primarily in Western Europe and America but also in Japan. The unique quality of the music satisfied "the world's thirst for global and New Age music exotica, and excitement over the end of the Cold War." (cf. Buchanan 1995, 408)

17 The vocal technique is described and exemplified meticulously in the works of Timothy Rice (1977, 1980 and 1994). See also Buchanan (1997, 139) and Buchanan (2001) for a more brief account. In a study by Haris Sarris and Panagiotis Tzevelekos (2008), the authors demonstrate a sonic relationship between the "mysterious Bulgarian voices" and the technical capabilities of the *gaida* (bagpipe), which originate in the sociocultural context of the pre-WWII agricultural societies of Thrace. (ibid., 38) I shall return to this in the following section.

According to Donna Buchanan (1997, 138), the "Mystère" brand became a successful marketing tool for several Bulgarian choruses in the beginning of the post-Cold War era, all exemplifying "stylized renditions of Bulgarian traditional music within discourses of feminine mysticism, ruralized authenticity, and cosmological phantasmagoria." (ibid., 134) Through rhetorical strategies in liner notes in CD booklets, including pictures of women wearing beautiful national costumes, fresh flowers behind their ears, white head scarves, and gold necklaces, the female singers, although highly professional, are depicted as "peasant girls endowed with raw and rustic talent of archaic vintage" (ibid., 151), "daughters of Orpheus's lyre," and "ancestral to contemporary life and cosmic in power." (ibid., 139) What seems interesting in the present context, though, is the association between the kind of forceful singing, ancient feminine mysticism, and the branding of Xena's personality and power, which is reinforced through her eerily ululating battle cry every time she decides to defend or attack somebody.[18] Moreover, the connection is verbalised (and made audible) directly in every single episode during the title theme and the opening credits through the alliteration, "The **p**ower," "The **p**assion," which is articulated by the voiceover as the female choir is heard in the theme's closing section. (fig. 3)

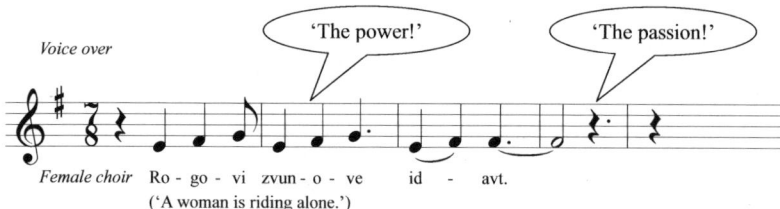

Fig. 3: Closing vocal section of the XWP title theme with the voice over.

Apart from "Main Title" (and its extended version), the number of tracks on Soundtrack 1 featuring Bulgarian (or Thracian) female voices totals

---

18 It should suffice to confirm that the ululation implicates an exotic "Other" through its association with the *Alala* cry of ancient Greeks warriors, Arab women expressing joy or sorrow, or perhaps even aggressive Plain Indian tribes attacking white settlers as they often do in American westerns.

MUSICAL EXOTICA AS DEVICES FOR FEMINIZATION

five;[19] they are "The Warrior Princess," "The Gauntlet," "Glede Ma Glede," "Burying the Past," and "Xena's Web."[20] The latter two, although predominantly instrumental, include vocal melodic sections, which are similar and almost identical, respectively, compared to the opening *recitativo* and the following choral section in the "The Warrior Princess" (figs. 4a-d).[21] In fact, the majority of vocal-melodic cues during the various episodes (including the shared "Main Title") are taken from either these two sections (including the derivations) or the main part of "The Warrior Princess" (0:31-2:11) with its irregular metric subdivision reminiscent of the "Main Title" theme, while cues from "The Gauntlet" and "Glede Ma Glede" are considerably rarer.[22] In figure 4,

---

19 It should be noticed that none of the two versions of "Main Title" are identical to the title theme used in the show. The changes involve primarily the addition of female voices (and lyrics) to the opening section, too.

20 Likewise, a few distorted samples of a solo voice (probably by means of pitch bending) "reminiscing" the initial phrase of "The Warrior Princess" appear on another track "Dreamscape," though very momentarily why it has been left out. So have "The Wrath of Calisto" and "Ladder Fight" (both from the episode "Calisto"), which include "exotic singing," too – an almost howling voice (without lyrics) personifying Caslisto (one of the show's main female "baddies"), her vindictiveness and mental illness, and a kind of antithesis to the controlled Thracian voices associated with Xena.

21 The solo voice melody in "Xena's Web," entering about the middle point (1:04-1:18), sounds like a tiny adjustment of figure 4a (probably acquired by studio mixing) while the following instrumental section (1:19-1:34) parallels figure 4b. Additionally, three segments (1:34-1:44, 1:53-2:01, and 2:02-2:12) in the conclusion (instrumental, choral, and instrumental respectively) are all similar to the last four tones of figure 4b, constituting the "β formula." I shall concentrate specifically on this in a moment.

22 Cues from "The Gauntlet" occur in the episodes "Athens City Academy of the Performing Bards" (20:30-20:47) and "The Greater Good" (23:34-24:47) – both points where we see Xena mortally wounded and close to death, though willful enough to survive and conquer. By means of close voicings (preferably major seconds), an intensely lamentational melodic line embellished with Oriental sounding melismas, and a sombre orchestral accompaniment (notably low tones with reverberation), the music – originally used in an earlier Hercules episode (cf. note 14) where Xena

Fig. 4:
a) 'The Warrior Princess' (0.00-0:18) • b) 'The Warrior Princess' (0.00-0:18)
c) 'Burying the Past' (2:12-2:35) • d) 'Xena's Web' (1:53-2:01)

despite surface (ornamental) differences,[23] I demonstrate the fundamental (structural) similarities between the vocal sections in "The Warrior Princess," "Burying the Past," and "Xena's Web," using the Greek letters α and β to pinpoint two essential musical "kernels" (i.e., organising ideas or "formulas"). Both serve as connotative signifiers and important attributive devices for the construction of a general melancholic atmosphere (corresponding to the sorrowfulness of Xena, and her regrets of her immoral past of terror), which is fundamental to the show. However, the melancholic mood is in-

---

is forced to run the gauntlet after her army mutinies – is closely associated with Xena's pain. "Glede Ma Glede" (a traditional Balkan harvesting song) occurs only once during the show's first season; that is in "Sins of the Past" (23:30-24:09) when Xena, visiting her home, rides past singing female villagers working in the meadow.

23 The reader should be on notice that the ornamentations in figure 4 are only rough estimations of what is actually sung. However, it is the fundamental notes of the melodies that hold importance. (The same holds true in figures 5 and 6, which are both transcriptions of *gaida* playing.)

terrupted frequently by energetic fighting scenes with Hong Kong-style whooshes (sonifying all quick movements and kicks) to the accompaniment of more traditional action-oriented orchestral music. As one will notice, the α formula is particularly dominant with the ubiquitous ascending and descending line (E – F♯ – G – F♯ – E) and E-minor tonality, most apparent in the episodes "Sins of the Past" and "The Path Not Taken." The β formula – a prominent attributional feature of musical exoticism, with its distinctive combination of Phrycian mode (the lowered second step) and tri-tone-harmonic relationship (the double leading notes F♮ and B♭, resolving to E and B♮) – seems to be connected distinctly to *instances of aggressive female agency*, an interpretative comment to situations in which Xena behaves in a hostile manner when encountering someone else (friend or enemy), either by pure communicative (verbal or nonverbal) means or through devastating physical violence.[24] Consequently, despite its brevity, the β formula represents one of the most significant constituents for bringing together the forceful singing style of the Bulgarian women and Xena's power; its distinctive *female vocality* (separating it from the pure instrumental score before and after), coupled with the tonal instability (notice the "mysterious" tritone chord progression E – B♭ – E with no thirds), make it a profound musical element, contributing thoroughly to Xena's psychology.[25]

---

24 The former is exemplified three times in "Sins of the Past," initially (8:06) when Xena warns Gabrielle not to follow her trail, saying "You don't wanna make me mad, now, do you?"; secondly (30:49) when Gabrielle nevertheless disobeys the warnings and manages to get Xena out of trouble, though Xena really does not want to be helped and looks suspiciously at Gabrielle; and thirdly when Xena surprises her enemy Draco (a ruthless warlord) from behind, saying "Hello Draco!" Alternatively, the latter can be observed in three other episodes; i.e., "Cradle of Hope" (30:52) when Xena, disguised as an exotic dancer and prostitute, eliminates a guard captain (Nemos) with a well-placed slap in his face; then "Prometheus" (11:58) when Xena, irritated by getting no information from a salesman (Falafel), grabs him by the collar and pulls him close, saying "I'm not going to ask you again"; and finally "Hooves and Harlots" (39:10) when Xena catches a deceitful traitor and stabs him just as he attacks her from behind.

25 The dissonant sound of the tritone chord progression was in the eigh-

DISTANT LANDS OF DANGER AND PLEASURE

The Sound of War in Exotic Places

In an article about the globalisation of Irish traditional music, McCann (2001, 89) refers to the "ethereal glances of uilleann pipe incidentals" in *XWP* as an example of how this music lends "its symbolic and commercial weight" to popular culture and media.[26] However, the bagpipe, featured in "Main Title" (fig. 5) as well as incidentally during the episodes, is not an *uilleann pipe* but a *gaida* (cf. Arenson 1998;

Fig. 5: The gaida introduction in 'Main Title'.

Rudnick 1998; and Perkins 1998), which – like the earlier mentioned "open-throat" vocalisation technique – comes originally from the Thracian and Rhodopian regions in Bulgaria and Greece. What seems important here, though, are the possible exotic and gendered connotations of the pipe caused by its timbral qualities as well as the melodic phrasing. Beginning with the issue of *exoticism*, Carolyn Bremer (1998) characterises the introducing bagpipe in "Main Title" as follows:

> The opening exotic bagpipe, sweeping up an uneven glissando tonic to dominant, engenders the duality of Western and non-Western music. But the Western tonal language, so clearly demarcated by the harmonic structure, is undermined by the ec-

---

teenth century commonly known as *diabolus in musica* ("the devil in music"), and therefore it was prohibited by various music theorists and banned by the church. Accordingly, judged by the function of the β formula in *XWP*, one might consider the vocal E-B♭-E progression as an agent for linking the "female mysteriousness" of Xena to reminiscences of her "diabolic" past as an evil "warlady."

26 The *uilleann pipe* – or *union pipe*, which is a bellow-blown bagpipe similar to the Northumbrian pipes and the Lowland Scottish bagpipe – has "evolved during the late seventeenth century." (McCullough 1978, 59) According to Schiller (1996, 201), it exemplifies instrumental Irish music in the eighteenth century par excellence, along with the antecedent *píob mhór* ("great bagpipes"); i.e., the so called "Irish Warpipe," which is a mouth-blown bagpipe.

MUSICAL EXOTICA AS DEVICES FOR FEMINIZATION

lectic timbre of the bagpipe and its ornamentation of each diatonic note descending back to the E minor tonic. (ibid.)

I certainly agree with the idea that notions of exoticism and Otherness can be associated with the distinct timbre of the bagpipe, which largely represents a sonic environment foreign to Western capitalistic urban societies – even though the bagpipe today has become a global commodity through the global commercialisation of Irish music as McCann said. (op.cit.) From being a prominent musical feature – not only of the British Isles, but also Eastern Europe, the Iberian Peninsula, North Africa, the Middle East, Central Asia, and India (Randel 1986, 65) – the bagpipe connotes exoticism. It is reinforced by a smooth panoramic shot of a beautiful coast with green hills, rugged cliffs in the wild ocean, and cloudy weather, dissolving immediately into another shot of Xena standing on the outer edge of a cliff, facing and praising Poseidon who rises from the sea with his trident, all implying a kind of ancient landscape far from modern urban societies. Indeed, the *gaida* is generally associated with the lonely female warrior appearing in the landscape by means of a recurring leitmotif from "Burying the Past." (fig. 6). While being introduced at length in the first episode ("Sins of

Fig. 6: The 'Lonely warrior theme', initial phrase.

the Past," 0:00-2:53), as Xena rides through a destroyed village and recalls her dark and violent past, the theme recurs briefly as a leitmotif later (23:13-23:32) and in subsequent episodes when Xena is travelling alone on a horseback.[27]

---

27 These are "Chariots of War" (29:43-30:03), "The Path Not Taken" (7:56-8:49), "Prometheus" (12:38-12:50), and "Death in Chains" (12:38-12:50), all representing situations when Xena takes action by herself. However, after the ninth episode ("Death in Chains," 1:41-2:19) the associative link between the *gaida* and lonely worrier seems to disappear as another theme from "Burying the Past" (1:44-2:12) achieve the same function. The latter is played by the *kaval* (an end-blown flute traditionally played throughout the Balkans and Anatolia),

Yet, bearing in mind Bremer's analytical description (op.cit.), the exotic flavour of the *gaida* is certainly not accomplished by its timbre alone; the exoticism is even more profound in the melodic ornamentation. In fact, the phrasing technique matches very well the elaborate vocal technique of *Les Mystère Des Voix Bulgares* (e.g., compare figs. 5 and 6 with figs. 4a and 4c). This is not mere coincidence. By means of acoustical analysis, Haris Sarris and Panagiotis Tzevelekos (2008) have demonstrated a strong similarity between traditional "open-throat" singing and *gaida* playing in Greek Thrace, which points towards a reciprocal influence. However, whether the former is derived from the latter or vice versa cannot be concluded unequivocally; however, it seems safe to conclude that the both kinds of traditional music making have grown out of a social context.

> In the pre-WWII context, you had to sing loudly in order to be heard in a noisy village square, and there was also a need for continuous sound to keep the dance going. Both men and women had to meet that challenge: women with their singing, and men with the gaida. The outcome seems identical, because the conditions were the same. (ibid., 55)

This brings us to the issue of gender: Historical and ethnomusicological studies of *gaida* playing report that "piping" is traditionally considered a performative art reserved for men. According to Rice (1980, 47f), there exists in Bulgarian musical thought a "functional and verbal division between *music* and *song*" (italics mine), which "is reinforced by a behavioural division of labour based on sex," (ibid., 48)

---

and contributes significantly to the melancholy of Xena and her personal attempt to expiate the dark deeds of her past (cf. "Chariots of War," 0:54-1:18; "The Black Wolf," 1:41-2:19; "Warrior... Princess," 0:00-0:27; and "Altered States." 7:16-7:35), although the theme is also used in "love scenes" according to the composer (Rudnick 1998). Examples of the latter would be "Sins of the Past" (39:35-40:38); i.e., Xena's reconciliation with her mother who finally forgive her after she proved that she has put the demons of the past behind her. Here, the *kaval* theme appears in an extended version, not present on Soundtrack 1.

MUSICAL EXOTICA AS DEVICES FOR FEMINIZATION

> Men are almost exclusively the instrumentalists (svirachi) and women are the main bearers of the song (pesen) tradition. The exceptions are the type that ultimately confirms the rule. Only a handful of female instrumentalists were reported in the literature before the recent advent of state-sponsored schools of folk music. (ibid.)

Similar descriptions are given by Sarris and Tzevelekos (2008) as well as Buchanan (2001), both of which I shall quote at length.

> [The *gaida*] was part of the men's world: young male shepherds spent their time in the fields playing the *gaida*, while the girls learned the song repertoire at home, in conjunction with house chores during their upbringing. This "gender separation" of music continued in adolescent life. The *gaida* was played almost exclusively by men, whereas women were the main carriers of the song repertoire. (Sarris and Tzevelekos 2008, 39)[28]

> The reason for this gender specificity derives from the division of labour in village life, which in turn prescribed the context and manner in which musical skills were acquired. Men were engaged predominantly with animal husbandry; women with domestic and agricultural work. As herders followed their livestock from pasture to pasture, they entertained themselves by playing music, especially on aerophones like the kaval or duduk, considered shepherds' instruments. ... Herding left men's hands relatively free to play instruments. ... Women's hands, however, were continually occupied with housework, food preparation, textile production and work in the fields.

---

28 The authors are here referring to "the old agricultural societies of Thrace" as "the cultural environment of the *gaida*"; i.e., the time before the population exchanges between Greece and Bulgaria in 1919, and Greece and Turkey in 1923. (ibid., 38-39) The *gaida* is still thought of as "the traditional companion of the solitary shepherd" in the Bulgarian (or Rhodopian) mountains. (Arenson 1998)

> They utilised their voices to accompany their work and express their emotions. (Buchanan 2001)

Schiller (1996) equally characterises the *uilleann pipe* as male dominated ever since its popularisation in the eighteenth century although for different reasons. Because of its "reputation of being extremely demanding as regards playing technique and maintenance," ... it was culturally regarded as unsuitable for female performers." (ibid., 201) Waldron (2006) further explores the gendered implications in traditional Irish music, drawing on studies by McCullough (1978) and Schiller (op.cit.) as well as in literature, by tracing the history of the *uilleann pipe*. Developed from the louder warpipe, which was used for military purposes, the uilleann pipe was traditionally associated with "maleness." (Waldron, op.cit.) As a matter of fact, the associative links to war and battles signify one of the main focal points in *XWP*: the inimitable fighting skills of the strong female warrior who defeats any male competitor or barbarian. Thus, though bagpipes have become typical wedding (not war) instruments in both the Balkans and the Gaelic societies, the connotation of war still might have an impact – at least on spectators accustomed to western culture and media.[29] Here the choice of the *gaida* for the *XWP* music appears curiously straightforward. Indeed, by the distinctive choice of instrument and melodic phrasing, the music's connotative signification potential is twofold: it combines the war theme with a sense of Otherness suggesting battle fights in exotic surroundings.

A Feminized Other or Another Kind of Feminization?

Having discussed the implications of exoticism, gender, and Otherness in the *XWP* music (via Bulgarian female voices and *gaida* play-

---

[29] Modern Hollywood movies exploiting war plots featuring Irish or Scottish scenery or people may support the notion of the bagpipe as a war instrument. For instance, *Braveheart* (Mel Gibson 1995) and *Rob Roy* (Michael Caton-Jones 1995) are prominent examples.

ing), we are faced with two complementary analytical perspectives. Thus, we might question if LoDuca's score must be considered a distinct *feminine variation* of musical exoticism and Otherness, or rather a *new kind* of musical femininity. As to the former, things turn out to be somewhat ambivalent. On the one hand the powerful and extraordinary vocalisation technique of *Les Mystère Des Voix Bulgares* appears to be a very convincing signifier of Xena as the vigorous Amazon woman from the primordial world. On the other hand, she is portrayed through the sound of "male war-making" and aggression due to the *gaida* and its warpipe undertone, certainly not consistent with "hegemonic femininity" (i.e., the western cultural industry's normative ideal of female behaviour). However, as I have already noted, the character of Xena clearly resists traditional gender stereotypification. As stated by Cathy Young (2005), *XWP* represents new temperamental and psychological standards of action heroines, which seem more current than similar characters on television shows of the 1990s:

> How was Xena a female pioneer? Let me count the ways. She had no male support or regular romantic interest. She didn't, unlike Wonder Woman or the Bionic Woman, have a conventionally feminine day-to-day alternate identity, though on a mission she could pose as a Roman matron, a virgin priestess or an exotic dancer. Xena was not "strong but feminine"; she was unapologetically strong and unapologetically female, sexy and powerful, unafraid to get sweaty and dirty on the job, and all the more beautiful for it. (ibid.)

Interestingly, while representing a momentous discursive change in modern fantasy television, this gender role modification is very much in line with a widely held (real historical or mythical) notion about strong Amazon women in ancient Greece. This notion, I believe, has been nourished recently by the latest thriller in the popular *Millennium* trilogy by the Swedish journalist and writer Stieg Larsson with its intermezzi of historic-anecdotal accounts of women warriors around the world throughout history.[30] This draws attention to the latter perspective, to the question of whether such a "modernized" (or rediscovered) femininity engenders a musical parallel (i.e., a new kind of "female music"). It seems natural to discuss the main features of the *XWP* music in relation to the music-parametric differences between "male" and "female" tunes (Table 1) as observed by Tagg (1989, 2003). In this way, one might consider adding "exotic constituents" to the female column, noting foreign instruments and singing styles as well as irregular metrics.

However, once again we are faced with two alternative views. Whereas Bremer (1998) – probably inspired by Tagg's "anthropological stereotypes" – associates metric irregularity with "masculinity" and lush string melodies with "femininity," Austern (1997, 26-27) takes a diametrically opposed position by characterising "irregular metrical accents" and "a deemphasis of the violin family" as a feminine feature. Such contrasting viewpoints, although disturbingly incompatible, demonstrate quite effectively that the link between musical exoticism and gender specificity is highly constructivistic and frequently a subject of ambiguity, controversy, and negotiation; the link is conditioned by the context of larger sociocultural discourses and ideologies as well as particular interactions between aural and visual modalities. Even so, in the case of the Bulgarian voices, the meaning potential is *essentially* female-oriented due to the vocal timbre. (After all, it is *only women* who sing!) Besides, even though the average Western audience does not understand the Bulgarian lyrics, the semantic and referential meaning potentials of the solo recitatives and choir sections are considerably direct (compared with the more connotational potentials of the *gaida* and *kaval*), and therefore I suspect that the vocal cues will capture the main attention. This is precisely why the α and β formulas seem so significant for the feminine angle of the *XWP* music.

---

30 The book was released in 2007 with the Swedish title *Luftslottet som sprängdes* ("The Air Castle That Was Blown Up"). The English translation is titled "*The Girl Who Kicked the Hornets' Nest*. (MacLehose Press. October 31st 2009)"

References

Arenson, Jill. "Songs of the Warrior Princess." *Whoosh!* 18 (1998).
Austern, Linda Phyllis. "Forreine Conceites and Wandring Devices": The Exotic, the Erotic, and the Feminine." In *The Exotic in Western Music.* Edited by Jonathan Bellman. Boston: Northeastern University Press, 1997.
Bremer, Carolyn. "Duality And Completeness: An Analysis Of The Xena: Warrior Princess Theme Music." *Whoosh!* 20 (1998).
Buchanan, Donna A. (1995) "Metaphors of Power, Metaphors of Truth: The Politics of Music Professionalism in Bulgarian Folk Orchestras." *Ethnomusicology* 39, no. 3 (1995): 381-416.
_____. "Review Essay: Bulgaria's Magical Mystère Tour: Postmodernism, World Music Marketing, and Political Change in Eastern Europe" *Ethnomusicology* 41, no. 1 (1997): 131-157.
_____. "Bulgaria – II. Traditional music." *Grove Music Online. Oxford Music Online.* 2 Dec. 2008. Article written in 2001.
Clément, Catherine. *Opera, or The Undoing of Women.* Minneapolis: University of Minnesota Press, 1988.
Damarell, Steve. *Xena: Warrior Princess.* Original Television Soundtrack. Vol. 1. Music Composed by Joseph LoDuca. Review on *Xenaville.com*, 1997.
Dunn, Dan. "Caught in Xena's Web Sites." *Real Edge Magazine* (March/April 2000).
Early, Frances and Kathleen Kennedy. *Athena's Daughters. Television's New Women Warriors.* Syracuse: Syracuse University Press, 2003.
Halfyard, Janet K. (2001) "Love, Death, Curses and Reverses (in F minor): Music, Gender and Identity in Buffy the Vampire Slayer and Angel." *Slayage: The Online International Journal of Buffy Studies* 1, no. 4 (2001).
_____. "An invitation to imagine: theme tunes and the construction of identity in contemporary US television series" Paper given at the University of Bristol, November 18, 2003.

Helford, Elyce Rae. "Feminism, Queer Studies, and the Sexual Politics of *Xena: Warrior Princess*." In *Fantasy Girls. Gender in the New Universe of Science Fiction and Fantasy Television*. Edited by Elyce Rae Helford. Lanham: Rowman & Littlefield, 2000.

Inness, Sherrie A. *Tough Girls: Women Warriors and Wonder Women in Popular Culture*. Philadelphia: University of Pennsylvania Press, 1998.

——————. *Action Chicks: New Images of Tough Women in Popular Culture*. Gordonsville: Palgrave Macmillan, 2004.

McCann, Anthony. "All That Is Not Given Is Lost: Irish Traditional Music, Copyright, and Common Property." *Ethnomusicology* 45, no. 1 (2001): 89-106.

McClary, Susan. *Feminine Endings. Music, Gender, and Sexuality*. Minneapolis: University of Minnesota Press, 1991.

McCullough, L. E. *Irish music in Chicago: An ethnomusicological study*. Ph.D. diss., University of Pittsburgh, 1978.

Meister, Melissa. (1997) "*Xena: Warrior Princess*. Through the Lenses of Feminism." *Whoosh!* 10 (1997).

Mills, Matthew (2005) "*Ubi Caritas?*: Music as Narrative Agent in *Angel*." In *Reading Angel: The TV Spin-off with a Soul*. Edited by Stacey Abbott. London: I. B. Tauris & Co Ltd., 2005.

Parakilas, James. "The Soldier and the Exotic: Operatic Variations on a Theme of Racial Encounter. Part I. "*The Opera Quarterly* 10, no. 2 (1993): 33-56.

Perkins, Heather. "The Music and Sound Design of *Xena: Warrior Princess*," *Whoosh!* 23 (1998).

Randel, Don Michael. *The New Harvard Dictionary of Music*. Cambridge, MA: Belknap Press of Harvard University Press, 1986.

Rice, Timothy. *Polyphony in Bulgarian Folk Music*. Ph.D. diss., Seattle: University of Washington, 1977.

——————. "Aspects of Bulgarian Musical Thought." *Yearbook of the International Folk Music Council* 12 (1980): 43-66.

——————. *May It Fill Your Soul. Experiencing Bulgarian Music*. Chicago: University of Chicago Press, 1994.

Ross, Karen, and Carolyn M. Byerly. *Women and Media. International Perspectives*. HobokenMaiken: Wiley-Blackwell, 2004.

Rudnick, Bret Ryan. "An Interview with Joseph LoDuca." *Whoosh!* 19 (1998).

Sarris, Haris, and Panagiotis Tzevelekos. "Singing like the Gaida (Bagpipe)": Investigating Relations between Singing and Instrumental Playing Techniques in Greek Thrace." *Journal of Interdisciplinary Music Studies* 2, nos. 1-2 (2008): 33-57.

Schiller, Rina. "Gender and Traditional Irish Music." In *Crosbhealach an Cheoil / The Crossroads Conference. Tradition and Change in Irish Traditional Music*. Edited by Fintan Valleley, Hammy Hamilton, et al. Cork: Ossian Publications, 1996.

Schubart, Rikke, and Anne Gjelsvik. *Femme Fatalities. Representations of Strong Women in the Media*. Gothenburg: Nordicom, 2004.

Schwartz, Jeff. "Feminism and Musicology: The Reception of Susan McClary's '*Feminine Endings*.'" Paper given at the Ninth Annual Midwest Feminist Graduate Student Conference, University of Toledo, February 17, 1995.

Silverman, Carol. "The Politics of Folklore in Bulgaria." *Anthropological Quarterly* 56, no. 2 (1983): 55-61.

Stokes, Martin. "East, West, and Arabesk." In *Western Music and Its Others. Difference, Representation, and Appropriation in Music*. Edited by Georgina Born and David Hesmondhalgh. Berkeley: University of California Press, 2000.

Tagg, Philip. "An Anthropology of Stereotypes in TV Music?" *Svensk tidskrift för musikforskning* 71 (1989): 19-42.

_____. *Ten Little Tunes. Towards a Musicology of the Mass Media*. Montreal. The Mass Media Music Scholar's Press, 2003.

Waldron, Janice L. "Gender and Uilleann Piping." *Gender, Education, Music, Society* 4 (2006).

Young, Cathy. "What We Owe Xena." 2005. Online text: http://www.cathyyoung.net/features/whatweowexena.html. Accessed 25 August 2009.

Index

Symbols
1001 Nights 133

A
Abenteuer 171
academe 90
Achilles 81
action chicks 14
Adam and Eve 130
A Discourse of Marriage and Wiving 131
Adorno, Theodor W. 145, 151, 154, 161
adventure tales 24
Aesop's fables 169
affect attunement 235
Age of Conan - Hyborean Adventures 102
Aladdin 169
Alan Quatermain 81
Alice 169
allegorical tale 174
allegory 11, 126
allusion 10, 63, 65
Ally McBeal 14, 259
alternative worlds 144, 145, 146, 157
Alton, Anne Hiebert 24
Amazon.co.uk 17
American Dream 11, 95, 96

A Midsummer Night's Dream 65
Andersen, Hans Christian 12, 167, 173, 176, 188
Angel 263
anticipation 17, 19, 26, 31
Appelbaum, Peter 35
Aragones, Sergio 102
architecture 117
Argosy magazine 90
Armageddon (film) 209
Armitt, Lucie 7, 11, 107, 108, 113, 143, 144, 146, 149, 152, 153
Arnold, Matthew 52
Aslan 186
Aubrey, John 50, 207, 215
Austen, Jane 130
A Witch Shall be Born 100

B
Bach, J.S. 239
bagpipe 267, 269, 274, 275, 278
barbarism 82
Barfield, Steven 22
Baroque, the 232
Barrie, James 5, 13, 193, 196, 213
Barthelme, Donald 11, 125, 135
Barthes, Roland 22, 94
Barth, John 134
Bartok, Béla 244
Batman 260

INDEX

Battle Hymn of the Republic 254
Baum, L. Frank 64, 75
Belgariad series 80
Bettelheim, Bruno 13, 49, 194, 201
Bildung 29, 30, 38
Bildungsroman 24, 50
Bloch, Robert 90
Bloomsbury Press 18
bobbits 50
Bolter and Grusin 221
Book of Revelation 150
Bordwell, David 13, 226
Botting, Fred 83
Boucicault, Nina 6
boxing tales 91
Brand, Neil 233
Braveheart 278
Bremer, Carolyn 264, 274
bricolage 120
Brooks, Terry 108
Browning, Robert 114
Budd, Robin 209, 215
Buffy the Vampire Slayer 14, 259, 260
Bulgaria 269
Burroughs, Edgar Rice 81, 90
Byatt, A.S. 21, 36

C

Campbell, Joseph 13, 224
cannibalism 89
capitalism 109
capitalist society 118
caricature 227
Carlyle, Thomas 51
Carmen 266
Carmina Burana 238, 244
Carpe Jugulum 63, 66, 67
Carpenter, John 101
Carroll, Lewis 29, 173
Carroll, Noel 7
catharsis 55
Chambers of Secrets 20
Chaplin, Charlie 169
Charmed 261
childhood 175, 178, 185, 207, 212, 215
childhood fears 146
children 99, 175, 186, 194
children's fantasy fiction 29
children's fantasy literature 19
Chimera 134
Chion, Michel 232
chivalric romances 52
Christensen, Johannes H. 155
Christianity 149, 155
Christology 150
Chronicles of Thomas Covenant 80
Cinderella 170
civilisation 82, 87, 95
Clark, John D. 94
Classical era, the 232
cliché 61
cognitive film theory 226
cognitive processes 13
cognitive theory 226
Coleridge, Samuel Taylor 172
Columbus, Chris 45, 245
comic relief 82
computer games 222, 225, 259
Conan 10
Conan the Barbarian 100, 102

Conan the Cimerian 79
Conan Unchained 91
Cooper, Susan 21
creational myth 149
crime 90
crime fiction 12, 84, 144, 148, 151, 154, 157
crime fighting stories 91
critical realism 45, 54, 56
critique of modernity 51
Csikszentmihalyi, Mihaly 226
culture 82, 87
Culture and Anarchy 52
cyberpunk 84

D

Dahl, Roald 21
Darwinism 152
David Copperfield 46
dead metaphor 10, 65, 71
De Camp, L. Sprague 94
degeneration 87
deixis 136
democracy 160
demonology 131
Deodato, Ruggero 101
Derleth, August 87, 90
detective fiction 25
Deus absconditus 153, 158
Dialectics of Enlightenment 151
dialectics of realism 148, 162
Dickens, Charles 174
Dies Irae 238, 242, 243, 252
Discworld 10, 61, 74
Disney 13, 205, 209, 211, 214
Doc Savage 91

Doložel, Lubomír 145
Donald Duck 169
Donaldson, Stephen 80
Don Quijote 169
double universe 12, 217
double worlds 167, 185
Dragonlance series 147
dreams 149, 213, 221, 227
Dr. Watson 169
Dumas, Alexander 81

E

Eco, Umberto 67
Edding, David 80
Electro 256
Elgar, Edgar 240, 251
elves 66, 172, 221
ending 28, 31, 33, 34
epistemology 127, 135, 143, 153, 159
Equal Rites 63, 64
Escape from New York 101
Euclidean room 235
evangelical realism 150
Eve 177
exoticism 278
expanded realism 23
extramural 67

F

fable 149, 174
fabula 226
fairies 8, 51, 172, 206, 214, 221
fairy stories 8, 172
Fairy Tale — A True Story 212
fairy tales 13, 108, 153, 174, 194, 196

INDEX

family discourse 10, 46, 48, 55
family values 209
fan fiction 19, 27, 32
fansite 18
Fantasia (music) 231
fantastic tale 172
fantastic, the 6, 11, 23, 126, 137, 141, 144, 146
fantasy 11, 12, 27, 45, 54, 86, 109, 125, 126, 130, 143, 146, 148, 151, 153, 154, 172, 178
fantasy fiction 21
fantasy film genre 223
fantasy films, 236
fantasy genre 22, 33, 75, 79, 127, 168, 175, 186
Fantasy Magazine 93
Fantasy (music) 231
fanzines 259
fascism 94, 97, 98, 151
father figure 47, 49
Faust 132, 133
Fazetta, Frank 102
female hero 211
female liberation 177
feminist discourse 260
Fennimore Cooper, James 81
feudalism 112
feudal society 111, 122
film 222
film music 232, 233, 234, 235
film score 234
film theory 225
Firebird 247, 252
folklore 67, 243
folk music 243

folk tale 174, 183, 194, 223
food 178
formulaic, the 63, 65, 70, 73
Forster, E.M. 49
French Revolution 122
Freud, Sigmund 132, 138, 153, 195, 201
frontier mythology 11, 95
Frye, Northrop 12, 149, 151

G

gaida 274, 276, 277, 278, 279, 280
Gaiman, Neil 118
Garden of Eden 52, 181, 187
gender 276, 278
gendered stereotypes 263
gender reversal 14
gender roles 13, 211
gender stereotypes 260
gender stereotypification 279
Genette, Gérard 10, 62
genre 75, 125
genre fiction 145
German Romanticism 173
ghost story 147
Gilead, Sarah 29
girl-power 261
Glockenspiel 246, 250, 253
Goblet of Fire 20
Goethe, Johann Wolfgang von 132
Gothic 82, 83, 87
Gothic literature 80
gothic romances 52
grail legends 52
grand narratives 63, 68, 70, 73
Great Depression, the 91

Great Ormond Street Hospital 213
Greece 266, 269, 274, 279
Green, Simon R. 12, 144
Grimm brothers 114, 171, 174
Groo the Wanderer 102
Gulliver 169

H

Haggard, H. Rider 81, 90
Hamlet 65, 127, 169
Hansel und Gretel 169
Hardy, Thomas 52
Harry Potter 9, 17, 45, 47, 54, 55, 56
Harry Potter and the Deathly Hallows 17, 25, 37
Harry Potter and the Halfblood Prince 23
Harry Potter and the Philosopher's Stone 20, 215
Harry Potter and the Philosopher's Stone (film) 14, 231, 245, 251, 253, 255
Harry Potter and the Sorcerer's Stone (film) 45
harrypotterfanfiction.com 32, 33
Harry Potter festival 19
Harry Potter phenomenon 19, 37
HarryPotterSeven.Com 26, 28
Hawk & Fisher 12, 144, 154, 157
Hein, Piet 129
Hejinian, Lynn 133
Helen of Troy 133
He-man 103
Hercules 81, 101, 103
hero 24, 224
heroic fantasy 80

hesitancy 147
hesitation 7, 23, 126, 134
high fantasy 84, 87
high mimetic 150
Hirstein, W. 227
historical criticism 151
historical tale 174
historicity 146
history of fantasy 171
hobbits 99
Hobb, Robin 108
Hoffmann, E.T.A. 171, 173, 175
Hogan, P.J. 211, 214
Holger Danske 179
Hollywood 225
Holst, Gustav 240, 251
Hook 208, 212
horizon 7, 9, 54, 57, 146, 157
Horkheimer, Max 151, 154, 161
horror 87, 88, 90
Hour of the Dragon 96
Howard, Robert E. 11, 79, 80, 90
Hughes, Thomas 49
Hugo Münsterberg 222
human folly 63, 67, 70, 73
humour 70
Hunt, Peter 144, 146, 152
Husserl, Edmund Gustav Albrecht 147
Hutcheon, Linda 67
hyperreality 35
hypertext 75
hypertextuality 62
hypotext 62

INDEX

I

identity 68
ideology 123
Iisjomfruen 167
imagination 130, 227
immediacy 221
immersion 222
incidental music 263, 265, 268
Indiana Jones 237, 250
industrialisation 51
Internet, the 32, 35, 37
intertextuality 62
intramural 73
Irish music 275, 278
Irish traditional music 274
Iron Council 112
ironic representation 72
irony 10, 71
Islam 149

J

Jackson, Peter 53, 227, 237
Jackson, Rosemary 11, 73, 108, 110, 144
James, Henry 7
Jeronimi, Clyde 205
Jones, Diana Wynne 21
Jones, James Earl 100
Judaism 149

K

Kane, Solomon 83
Kermode, Frank 28, 31, 33
Kiley, Dr. Dan 209
King Conan 102
King Kong 81
King Rat 11, 107, 111
Kipling, Rudyard 49
Knight, George 80
knowledge 128
Korgoth of Barbaria 103

L

Lakmé 266
Langer, Susanne K. 235
Larsson, Stieg 279
legend 161, 174
Leiber, Fritz 80, 84. Se
leitmotif 242, 255, 275
lesbianism 89
Lethem, Jonathan 155
Lewis, C.S. 12, 79, 97, 108, 167, 175, 176
Lilith 177
limbic system 228
Lindgren, Astrid 173
literary fairy tale 174
literary immortality 169
Little Mermaid 169
Little Red Ridinghood 169
LoDuca, Joseph 266
London 11, 111, 115, 123
London, Jack 81
Lords and Ladies 63
Lovecraft, H.P. 82, 87, 90, 97
low mimetic 152
L-space 62
Lukács, Georg 10, 54
Luther, Martin 152, 156

M

Macbeth 65, 169
MacDonald, George 173, 176

MAD Magazine 102
Mad Max 101
magic 158, 172
Magritte, René 129
map 118, 147
mapping 11
marcato 238
Märchen 171
Margaret Ogilvy 196
Marin, Louis 7, 54, 57
Marvel Comics 102
marvellous, the 6, 23, 38, 172
Marvel Super Heroes 34
mask 68
Maskerade 63, 64, 68, 70
Massive Multiplayer Role Playing Game 102
materialism 162
Matthews, Richard 90
McCaughrean, Geraldine 213
McClary, Susan 261
Mephistopheles 132, 133
meta-fiction 74
metanarratives 168, 170
metaphor 65, 111, 115, 119
Mickey Mouse 169
Middle Earth 85, 147
Miéville, China 11, 107
Milius, John 100
Millennium trilogy 279
mimetic, the 23
Minimalism 256
Mirror of Erised 45
mise-en-scene 227
misogyny 94
modality of fiction 12, 144, 145
Model, Ben 233
modernism 54, 243
modernity 53, 54, 56, 109, 215
modernity discourse 10
Moorcock, Michael 81, 84, 86, 87
morphology of the folktale 223
Mortal Kombat 102
Motherless Brooklyn 155
Münsterberg, Hugo 222
music 13, 14
musical exoticism 273, 280
musical femininity 14
mystery 27
mystery genre 25
myth 65, 144, 148, 151, 153, 156, 157, 174, 221
mythic 150

N

narcissism 10, 13, 48
narcissist 208
narration 139
narratology 222
naturalism 152, 153, 156
nature 95
Nazis 86
Nesbit, Edith 173
neuroscience 127
Neverwhere 118
New Age 243, 269
New Fairy tales 175, 179
New Testament 12, 144, 148, 149, 150, 154
Niccholes, Alexander 131
Nietzsche, Friedrich 100
nightmares 221, 227

INDEX

Noble Savages 82
non-diegetic music 235
Norse mythology 85
nostalgia 243
Notes on the English Character 49
nuclear family 13, 47, 209, 210, 214
Nünning, Vera 135
Nussknacker und Mausekönig 173

O

Odysseus 81
Oedipus 169
Oedipus conflict 13, 47, 48, 198, 201, 202, 214
Old Testament 12, 144, 148, 149, 151
Oliver Twist 46, 56
On Fairy Stories 8, 172, 175
opera 71, 237
orcs 221
Orff, Carl 238, 244
Orientalism 14, 266, 267
Otherness 278, 279
oxymoron 67
Oz 146

P

parable 174
paranormal phenomena 127
parodic distance 75
parody 10, 61, 63, 67, 68, 69, 70, 71, 72
pastiche 10, 63, 70, 208
peak shift 228
peer group 48, 49, 208
perception 228

Perdido Street Station 112
Peter and Wendy 200
Peter Pan 5, 13, 29, 193, 197, 200, 208, 209, 214, 217
Peter Pan, Disney 205
Peter Pan, Hogan 211, 214
Peter Pan in Kensington Gardens 200
Peter Pan in Scarlet 213
Peter Pan or The Boy Who Would Not Grow Up 198, 200
Peter Pan Return to Neverland 209, 215
Phantastes 176
phenomenology 126, 147
Philistines 53
philosophical realism 151, 157, 162
Photographing Fairies 212
Pied Piper 11, 111, 112
Pippi Långstrump 173
Plato 158
pleasure principle 195
Poe, Edgar Allen 81
pornographic fiction 84
Poseidon 275
positivism 150
postmodern 35, 74, 138
postmodern fiction 86
postmodernism 75
Potter phenomenon, the 19
Pratchett, Terry 10, 61, 64
prediction 27
prequel 27
primary and secondary worlds 54
primary world 9, 35, 167, 177, 185, 186

primitivism 243
Prince Caspian 188
Prisoner of Azkaban 20
procedures 226
professional wrestling 103
Propp, Vladimir 13, 223
protagonist 223
protofascism 11
prototypes 226
psychoanalysis 153, 194, 200
psychology 127
puberty 211
public school 49
pulp fiction 88
pulp magazines 89, 90, 91

Q

quasi-secondary world 22
Queen of the Black Coast 99
quest 24, 184
quest romance 24

R

racism 94, 97
Rackham, Arthur 200
Ramachandran, V.S. 227
rationalism 152
rationality 148, 158, 159
Raymond, Bradley 214
R&B 256
reader response 126
realism 12, 22, 24, 38, 45, 54, 110, 127, 144, 147, 148, 149, 150, 151, 153, 154, 157, 159
realistic focalizer 146
reality 35, 38, 143, 145, 172

reality principle 196
reason 12, 148, 167, 185
Red Nails 89
Red Sonia 100
regression 235
relative autonomy 145
religion 68
remediation 221, 227
Renaissance, the 152, 231
repression 199
retold stories 170
Ricaeur, Paul 145
Robin Hood 170
Rob Roy 278
romance 27
Romantic era, the 232, 237
romanticism 152
Romantic Period, the 232
Romantics, the 132
Rose, Margaret 74
Rousseau, Jean Jacques 82
Rowling, J.K. 17, 20, 26, 27, 34, 38, 39, 47, 54, 56, 79, 99, 245

S

Saarinen, Risto 155
Sabrina, the Teenage Witch 14
sadomasochism 89
Sancho Pancha 169
Santa Claus 169
satire 61, 63, 67, 70, 71, 73
satirical fantasy 19, 36, 38
satirical fantasy fiction 31
Scheherazade 12, 133
schemata 226
schoolboy novels 49

INDEX

school stories 24
Schubert's Lieder 237
Schwarzenegger, Arnold 100
science fiction 88, 90
Scott, Walter 81
Sears Tower 8
secondary secondary world 21, 35
secondary world 9, 21, 23, 35, 54, 113, 167, 177, 185, 186
Second World War 210
secular theodicy 156
Seduction of the Innocent 99
Seven Dwarfs 169
sexuality 88
Shadows in Zamboula 89
Shakespeare, William 65, 75, 127
Sherlock Holmes 90, 169
Shore, Howard 237, 245
sibling rivalry 47
Signs of the Times 51
silent movies 233
Sir Gawain and the Green Knight 176
Slotkin, Richard 95
Snow White 169
Social Darwinism 11, 97
Socialist Workers Party 107
social psychology 145
social transgression 118
Socrates 128, 129
Sørensen, Villy 180
Soya, Carl Erik 168
Spielberg, Steven 208
Spies, Johann 132
splatter-punk horror 84
Stalky & Co 49

Star Wars 21, 237, 250
stereotypes in music 14
Stern, Daniel 234
Stravinsky, Igor 244, 247, 252
sub-creator 9
subculture 119
subversion 11, 74, 75
subversive literature 108
superheroine 260
Superman 260
surrealism 227
suspense 34
suspension of disbelief 9, 85
Sword & Sorcery 10, 79, 80
syuzhet 226

T

taboo 80, 88
Tagg, Philip 14, 261
Tarzan 81, 85, 169
teenager 216
templates 226
texts 63, 73
Thanatos 198, 214
The Ants and the Grasshopper 195
The Balloon 12, 135
The Barbarians 101
The Barbaric Triumph 93
The Bible 12, 149
The Boy Castaways of Black Lake Island 198, 200
The Country and the City 52
the Cthulhu Mythos 87
The Dark Barbarian 82, 93, 94
The Devil in Iron 87

The Devil in Iron & People of the Black Circle 96
The Dreamthief's Daughter 86
The Farseer Trilogy 108
The Fellowship of the Ring 50, 252
The Fellowship of the Ring (film) 255
The Frost-Giant's Daughter 85, 89
The God in the Bowl 87
The Hero with a Thousand Faces 225
The Hobbit 85
The Horse and his Boy 188
The Hyborean Age 96
The Lion, the Witch and the Wardrobe 108, 176, 177, 186, 187, 188
The Little Match Girl 174
The Little Mermaid 174
The Little White Bird or Adventures in Kensington Gardens 200
The Lord of the Rings 45, 51, 53, 56, 64
The Lord of the Rings: The Fellowship of the Ring 13
The Lord of the Rings The Fellowship of the Ring (film) 231, 237
The Lord of the Rings: The Return of the King 50
The Lord of the Rings: The Return of the King (film) 227
The Magician's Nephew 176, 186
theme park 34, 37
The Narnia Chronicles 12, 167, 176, 186, 188
The New Barbarians 101
The Nightingale 179
theodicy 156
theology 150, 153
The Peter Pan Syndrome: Men Who Have Never Grown Up 209
The Phantom of the Opera 64, 67, 69, 70, 71, 72
The Pied Piper of Hamelin 114
therapy 30
The Red Shoes 179
The Return of the King 51
The Savage Sword of Conan 102
The Scar 112
The Shadow 91
The Shadow Kingdom 80
The Shepherdess and the Chimney Sweep. 179
The Silver Chair 176, 178, 179, 186, 188
The Snow Queen 12, 167, 179, 188
The Sword of Shannara 108
The Three Little Pigs 195, 205
The True Story of my Life - A Sketch 174
The Turn of the Screw 7
The Ugly Duckling. 179
The Voyage of the "Dawn Treader" 178, 186
The Wonderful Wizard of Oz 29, 64
The World of Warcraft 102
The Writer's Journey: Mythic Structure for Storytellers and Screenwriters 225
The X-Files 14
Thrace 266
Tickell, Thomas 206

INDEX

time 177
Tinker Bel (film) 214
Toccata and Fugue in d-minor 239
Todorov, Tzvetan 6, 12, 22, 125, 134, 137, 144, 147
Tolkien, J.R.R. 8, 22, 36, 51, 52, 53, 56, 64, 74, 75, 79, 85, 97, 108, 147, 172, 175
Tom Brown's Schooldays 49
topography 136
Torrance, Thomas F. 150
Tower of the Elephant 87, 96, 100
transtextual cues 229
transtextuality 10, 62, 70, 73
tween-generation 211
tweening 13
tweens 216

U

uilleann pipe 278
uncanny, the 6, 136
underscoring 14
Unheimliche 221
urban space 118, 122
Utopia 7, 8

V

Valhalla 85
vampires 66, 72
Victorian culture 174
Victorian literature 174
Victorian quest romance 11
videogames 101, 221
Virtual Reality 222
vocal motet 231
Vogler, Christopher 13, 225

Volgsten, Ulrik 234

W

Walt Disney 254
War of the Worlds (film) 209
Webber, Andrew Lloyd 64, 72
Weird Tales 87, 90, 91
welfare society 155
Wertham, Frederic 99
western, the 90, 91, 95
Wicked Queen 169
Wild West 88
Williams, Charles 97
Williams, John 237, 245, 249, 254
Williams, Raymond 52
Williams, Vaughan 240, 251
Winfrey, Oprah 21
witch 132, 169, 176
witchcraft 131
witchcraft trials 131
Witches Abroad 63, 64
Wolf 169
Wonderful Stories for Children 173
Worms of the Earth 87
Wyrd Sisters 63

X

Xena Warrior Princess 14, 101, 103

Y

young adult genre 27

Z

Ziehe, Thomas 10, 48
Zipes, Jack 110
Zola, Émile 152